THE ENGLISH WARRIOR

from earliest times to 1066

Stephen Pollington

Anglo-Saxon Books

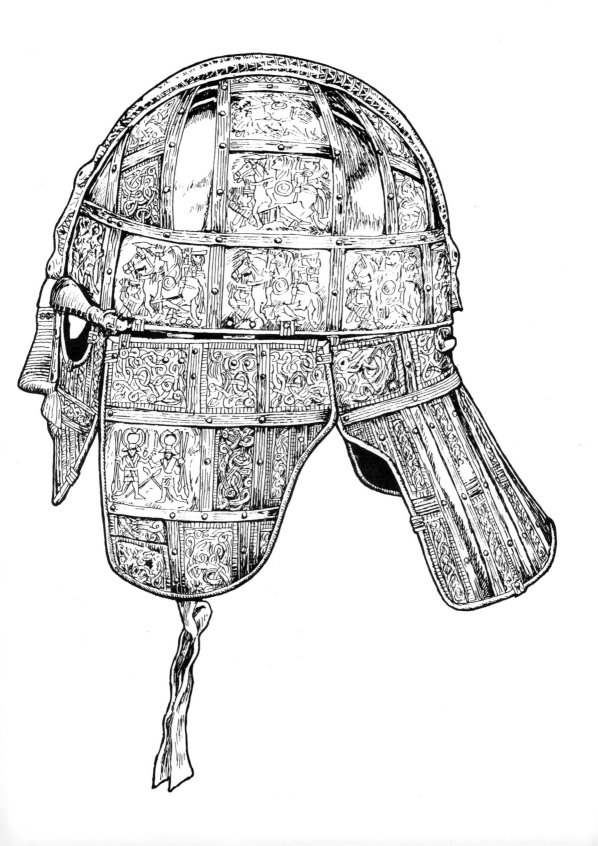

For my mother and the memory of my father

THE ENGLISH WARRIOR

from earliest times to 1066

ac hit þæſ mæſt eallan lað to ƒeohtanne ƿið heoρa aȝenneſ cẏnneſ
mannum ƒoρðam þæρ pæſ lẏtel elleſ þe aht mẏcel mihton
butan enȝliſce on æȝðρe healƒe

but it was most hateful to all to fight against their own race's men,
for there was little else who could achieve anything much on either side
except for the English

(Anglo-Saxon Chronicle, s.a. 1052)

BY THE SAME AUTHOR

Wordcraft: Concise Dictionary and Thesaurus, Modern English – Old English
Heart shall be the Keener – the argument of courage at Maldon
An Introduction to the Old English Language and its Literature
Rudiments of Runelore
The Warrior's Way

Published 1996 by
Anglo-Saxon Books
Frithgarth
Thetford Forest Park
Hockwold-cum-Wilton
Norfolk England

Printed by
Redwood Books
Trowbridge
Wiltshire
England

British Library Cataloguing-in-Publication Data. A catalogue record for this book is available from the British Library.

ISBN 1–898281–10–6

Contents

Contents

List of Figures

List of Figures

The cover illustration is based on the lid of the Franks Casket (first half of the 8th century) believed to be of Northumbrian origin. This and the drawing of the Sutton Hoo helmet shown overleaf are both byCharles W. Evans-Günther. Other original drawings are by the author.

List of Tables

Foreword

This book stems from my long interest in military themes in both Old English literature and Anglo-Saxon archaeology. Much has been written about the various topics discussed in these pages, but very little has been done to synthesise the information available: it remains scattered in dozens of different books, articles and treatises. The aim of this study, therefore, is to bring together the various types of evidence, and to interpret and present them in a readable and non-specialist manner.

The book is not intended to be a bald listing of the battles and campaigns from the Anglo-Saxon Chronicle and other sources, but rather it is an attempt to get below the surface of Anglo-Saxon warriorhood and to find out what is recoverable of the rites, social attitudes, mentality and mythology of the warfare of those times, as much as of the weapons and armour. For this reason the narrative may seem to change rather abruptly, from archaeological to literary evidence, from Iron Age Scandinavia to Anglo-Saxon England, from Iceland to Asia. This is to some extent inevitable working with the material to hand.

The sections of the book are sub-divided into what I hope are manageable chunks of information. I have tried throughout to achieve two aims. The first is to offer answers to questions which have bothered me - for example, why were swords made by pattern-welding?, what was the background and nature of the special relationship between maternal uncle and nephew? how did the warrior relate to his leader and to the rest of his society? The second is to provide as broadly encyclopaedic a treatment of Anglo-Saxon military topics as space would allow. It is immensely frustrating to read that spears of Swanton Type C1 were recovered from a grave, without having any idea as to what such spears look like or what their presence means. For that reason, the sections dealing with weaponry are a little like a standard reference work on the archaeological aspects of military hardware, in order that the reader will have a brief summary of the various technical terms involved in discussing these subjects. In my view, a single book dealing with these topics in a brief, accessible and comfortable way is long overdue.

The early period of Germanic warriorhood is dealt with at some length in terms of what it meant to be a warrior within such a society. Did a young man choose to be a warrior in the same way he might choose to be a smith or a carpenter or a seaman? Were sword, spear and shield the tools of his trade in just the same way as the chisel, saw, adze and axe were of the woodworker's? I think not; indeed, I take the view that those who were to become warriors were singled out in certain ways, as I explain, and that their weapons were from earliest times charged with a heavy symbolism far greater than that surrounding any other equipment, even that of the semi-divine smith.

The book is divided into three sections. In the first, I consider what it meant to be a warrior in the earliest English society, and how that changed with the passage of time, the first agrarian culture giving way to a warrior-cult which in turn was replaced by a

13

strong central authority which, in effect, the military merely served and upheld; this progress mirrors the political development from tribal community to nation-state. The second section is concerned with the weapons and equipment of the warrior, their manufacture and use, and their users' attitudes to them. Finally, I turn to military organization, from battlefield tactics to the social structures which gave rise to the various forms of warriorhood known from the period. It hardly needs saying that the changes observed from the times of the Germanic inroads into Central Europe to the last gasp of the native English military structure at Senlac, were so far-reaching as to have totally transformed the host society not once, but two or three times.

One of the paradoxes of Anglo-Saxon studies as a whole is the inverse proportions of documentary to physical evidence: the earlier, pagan period yields copious finds in the form of grave-goods, but the sporadic textual evidence is unreliable, difficult to interpret and mostly only survives in later copies; with the adoption of Christian literate culture, the documenting of even relatively humble aspects of society begins, but Christian burial practice denies us the corresponding material remains.

In researching the subject I have picked the brains of many acquaintances and I wish to record here my thanks to them collectively, as well as to the following who have allowed me to read their work before publication: Terry Brown for *English Martial Arts*; Kathleen Herbert for *Peace-Weavers and Shield-Maidens*; Alan Haymes for *Anglo-Saxon Kinship*. [The drawings of the Franks casket detail (cover) and the Sutton Hoo helmet (frontispiece and p. 144) were produced by Charles Evans-Günther.] And finally to John and Georgina Quadling for their time and friendship. It is a commonplace of any project such as this, involving many man-hours of research, that the truly crucial piece of evidence which brings the whole subject into focus only turns up once the manuscript has been delivered to the publisher. I have no reason to believe that this work will prove an exception! In my defence, I can only say that I have tried to bring together as many different threads of the story as I could find and hope to incorporate into such a work: if the overall design has occasionally been lost in the welter of tiny detail, this is only to be expected when working on so large a canvas.

Steve Pollington
Essex, August 1995

N.B. Throughout the book, words and text excerpts are given in Old English or Old Norse, the translations of which are my own unless otherwise stated. The wording of different translations of the same text may occasionally vary according to the point being illustrated.

In Old English texts, the letters 'thorn' Þ, þ and 'eth' Ð, ð are interchangeable, both standing for the sounds we now write 'th' as in 'this' (voiced) and 'thin' (voiceless). In Old Norse, 'thorn' always has the voiceless ('thin') sound and 'eth' the voiced ('this') sound. The letter 'ash' Æ, æ has the 'a' sound of 'cat', 'sack'. This is not a book on linguistics, so readers will have to consult a grammar for more details of the pronunciation of other letters (ȳ, etc.)

List of Abbreviations

OE	Old English (language)
ON	Old Norse (language)
ASC	Anglo-Saxon Chronicle (Manuscript identifier letter is given after)
s.a.	*sub anno* (reference appears under the entry for this year)
AS	Anglo-Saxon

Glossary

A brief tabulation of some of the less familiar words (OE, ON and modern) used in this book. Words given in italics are also glossed here. The letters Þ/þ and Ð/ð come after the normal alphabetic run.

æðeling	member of the king's kindred, hence hereditary nobleman
Angelcynn	the English nation
Anglii	tribe living in eastern Jutland from whom the *Angelcynn* sprung
atheling	modern spelling of *æðeling*, member of the king's kindred, hence hereditary nobleman
bana	killer, slayer (bane)
berserkir	Scandinavian warrior group who wore ritual bearskins in battle
bind-ring	a metal ring fixed round the socket of a spearhead to secure it to its staff
bookland	(OE *bócland*) land held in perpetuity by charter
burh	a fortified site; under Alfred and his successors, one of a series of such sites providing static defence in depth across the English-held parts of the country
cumbol	banner or standard used in warfare for identification
cynn	kindred, family
drihten	'lord', master of the *gedriht*
duguð	'doughty men', veterans
ealdordōm	territory subject to an *ealdormann*
ealdormann	provincial governor
ēam	maternal uncle, a crucial relationship in Germanic society
eorl	(i) early and poetic, a hero (ii) later, an *ealdormann* (ON *jarl*)
fiend	the enemy
folc	the military forces of a region, an army
fyrd, fierd	defensive forces levied by a king
gedriht	band of warriors sworn to stay together
gēogoð	'youths', young warriors
Germania	(i) the territory of the Germanic peoples, north west Europe and southern Scandinavia; (ii) the literary work by the Roman writer Tacitus describing the Germanic tribes of his day (C.1 AD)

giedd	lament, sorrowful song
gift-stool	(OE *giefstōl*) place where the lord sat to distribute rewards to his followers on ritual occasions
grip	central part of a sword's hilt which is held in use
griþ	the king's peace
guard	upper and lower bars between which the grip lies
Heptarchy	the relatively stable arrangement of seven Anglo-Saxon kingdoms during the 7th and early 8th centuries
here	attacking troops, raiding force
heriot	a payment of death dues to the king, taking the form of weapons and armour (OE *heregeatu* 'wargear')
hide	unit of land sufficient for a single family; multiples of this unit were used for tax assessment of larger estates
hilt	part of a sword which covers the tang, forming the handle
jarl	Norse name for an 'earl' or leader
lāf	an heirloom, something of value left by an ancestor
languet	a thin tongue of metal extending from the bottom of a spearhead's socket to provide a more secure fit
lēoð	song, ballad
māððum	an item of value through its association with the past
Óðinn	Norse god of inspiration, magic and death
Olmerdiget	Jutland earthwork, perhaps an early Anglian boundary
ombeht	a royal official
ord	(i) point of a weapon (ii) vanguard of an army
ōretta	challenger, duellist
pommel	upper part of a sword's *hilt* which acts as a counterbalance to the blade
quillons	lower guard between a sword's grip and the blade
ring-giver	(OE *bēahgiefa*) poetic name for the lord as distributor of treasures to his followers
scegð	a light, English warship
scop	poet, travelling verse-maker
seax	single-edged sword
skáld	Norse equivalent of a *scop*
symbel	ritual involving strong drink

tang	thin metal prong to which a sword's *hilt* is attached
Tīw	Anglo-Saxon god associated with victory
Tīwaz	Germanic god, ruler of heaven, lord of battle, also called *Tīw* and *Týr*
tōthyll	a beacon or vantage point
Týr	Norse god associated with victory and the binding of the wolf
ulfheðnir	Scandinavian warrior group who wore ritual wolfskins in battle
weorþ	'honour', good reputation
werod	bodyguard, a lord's personal followers
wōð	(poetic) inspiration
Wōden	Anglo-Saxon god of inspiration, magic and death
Wōðenaz	Germanic god of inspiration, magic and death, also known as *Wōden* and *Óðinn*
þēod	tribe, folk, nation
þēoden	lord of a people, leader
Þórr	Norse god of thunder and protection, also spelt Thor
Þunor	Anglo-Saxon god of thunder and protection, also called *Þórr*
þyle	spokesman, ritual speaker, poet or narrator

I. The Warrior

Bravery belongs to a hero...

(Exeter Book *Gnomic Verses*, line 15)

Ellen sceal on eorle...

1. The Warrior

Figure 1 The main English shieldwall at Hastings from a detail in the Bayeux tapestry. This wall is in 'close order' with the men packed in together, but facing outwards in two directions, each division having its own standard carried by a 'cumbolwiga' behind its 'ordwiga' – the men on the extreme left and right, who will bear the brunt of any attack.

Although the warrior occupied an almost central position in the pre-Christian English social scheme, and was the focus of many of the greatest early artistic endeavours of the people (splendid war-gear, splendid war poetry) his attraction for the modern scholar has been lessened by a climate which is, in the main, unfavourable towards military subjects. It has been acceptable for some time to praise early English Christianity and learning, but not to take due note of the political and military success which made possible the performance and preservation of these other accomplishments. This is an extraordinary double-standard.

As an example of the atmosphere and *milieu* in which the early English warrior lived, one could do no better than to look to the early, heroic verse for what it can tell us of the early English viewpoint on such matters. There is no great amount of such verse surviving, sadly, but there is just enough for us to be aware of the majesty of the native treatment of the *genre* and to regret its loss the more keenly.

The heathen warrior-hero Bēowulf is presented, in the text of the only surviving English poem to deal with his story, as a bold yet moderate figure; a fighter able to wrestle the arm off a monster yet not given to violence towards his fellows even when drunk; a counsellor able to look behind fair words to the foul deeds they mask; a fierce, uncompromising and noble leader whose bad luck it is to fight alongside men who will fail him at the test. It is remarkable that the principal aim of most scholarly work on the poem over the last twenty years has been devoted to showing that virtually every aspect of the poem must have its source in biblical, especially Patristic, literature, even though all these aspects of Beowulf's character as presented in the poem are perfectly consistent with the picture of a (somewhat idealized) Germanic hero; in other words, it seems to me that scholars have decided that a theme so noble and fine as this poem undoubtedly conveys cannot have been the product of the benighted English imagination – it must have been brought in, borrowed from some older, wiser culture. Yet the atmosphere of the poem is so vividly true to what we know of the ancient north, so consistent with the preoccupations of the Germanic warrior mentality, that it seems the only explanation for this modern attitude is a wilful refusal to take a fresh, unbiased look at the text and the culture it represents. This perhaps stems from a tacit supposition that the poem – which few would deny has its roots in pre-Christian times – has been 'transformed' into a substantially new and nobler Christian poem from something older, wilder and grislier. But what evidence is there for this? The Christian references are throughout the poem specifically to the Old Testament and are seldom intrusive, probably because the tribal mindset and *milieu* in the Old Testament is closer to that of Germanic Europe than anything in the New. *Beowulf* is very much a window onto a vanished world (albeit a slightly opaque one), and deserves closer attention in that regard than has been given to it in recent times.

Status of the Warrior

>...Warfare is proper for a nobleman...
>
> (*Maxims* I, line 83)
>
> ... *Gūð sceal in eorle* ...

The belief was once widespread, and perhaps lingers to some extent still, that the Anglo-Saxon army was composed of all the able-bodied men (whether of tribe, shire or nation) of military age (say fourteen upwards) and that when it took to the field, defeat meant disaster – a whole generation cut down or enslaved. This idea is misleading in various different ways, as I hope to show.

First off, then, what was an army and who could be in it? Did the call to arms leave entire kingdoms unprotected? Evidence for this is varied, and much is based on inference, but tends to point to one thing: warrior status was somewhat elevated in social terms, and was open only to certain classes of individual. Moreover, though membership of the 'right' social class was the first requirement for the aspiring warrior, only the fit and able were eligible to undergo military training: the deaf, dumb, blind and crippled, the very short and very weak, those afflicted with disease and those lacking the intellectual and temperamental qualities likely to produce a successful fighter – none of these would warrant the expense and trouble which arming and training entailed. This much seems obvious. Presumably those who were physically strong but otherwise unsuited to military life (e.g. through deafness, poor eyesight, asthma, or plain laziness) could exercise their skills elsewhere as smiths and craftsmen, while the very weak would probably not normally survive childhood.

King Alfred of Wessex, setting out the requirements for a king to govern in the prose translation of Boethius's *de Consolatio Philosophiæ*, says that he needs *gebedmen ๆ fyrdmen ๆ weorcmen* "praying men and fighting men and working men", and this division is an ancient one.[1] The noted French scholar, Georges Dumézil, has proposed a three-way[2] division in all societies of the Indo-European type, based on a set of oppositions: free men versus unfree men, free men being divided into commoners and nobles, nobles divided into warriors and rulers, and rulers further split between priests and kings (i.e. holders of religious and secular authority respectively). This pattern, which dates back to Neolithic times at least and is found across much of Europe, India and the Near East, can be represented thus:

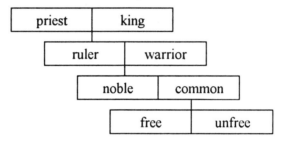

Figure 2 Schematic representation of reconstructed social structure

The warriors in such societies constitute a defined grade in the social hierarchy and are often proud of their status and the enormous resources the society invests in them. The corresponding benefit which makes this worthwhile for both farmers and rulers is that the warrior class acts on behalf of society as a whole, enforcing the will of the rulers on the society and its neighbours through aggression and show of force, while protecting the farmers, their crops and livestock from attack.

Early warfare was mostly about power of various kinds: cattle-raiding is a means of acquiring valuable goods at little expense, similarly slave-raiding and general plundering. Territory is another kind of wealth which may be won through war,

---

[1] Alfred's immediate source is not known, although this idea of a tripartite division of society had some currency in the ancient world. Alfred is usually considered to be the first mediaeval writer to use the concept.

[2] Dumézil himself usually refers to 'functions', by which he means areas of activity within the social system. The system may be summarized as:

First function	Regulation – kings and priests
Second function	Protection – warriors
Third function	Production – farmers, hunters and merchants

though it is harder to keep than it is to acquire.[3] The economic factor which figures in war is usually a state of extreme competition for scarce resources, whether these are of livestock, women, territory or the economic output of a subject population – all resources which can run short in a community, and can cause rivalry between neighbouring folk. Less tangible is the resource of prestige or honour (OE *weorþ*) which can prompt highly competitive groups to enter into a state of war with each other, whereby the victorious warrior stands to gain much prestige from his glorious martial deeds against the enemy – rehearsed before his fellow warriors and his superiors – while sometimes also acquiring a certain amount of economic benefit in the form of booty and the rewards of a grateful leader.

If prestige is a highly-prized commodity, its converse – infamy or ill-fame – is something to be avoided. In this respect, many societies heap praise upon praise on their own warriors while deriding their rivals, belittling their strength, mocking their achievements. This phenomenon occurs in the early English epic poem *Beowulf*, where on his arrival at the court of the Danish king, the hero exchanges words with the king's champion (*ðyle*) Unferth,[4] whose reputation was impugned by the arrival of the youngster, implying (quite correctly) that Unferth was not man enough for the task:

> Unferth spoke, the son of Ecglāf
> who sat at the feet of the Scyldings' lord,
> he unbound a battle-rune – to him was Bēowulf's journey,
> the brave man's sea-trip, a great displeasure
> for he would not allow that any other man
> ever greater fame in middle-earth
> had earnt under the heavens than he himself:
> "Are you the Bēowulf who fought with Breca
> over the broad sea in a swimming contest,
> where you both tested the waves for your pride,
> and in deep water, for foolish boasting
> you risked your lives? ..."

(lines 499–510)

> *Hunferð maþelode, Ecglāfes bearn,*
> *þe æt fōtum sæt frēan Scyldinga,*
> *onband beadurūne – wæs him Bēowulfes sīð,*
> *mōdges merefaran, micel æfþunca*
> *forþon hē ne ūþe þæt ænig ōðer man*
> *æfre mǣrða þon mā middangeardes*
> *gehēdde under heofenum þonne hē sylfa:*

---

[3] Wars of extermination are not unknown from the period, as we shall see, but these are mostly religious-inspired and demonstrate the power of religion and the priesthood as against the more materialistic, temporal power of the king.

[4] Misspelt *Hunferð* in the poem, but clearly alliterating with initial vowels.

> *"Eart þū se Bēowulf sē þe wið Brecan wunne*
> *on sīdne sǣ ymb sundflite*
> *ðǣr git for wlence wada cunnedon*
> *ond for dolgilpe on dēop wæter*
> *aldrum nēþdon? ... "*

Bēowulf was not a man to leave a challenge to his integrity unanswered, however, and replied in similar tones of calculated insult:

> Bēowulf spoke, Ecgþēow's son:
> "Hark! My friend Hunferð, much you
> have spoken about Breca, drunken with beer,
> have said of his journey. Truly I tell
> that I had greater sea-strength,
> might in the waves, than any other man...
> ...About you nothing have I
> heard tell of such deeds of warfare,
> strife of swords; neither you nor Breca yet,
> neither of you in battle-play
> have performed such brave deeds
> with ornamented swords – I do not boast of the match
> – although you were the slayer of your brothers,
> your close kinsmen, for which you shall in hell
> undergo damnation, though your wit is sharp ..."

(lines 529–34 and 581–9)

> *Bēowulf maþelode, bearn Ecgþēowes:*
> *"Hwæt! þū worn fela, wine mīn Hunferð,*
> *bēore druncen ymb Brecan sprǣce,*
> *sǣgdest from his sīde. Sōð ic talige*
> *þæt ic merestrengo māran āhte,*
> *earfeþo on ȳþum, ðonne ǣnig ōþer man...*
> *...Nō ic wiht fram þē*
> *swylcra searonīða secgan hȳrde,*
> *billa brōgan; Breca nǣfre gīt*
> *æt heaðolāce ne gehwæþer incer*
> *swā dēorlīce dǣd gefremede*
> *fāgum sweordum – nō ic þæs geflites gylpe*
> *– þēah ðū þīnum brōðrum tō banan wurde,*
> *hēafodmāgum, þæs þū in helle scealt*
> *werhðo drēogan, þēah þīn wit duge... "*

In both these speeches, the poet's introductory remark names both the speaker and his father. This accent on ancestry is another common feature of societies in which reputation is important – by knowing the man's kin, one knows his background and his social position, his hereditary enemies and allies. This attitude is bound up with the Germanic view of time, whereby the past had a palpable effect in the present and ancient deeds could have repercussions in the here and now. We shall look further at this when we review the *māððum* below. (See page 35)

Military service was confined to the free, and the right to bear arms was the mark of free status. In the Norse poem *Rigsþula*, the god *Rígr* engenders the various grades of mankind – sets up the social system, in fact – one of which is the *jarl* 'earl, leader' whose special accomplishments are with shield, bow, dart, spear and sword in warfare and in hunting. This Scandinavian evidence points quite clearly to warfare as a way of life for the *jarl*, his social role, just as it falls to others to tend to animals and plough the fields, or to produce the tools and artefacts which make both agriculture and warfare possible. The son of Jarl is *Konr Ungr* 'Kon the Young', a hypostasis of *konungr*, 'king'; his remit is wider than mere warriorhood for he learns runes and spells which enable him to overcome his foes, calm storms at sea and understand the speech of birds (who normally warn of impending danger). The emphasis here is on secret knowledge to which only kings are privy, and which enables them to take care of their people.

From the time of King Ine of Wessex at least, warfare in England became increasingly the legal prerogative of kings; that is to say, only a king could undertake a legitimate campaign, and only a king's followers could take part.[5] The motive for this attempt to limit warfare to a certain group was two-fold: first, it made the wide-spread and endemic feuding of families and villages with their neighbours unlawful (and therefore an offence punishable by fines, payable to the king); second, it meant that only those the king selected could hope to profit legitimately from war. That these measures were an attempt to strengthen the royal authority of Ine and his descendants is obvious, since a form of small-scale 'ritual' warfare was inherent in English society.

Warriors of the English Conquest

… to a hero belongs good faith,
wisdom to a man …

(Exeter Book *Gnomic Verses*, lines 32–3)

… trēow sceal on eorle,
wīsdōm on were …

The English people did not come into being in Britain. Their story begins in southern Denmark, and they continued for many generations after their arrival in the 3rd, 4th and 5th centuries AD, to look to the northwest Continent as their homeland, to the lands at the neck of the Jutland peninsula and to the islands of Fyn and Sjæland –

---

[5] However it was illegal for anyone to fight within the king's *grið*, a distance of some three miles around his person. Breach of this custom was punishable by death if the king chose to enforce it.

modern England is effectively 'New England', since that other, older 'England' across the North Sea was our earliest home. The acquisition of land and, ultimately, political mastery of lowland Britain is a much-debated subject into which there is not space to delve here. Nevertheless the image conveyed by such emotive terms, found even in quite sober works, as 'the Anglo-Saxon invaders' or 'raids of the Saxon pirates' and the like, is of marauding bands of bloodthirsty cut-throats roaming aimlessly through the ungoverned and unprotected post-Roman countryside murdering and pillaging at will. Finally tiring of this strenuous life, they are then supposed to settle down to farm, turning their swords into ploughshares and raising broods of warlike sons whose inherent aggression leads them to begin the process anew.

There is, however, no factual basis for such a picture of defenceless Romano-Britons driven like sheep before the English wolves. Probative evidence is found in the rapid and total replacement of British (a Celtic language) by various Germanic tongues in the lowlands, beginning in East Anglia and along the Thames valley and spreading quickly north and west. To effect this transformation, the Anglo-Saxons must have either replaced the pre-existing population entirely (which is possible only in the areas of earliest settlement, where the English immigrant population was densest – but unlikely, given that Roman administrative forms continued in use well into Saxon times) or have quickly gained the upper hand in political, commercial and social life so that British (the ancestor of Welsh, Cornish and Breton) became a low-status language which there was no incentive to use or learn. In any event, the British language, culture and way of life were replaced virtually in their entirety by the Germanic equivalents, a process requiring the movement and re-alignment of whole populations,[6] not just groups of raiders and warbands. To see the English takeover in Britain as a purely military affair confined to the aristocracy and its élite is to underestimate the breadth of vision, tenacity and vigour of the people involved.

The earliest Germanic warbands[7] are presumed to have arrived in these shores – in advance of the later migration – in groups under the command of men who would later

---

[6] The wholesale abandonment of settlements in southern Denmark and northern Germany in the late 400s supports the assumption that the Germanic population of Britain was not solely made up of warrior-adventurers, but also of farmers and craftsmen.

[7] John Haywood proposes that the beginnings of England lie on the eastern seaboard between the estuaries of the Humber and Thames. We may suppose that Germanic seafarers established themselves in good vantage points to control passing shipping, and either exacted a toll or raided the more recalcitrant vessels. In time, the 'pirates' spread along the south coast and began to penetrate inland to the centre of the island, becoming so firmly entrenched that the sub-Roman authorities had no choice but to recognize these emergent states and deal with them as neighbouring polities, much as the Romans had had to do, and the Franks would later have to deal with the Norsemen of Normandy. Despite later English tradition as recorded by Bede, the notion that the English were invited into Britain to deal with the threat posed by the Picts and Irish is not tenable, in view of the fact that the first Germanic bases (e.g. Mucking on the Thames) were sited in areas as far away as possible from those under threat, and furthermore in strategic locations for controlling the waterways of eastern Britain – a tactical mistake the Britons could hardly have failed to foresee. The tradition of 'invitation' may be more realistic in connection with the later leaders, such as Hengest, who make their appearance from the mid 5th century onwards.

be styled by their descendants as 'kings'[8] and accredited with divine ancestry. The remit of these early commanders was to acquire wealth and booty, whether in the service of Rome or of local authorities, with which to reward the bands of young men who followed them in the hope of rich pickings. 'Wealth' in this context could mean either chattels or territory, and the more far-sighted (and long-lived) could evidently see the benefits of taking control of areas of the land they had been brought in to protect. Within a short period of time the whole of the east and southeast of Britain was Germanic-dominated, partly due to English military successes and partly due to the replacement of Latin by Frisian[9] as the language of trade and commerce along the North Sea coasts with the regeneration of market towns in the 600s.

The warbands themselves were not large, probably normally numbering dozens of men and exceptionally a hundred or more; if we trust the poem *The Battle of Finnsburh* the force with Hnæf at the Frisian stronghold was sixty[10] strong. They were well-trained, well equipped and well-motivated; Continental Germanic tribes numbering two or three thousand free men could hardly field armies of more than one tenth of their of number without seriously overburdening the farmers who produced the agricultural surpluses which made warriorhood a viable proposition. Although the testimony of the *Anglo-Saxon Chronicle* for the Germanic invasion is seldom better than retrospective hearsay, the references there to the size of armies are consistently modest:

495. "Here (at this point in the annals) two leaders came to Britain, Cerdic and Cynric his son, with five ships..."

> *Hēr cōmon twēgen ealdormenn on Bretene, Cerdic and Cynric his sunu mid fif scipum...*

501. "Here Port came to Britain, and Bieda and Mægla his two sons, with two ships..."

> *Hēr cōm Port on Bretene, and his twēgen suna Bieda and Mægla, mid twǣm scipum...*

While the historicity of these early accounts is at best questionable, there is nevertheless the underlying assumption that a force of a few ships was a credible military presence, at least for a newcomer in post-Roman Britain. Each ship could transport between forty and sixty men (judging by the evidence of the Sutton Hoo ship burial and later Viking interments) so a maximal five shiploads of sixty men each would enable a warlord to field a force of three hundred men, allowing no margin for non-combatants and ship-guards. (In passing, we may mention that the later resistance

---

[8] For more on the relationship between kingship and kinship, see p. 32 below.

[9] Frisian is a North Sea Germanic language, the closest recorded relative of English and no doubt spoken by many of the earliest newcomers, whose tribal origins were certainly mixed.

[10] See Appendix II. The reference is in line 40, *sixtig sigebeorna*.

to the English in the north east, as recorded in the early Welsh poem *Y Gododdin*, involved a battlefield strength of just three hundred horsemen on the British side.)

Weapon graves in early English pagan cemeteries (which obviously do not paint a complete picture of even contemporary warriorhood) are usually small in number from the early period, but the danger of drawing inferences about weapon distribution within any society from grave-goods is that the swords, shields and spears which ended up in graves had been deliberately selected for that fate, which was not their primary purpose: there may have been religious or cultural reasons for this practice. Obviously, those societies which are in greatest need of weapons for the acquisition of resources are the very ones least likely to have good weapons, due to their relative poverty; they may, however, decide that it is worth their while to transfer proportionately more of their resources into the training of warriors and making of weapons to compensate, though in this case they are the less likely to bury them as grave-goods and so deny their use to others. Moreover, to what extent are the weapon sets found in graves the same as those in use on the battlefield? Does the fact that a man was buried with a spear and shield necessary imply that he did not possess a seax, francisca or sword? Is the burial of a man in an orderly graveyard beside his settlement likely to have been that of a fallen warrior – isn't it more likely that he would be the victim of disease or old age or accident? Are there any certain battlefield graves which might give us a clue to the quantities of war-gear in use? The whole subject is fraught with uncertainties, for which only our only guide is common sense. However, without making any great claims as to the representative nature of the evidence, here are some figures for the distribution of swords as grave-goods in the south-east of England during the pagan period:

Cemetery	Graves/ Grave-groups	Swords	% of total i.e. nº of swords per 100 graves
Kingston, Surrey	308	2	0·6
Bifrons, Kent	150	7	4·6
Holywell Row, Suffolk	100	1	1
Burwell, Suffolk	123	0	0
Springfield Lyons, Essex	103	0	0
Prittlewell, Essex	34	5 (6?)	17·6

Table 1 Distribution of swords in some early cemeteries

Nicholas Brooks quotes an average ratio of swords to spears of 20:1 (i.e. 5%). The Prittlewell cemetery was thus probably an exceptional burial ground,[11] and the high

---

[11] We shall be returning later (p.115) to the Prittlewell warriors.

frequency of sword burials may reflect a strong 'aristocratic' presence in the graves. In England generally the incidence of weapon graves within a cemetery is higher than in the Continental territories, which rather suggests that warriorhood was more important in the new English states than back in the homeland, and that the young, strong and brave were attracted by the possibilities of the 'frontier territory' of Britain. Research has shown that the more splendidly-equipped burials of the early pagan period are quite often of young males – some were adolescents, in our terms, though in turbulent times such as the fifth century a lifespan of twenty or thirty years might be considered normal among the warrior class.

We may note in passing that Tacitus mentions (*Germania*, ch.6) that Germanic tribes traditionally fielded armies of one hundred men from a given region, and that there have been attempts to link this unit of a hundred warriors with the administrative unit of the 'hundred' as a division of a modern shire or county, in the English south east at least. But the evidence for the 'hundred' as a discrete area is virtually non-existent before the tenth century, and can hardly be adduced in connection with Continental practices of a thousand years before.

The English, according to Bede and his sources, were invited into Britain by Vortigern on behalf of the post-Roman authorities here, and fought well on behalf of their employers before the policy change which was to lead to their dominance. The status of the warriors who fought here is disputed – terms such as *læti* and *numeri* for regular troops fighting with their own weapons for Roman paymasters, or *foederati* for men granted land on condition that they perform military duties in exchange, appear in the vast literature of the subject – yet their effectiveness and swift success is not. These men could well represent the military élite which the Anglii[12] had developed in their long history of warfare, and which was poised and well-placed to exploit the opportunity presented by the collapse of even vestigial post-Roman power in Britain and the military vacuum created by successive Roman recruitment campaigns among the Britons. Conditions in fifth century Germania were hostile and uncertain – a state of constant and intense competition was normal between late Iron Age Germanic polities, and *Britannia* may have seemed all the more attractive for what transferring there enabled the English military to leave behind.

King, Warrior and Tribe

> A young nobleman his good followers must
> encourage to battle and to ring-giving…
>
> (Exeter Book *Gnomic Verses*, lines 14–5)
>
> *Geongne æþeling sceolan gōde gesīðas*
> *byldan tō beaduwe and tō bēahgife…*

---

[12] *Anglii* is the earliest recorded form of the folk-name which gave rise to <u>England</u>.

We have the testimony of the Roman historian and writer Tacitus that the Germanic folk chose their kings for good family and their leaders for their good qualities (*reges ex nobilitate duces ex virtute sumunt*) and there has been some blurring of the original distinction in function between the high-born, law-giving king and the middle-class leader chosen to undertake a given project (e.g. mount a raid or a defensive campaign, etc.) on behalf of his people.

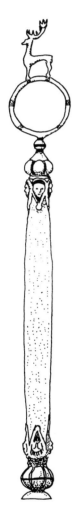

The early social structure of the English in Britain, as reconstructed from the available evidence, centred on the local leader, called variously *cyning, drihten, hlāford, þēoden*. The leader kept a band of men with him – later called variously *heorðgenēatas*, 'hearth-companions' or *heorðwerod* 'hearth-troop' – who were his personal retinue. They may be presumed to have eaten with him, slept in his halls, ridden with him on his travels and shared his fortune, for good or ill. These men were called *gesīþas* 'with-travellers, companions' or *ðegnas* 'serving men, officers, thanes', and it was their duty both to protect and to serve their lord. They acted as bodyguards and a private army, in practice, and in those times as the nearest equivalent to a police force, putting the king's laws into effect and enforcing the king's decisions throughout his domain.

Anglo-Saxon kings were 'chosen' (*gecoren*) not by democratic secret ballot, but by virtue of being accepted as overlord by the leading men of the nation. Naturally, the newer the king, the weaker his position was while he tried to enlist the support of the nobles and his predecessor's favourites; more than once, a disgruntled relative led a rebellion against a king whose position had not been consolidated. In these struggles, the king could count on his own followers only – a group of men with whom he had grown up, supplemented with others who had decided to throw in their lot with him – while the contender mounted his challenge with a similar small troop. The numbers involved in these factions seem to have been very small, perhaps only a few dozen.

The 'band of retainers', the *heorðwerod*, was conventionally split into two factions: the youths and the tried men. Presumably groups of sworn friends would swear to serve the king as they came of age.[13] These men, eager to gain glory and booty, formed the *geoguð* 'youth', supplying the zeal and the greater part of the muscle behind

Figure 3
The ritual whetstone from the Sutton Hoo ship burial, 7ʰ century

---

[13] On the age for military service, see below, p.65.

the army. No doubt it fell to them to carry out the audacious plans, to mount fast, hard-hitting raids, to undertake the most dangerous missions, and to distinguish themselves in the clash of spears, trading blows with the foe. The other faction in the warband was the *duguð*, the 'doughty men', the warriors who had proven themselves in war and had had enough intelligence, skill or luck to avoid death or serious injury. These men were the skilled and experienced core of the king's force, probably of an age with him and forming his closest companions, his *witan* 'wise men, those who have seen' or advisers.

The Danish writer Saxo Grammaticus, writing in the eleventh century, describes the normal deployment of forces, whereby the foremost men (OE *ord* 'point, vanguard') formed a wedge at the front of the army, backed up by the youths armed with throwing spears, while behind them stood the older, more experienced warriors – in a position to give advice and encouragement to the others and to take in the tactical aspects of the fight. We may imagine an arrangement something like Figure 4.

		fierd			
		fierd			f
werod	duguð	geogoð	ord		ī
ðēoden	duguð	geogoð	ord	ord	e
werod	duguð	geogoð	ord		n
		fierd			d
		fierd			

werod – the leader's sworn followers;
ðēoden – leader or king;
duguð – veteran warriors;
geogoð – younger warriors;
ord – front-line men;

fierd– the rest of the forces (often drawn up in similar formations around individual leaders' supporters);
fiend – the enemy.

Figure 4 Schematic arrangement of forces

The king's various titles reflect aspects of his role. He held the national lands, the tribal territory, and had responsibility for its protection and welfare. The title *cyning* ('king') means 'scion of the kindred' – the 'kindred' being one family (*cynn*) which represented and embodied the national spirit, and the luck[14] of the people. As the *cyning*, he was the leading adult male member of that family, though in some kingdoms more than one man could bear the rank simultaneously and it may be that at one time any adult male from that line could claim the title *cyning*. In West Saxon

---

[14] King Sigeberht of East Anglia had renounced the world and withdrawn into the life of a religious recluse when his people were threatened with war; the leading men entreated him to come out of retirement and lead them once more to victory. The king finally relented and, armed with only a staff, took to the field, where he was killed and his army routed. Clearly the East Anglian nobility thought that the luck of the nation resided in the person of the king, and that without his support they were doomed.

sources, these collateral males are called *æðelingas*[15] which is often translated 'princes', although it lacks the suggestion of (comparative) youth the modern word usually implies. It seems that any *æðeling* could raise and maintain his own troop, and that many men of this rank did so and were able to challenge successfully for the throne because of this.

Destruction of the tribe (*ðēod*) and acquisition of its assets was only possible for a rival after first destroying the *cynn* (symbol and rallying point of the *ðēod*) – hence the rather severe treatment of defeated kings in many of the early stories. The king's symbolicrelationship with the tribe gives rise to one of his titles, *ðēoden* (master of the *ðēod*). As the lord of the bands of sworn friends who served and supported him (the *gedriht*), he also had the name *drihten* (master of the *gedriht*). Clearly the latter of these names refers to the *dux* rather than the *rex* proper (the 'leader' rather than the 'king') and relates to both leader and men having sworn to stick together through thick and thin; *gedriht* is based on the verb *drēogan* 'experience, undergo' especially referring to living through hardships. The last term, *hlāford*, the source of our word 'lord', defines a complex social arrangement: the word means 'loaf-keeper' (*hlāf weard*) while the related term 'lady' (*hlāfdīge*) means 'loaf-kneader', exhibiting the dual administrative roles of food-production and food-protection according to sex. There is a connected term *hlāfǣta* 'loaf-eater',[16] meaning 'henchman, dependant, retainer' which likewise shows that the lord's underlings expected him to provide the food which the lady made for their consumption. This model of social relationships must be very old indeed, since by historical times the 'lord' and his 'lady' are no longer the administrative heads of farming communities, but somewhat idealized terms for the nobles of the folk.

Warrior Rituals

> ... in the hall a king must
> hand out rings ...

> (Exeter Book *Gnomic Verses*, lines 28–9)

> ... *cyning sceal on healle*
> *bēagas dǣlan* ...

Ritual, ceremony and traditional behaviour formed an important part of military life in the Anglo-Saxon period; it was one of the bonding agents used to hold together the groups of individuals who constituted the warband. Ritual also lent a sense of timeless permanence to the group – the king gave out gifts on such-and-such a day every year, as his predecessors had before him and his successors would in the future; these events

---

[15] The singular is *æðeling*.

[16] This word became 'beefeater', now confined to the Yeomen of the Guard at the Tower of London, but originally any 'henchman'.

were in a sense 'outside time'[17] in that they were unchanging, identical on every occasion, a link in the here-and-now to a mythic and symbolic prototype. Ritual is always an enactment of myth, whether the myth is consciously acknowledged as such by the society or group enacting it or not.

The Gifts Ritual

The lord kept his band of companions together by sharing his hospitality with them. They in turn constantly reinforced their vows of loyalty, bolstering the king's power and good name. Central to this system of mutual obligation was the notion of the gift. We will be looking later at the role of the sword in gift-giving, but it as well to note here that ritual honouring of supporters by public gifts formed part of the duty of a successful king. The treasures handed out at the ritual oath-taking[18] had strong associations of valour, honour and reputation, more-or-less as medals and titles have had in our culture, except that the objects used to show honour were valuable in themselves: weapons, armour, drinking vessels, horse-furniture, jewellery and land. It is a commonplace of such societies that gift-giving creates a 'debt' between the recipient and the donor – a moral bond which takes the form *gift ~ counter-gift* (= reward); if the recipient of the gift is of higher social status than the donor, the proper reward for the gift is favour; if of lower status, it takes the form of loyalty; where the partners are equals, a return gift is expected. The second-rank warrior receiving a sword from his (higher-rank) lord swears to perform further deeds of courage in his lord's name (loyalty); the lord, receiving war-booty from his warriors, promises them advancement and the opportunity for greater gains (favour); a king wishing to secure an alliance with one of his neighbours uses a rich gift as a means of opening peaceful relations in which gift-exchange, as between friends, can take place. In pre-Christian times this relationship extended even to the gods: the king's offerings to the gods constituted a petition which they could not requite except with favours (the king was not their social equal, after all!).

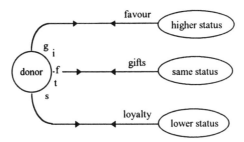

Figure 5 Schematic representation of the social value of gift-giving

---

[17] Ritual is generally said to occupy 'sacred time', which exists alongside normal 'quotidian' time and which can be entered by those taking part. Likewise, the ritual takes place not within the terrestrial geography but in a 'sacred landscape' set apart from the normal three-dimensional world.

[18] For more on the oath-ritual or *symbel*, see p. 36.

Such ritual exchanges are characterized by the *māððum*,[19] a valuable article such as a sword or cup or piece of jewellery, which often has some intrinsic value but greater symbolic value. A sword may be valued as worth a fixed amount of gold; but as a *māððum* its worth may be incalculable – it is the stored up history of the object which gives it its power. Every warrior who has used it, every battle it has been used in, every oath sworn upon its naked edge, every feud it has caused or settled, all these past events have contributed to the tale of the sword, its 'worth' (but not its monetary value, necessarily) and meaning. The idea of a *māððum* is perhaps close to our idea of 'sentimental value' where, for example, a small item of jewellery, a cigarette lighter, a watch, a pen, or some such trifle can take on immense significance as a tangible link with a loved one or a particular event. But whereas our 'sentimental value' is usually deeply and exclusively personal, 'worth' in this sense was public and common to all.

As an example of the rewards a warrior could expect from a generous lord, we have the testimony of *Beowulf* where the Danish king Hrōðgār rewards the victorious hero as follows:

> Then Healfdene's son gave to Bēowulf
> a golden standard as a reward for victory,
> an ornamented banner, a helm and mailcoat;
> many saw a famed ancient sword
> brought before the warrior. Bēowulf received
> a cup on the hall-floor, of that gift of wealth
> he had no cause to be ashamed before the warriors;
> I have never heard of four treasures more nobly,
> decorated with gold, by many men
> being given to another on the ale-bench.
>
> (lines 1020–9)

> *Forgēaf þā Bēowulfe bearn Healfdenes*
> *segen gyldenne sigores tō lēane,*
> *hroden hiltecumbor, helm ond byrnan;*
> *mǣre māðþumsweord manige gesāwon*
> *beforan beorn beran. Bēowulf gebāh*
> *ful on flette, nō hē þǣre feohgyfte*
> *for scēotendum scamigan ðorfte;*
> *ne gefraægn ic frēondlīcor fēower mādmas*
> *golde gegyrede gummanna fela*
> *in ealobence ōðrum gesellan.*

While *Beowulf* is not a historical work, the idea of such rich rewards being given – publicly awarded – to a successful volunteer is entirely consonant with what is

---

[19] Plural *māðmas* or *mādmas*.

recorded elsewhere. Note also that the gifts are specifically called *fēower mādmas* 'four ancient treasures', charged with power and significance.

Figure 6 Two advancing warriors from the detail of a helmet plate from Vendel, Sweden. The warriors wear imposing helmets surmounted by eagle crests, that on the right bearing a striking similarity in its overall design to the example from Sutton Hoo Mound 1. The left-hand figure's helmet is apparently fully enclosed and has a prominent 'beaked' faceplate. Both men have sheathed swords slung on baldrics and broad, lugged spears with carrying straps

The Ale Ritual

The warrior ritual of greatest significance was the *symbel*, which is often translated 'feast'; yet there is no certain evidence that it was what we would call a feast – with eating, drinking, conversation and entertainment – but it seems rather that it was a solemn ritual occasion.[20] No eating took place, but the rite was characterized by three things: strong drink; ritual speech; gifts. At the *symbel*, warriors drank alcoholic drinks,[21] probably from the lord's collection of drinking-horns, goblets or glass beakers. There was then an exchange of words: the warriors individually stood before the lord, who thanked them for their past deeds and handed out the valuable gifts (*mādmas* or *māðmas*) which recognized their high status; they in turn spoke the *bēot*, a kind of boast or promise to perform some feat, such as to slay such-and-such a foe of the people, or less specifically to stand beside their lord and never flinch from his protection, though their lives depended on it. By means of such exchanges the bonds of

---

[20] *Symbel* may be derived, according to Paul Bauschatz, from reflexes of the root *som-* 'together' and *alu* 'ale' – a 'drinking together of alcohol'.

[21] The drinks referred to in later literature were ale, beer, mead, cider and ('for the old and wise') wine. There is some suggestion that beer flavoured with wild rosemary may have been reserved for such ritual occasions, due to the plant's psychedelic effects which would help loosen the tongues of the less eloquent.

friendship, loyalty and inter-dependence were reinforced. Small wonder that those who failed their companions were reviled.[22] One thing the Germanic warrior could not promise, however: success, which was not his to bring to the *symbel*; he could only promise to achieve such-and-such or avenge the slaying of so-and-so *or die in the attempt.*

Having received his due allocation of *māðmas* the warrior expressed his loyalty to his lord with words and gestures, among which may have been the ritual embrace and kiss, and the laying of his head and hands on the lord's knee as mentioned in *The Wanderer*:

> … it seems to him in his mind that his lord
> he clasps and kisses, and on his knee he lays
> hands and head as sometimes before
> in days of old he enjoyed the gift-stool…

(lines 41 – 44)

> *þinceð him on mōde þæt hē his mondryhten*
> *clyppe ond cysse and on cnēo lecge*
> *honda and hēafod swā hē hwīlum ǣr*
> *in geārdagum giefstōles brēac…*

where these rituals are explicitly referred to in connection with the *giefstōl* 'gift-stool', the place the lord sits when distributing treasure. If, as may have been the case judging from other references, the lord had his sword drawn and laid across his knees, the symbolic placing of head and hands beside the weapon might betoken obedience up to and beyond death.

An example of a *symbel* and the following entertainment in *Beowulf* occurs in the hero's report of his reception and reward at the Danish court to his own king:

> "For that fight the Scildings' lord
> rewarded me well with gold plate,
> many old treasures once morning came
> and we had sat at *symbel*.
> Song and mirth were there. The old Scilding,
> knowing many things, told of long ago;
> at times with joy the bold-in-battle
> greeted the harp, the play-wood, at times he made a lament,
> true and touching; at times a wondrous tale
> the great-hearted king told truly;
> at times he began again, bound by great age –
> an aged warrior – to mourn for his youth,
> his war-strength; his heart surged within him
> when he, old in years, remembered much.

---

[22] For more on the exiled warrior, see p.85.

So in that place for a whole day we
took our pleasure, until a second night came
to men..."

(lines 2101–17)

"Mē þone wælrǣs wine Scildunga
fǣttan golde fela lēanode
manegum māðmum syððan mergen cōm
ond wē tō symble geseten hæfdon
Þǣr wæs gidd ond glēo. Gomela Scilding,
fela fricgende, feorran rehte;
hwīlum hildedēor hearpan wynne
gomenwudu grētte, hwīlum gyd āwræc
sōð ond sārlīc; hwīlum syllīc spell
rehte æfter rihte rūmheort cyning;
hwīlum eft ongan eldo gebunden,
gomel gūðwiga gioguðe cwīðan,
hildestrengo; hreðer inne wēoll
þonne hē wintrum frōd worn gemunde.
Swā wē þǣr inne ondlangne dæg
nīode nāman, oð ðæt niht becwōm
ōðer tō yldum... ".

Here it is clear that the *symbel* has taken place the night before, and that the gift ceremony takes place the following morning, perhaps before the entire company in the hall; only then does the entertainment begin: songs are sung, harps are played, tales are told, old memories revived.

Nevertheless, particularly in the matter of old memories, the ale ritual could be something of a gamble since the feelings of friendship and cohesion it was meant to foster could be subverted by lingering jealousies and resentment. The *Beowulf* poet clearly understood the dangers involved, when he told of a wedding bridal meant to celebrate a political marriage to seal an alliance between former foes:

Then he who sees a ring speaks over the beer,
an old spear-fighter who remembers the whole
spear-death of the warriors – his mind is grim –
against a young warrior, in sorrowful mood he begins
to test the courage through the feelings of his heart,
to waken deadly hatred, and he speaks those words:
"My friend, are you able to recognize the sword
which your father bore to battle
wearing his helmet for the last time,
– a precious weapon – where the Danes slew him,
they ruled the battlefield when Wiðergyld lay dead,

38

after the heroes' fall, those brave Scyldings?
Now here a son of one of the killers
proud in his war-gear walks the hall's floor,
boasts of the killing and bears that very *māððum*
which by rights you should possess."

(lines 2041–56)

Þonne cwið æt bēore se ðe bēah gesyhð,
eald æscwīga se ðe eall geman
gārcwealm gumena – him bið grim sefa
– onginneð geōmor mōd geongum cempan
þurh hreðra gehygd higes cunnian
wīgbealu weccean ond þæt word ācwyð:
"Meaht ðū mīn wine mēce gecnāwan
þone þīn fæder tō gefeohte bær
under heregrīman hindeman sīðe,
dȳre īren, þær hyne Dene slōgon,
wēoldon wælstōwe syððan Wiðergyld læg
æfter hæleþa hryre, hwate Scyldungas?
Nū hēr þāra banena byre nāthwylces
frætwum hrēmig on flet gæð
morðres gylpeð ond þone māðþum byreð
þone þū mid rihte rædan sceoldest."

The references to ancestors and ancient family possessions – the buzz-words *cynn* and *māþþum* – being flaunted by the murderer's kin would be enough to kindle the vengeance of an ambitious youngster who had had too much to drink.

Ritual Warfare – Challenging and Duelling

We have already seen that reputation was everything to the early warrior, and that anyone who impugned his name could expect harsh treatment: either a counter-insult, or even a challenge to fight. Such single-combat was a form of 'ritual warfare' in that it was governed by very strict rules, the breaking of which meant loss of honour. Some early Germanic groups used to use this form of ritual fighting to test their war-luck before entering into battle, by capturing one of the enemy and forcing him to fight one of their own men; Tacitus says (*Germania*, Ch.10) that the outcome of the duel could be used to settle the differences between whole nations, implicitly therefore without further loss of life.[23] Yet an army who found that its luck was out, that the gods were favouring the other side, would still have to choose whether to fight or buy peace with tribute.

---

[23] Procopius mentions a similar idea among the Goths, one of whom challenged a Roman army to send out a man of theirs against him; Paul the Deacon likewise records a situation where the Langobards were prevented from passing through the territory of the Assipitti, and the two sides each sent a representative warrior to settle the issue.

This tradition of settling scores by single-combat has a long history among the English. Indeed, the earliest English king of whom we have more than just a name is *Offa*, who is presumed to have lived in Angeln, southern Jutland, in the 400s AD some generations before the English transferred to *Britannia*. Part of his story concerns his slothful youth and the despair of his aged, blind father *Wærmund* at his heir's lack of spirit. When a neighbouring Swabian tribe detect that the king is too old to fight and his son too slack, they issue a challenge whereby the king must either find a champion to face them in single combat or surrender his throne. Wærmund intends to meet the challenge himself; the Swabian king refuses to fight an old, blind man but will consent to settling the affair with his son, fully expecting that Offa will run from the match. However, in contrast to his previous behaviour, the young prince agrees to the contest which is to take place on an island in the river Eider. On the appointed day, Offa goes to the eyot where he finds he must face both the Swabian prince and a chosen champion; nothing daunted, he engages both in combat and slays the pair single-handed. This legend survived in lower Jutland into mediaeval times at least, but we can be sure that it was brought to England with the incoming Anglian settlers as it is alluded to in a very early poem called *Wīdsīþ* (written down about 1000 AD but betraying its early date through its language and verse forms):

> Offa ruled the Angles, Alewih the Danes,
> who was the bravest of all those men
> yet he did not outdo Offa in heroism
> but Offa, foremost of men, won by warfare
> the greatest of kingdoms, being still a youth,
> none of equal age [did] greater deeds of courage
> in battle with his single sword
> he set out the boundary against the Myrgings
> by Fīfeldor, ever thereafter [they] held [it]
> the Angles and the Swabians, as Offa struck it.
>
> (lines 35–44)

> *Offa wēold Ongle, Alewih Denum:*
> *se wæs þāra manna modgast ealra*
> *nohwæþre hē ofer Offan eorlscype fremede,*
> *ac Offa geslōg ǣrest monna*
> *cnihtwesende cynerīca mǣst,*
> *nǣnig efeneald him eorlscipe māran*
> *on ōrette āne sweorde*
> *merce gemǣrde wið Myrgingum*
> *bi Fīfeldore,[24] hēoldon forð siþþan*
> *Engle ⁊ Swǣfe swā hit Offa geslōg*

---

[24] Fīfeldor is a river name made up from *fīfel* 'terrible monster' and *duru* 'door'; the name of the Eider is believed to be derived from *ege duru* 'terror-door' and the identification of the two seems secure.

Here we see the archetypal Germanic hero, prepared to fight for his folk and even to face unfair odds for the sake of his personal honour, and that of his kin and his people. Overwhelming odds seem to play an important role in traditional Germanic military literature, and the theme recurs in the Old English poem *Waldere* where the hero, pursued by foes, has positioned himself in a narrow gully between two cliffs so that his enemies must come at him in single file, one by one – much in the manner of duelling. The poem describes his lover's words of encouragement to the struggling hero thus:

> I shall not speak words of blame to you, my love,
> that at the sword-play I saw you,
> give way through lack of courage to any man's
> attack or flee to the wall
> to protect [your] life, though many foes
> were hewing at your mailcoat with swords
> but you always sought to fight,
> [your] sword across the boundary – hence I dreaded the outcome for you
> – but you vigorously sought to fight
> in the position of [the]other man
> in the way of warfare. Do honour to yourself
> with valiant deeds, while God takes care of you!
>
> (I, lines 12–23)

> *Nalles ic ðē, wine mīn, wordum cīde*
> *ðȳ ic ðē gesāwe æt ðām sweordplegan*
> *ðurh edwitscype ǣniges monnes*
> *wīg forbūgan oððe on weal flēon*
> *līce beorgan, ðēah þē lāðra fela*
> *ðīnne byrnhomon billum hēowun*
> *ac ðū symle feohtan sōhtest*
> *mǣl ofer mearce, ðȳ ic ðē metod ondrēd*
> *þ ðū tō fyrenlīce feohtan sōhtest*
> *æt ðǣm ætstealle ōðres mōnnes*
> *wīgrǣdenne. Weorða ðē selfne*
> *gōdum dǣdum ðenden ðīn god recce.*

Hilda Ellis Davidson has taken the phrases used here to describe the method of fighting in terms of single-combat, and the puzzling phrase *mǣl ofer mearce* 'sword over boundary' to refer to the striking across the formal boundary line between opponents in a duel, behind which they must stand to deliver blows, while the *ætsteall* 'counter-position, standing-place' is the 'marked' location of the opposing duellist, the territory on his side of the line. (In the shieldwall, the immediate neighbours may have been those called *eaxlgestellan* "shoulder-placed (men)", implying that *eaxl[ge]steall* was the position to either side of a man, and *ætsteall* the opponent's position in front of him.)

41

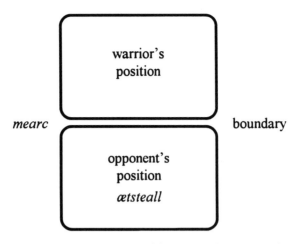

mearc   boundary

Figure 7 Schematic representation of the 'wīgrǣden' (way of warfare)

She also suggests that the unique word *wīgrǣden* should be considered to mean 'battleground' or even 'customs of duelling', which is a possible reading, although I have used the more general 'way of warfare' since her narrower translation suggesting regulated conduct does rather imply something artificial, imposed by human behaviour and mental attitudes on the events, whereas this meaning is not entirely supported by the text.[25] In any event, his lover's speech is meant to indicate that Waldere has not hung back from fighting but has rather been a little too bold in his attacks and exposed himself to danger unnecessarily.

In the Old High German poem *Hildebrandslied* a duel is fought between two warriors who begin by hurling spears from horseback, then dismount and advance against each other with drawn swords for the serious combat. There is little evidence of duelling in this manner outside this one poem, however, and it may reflect a peculiarly East Germanic (Gothic and Langobardic) development in which the increased importance of the horse to their normal military operations has spilt over into their method of single-combat.

A warrior who habitually issued challenges was called in Old English an *ōretta*, a word based on the elements *ōr-* 'out' and *hāta* 'one who calls', i.e. a man who calls to another to come outside and face him. The hero Bēowulf going to fight the dragon in its lair is so described:

> Then by his shield rose the valiant *ōretta*
> hard beneath his helmet, his mailshirt he bore
> under the rocky cliff, he trusted to the strength
> of a single man ...

> (lines 2538–41)

---

[25] The 'dictionary' meanings of *rǣden* include 'conditions, rules' which supports the reading 'rules of combat', but other uses of the word in compounds suggest something vaguer, more arbitrary than a set of rules, as for example *woruldrǣden* 'way of the world, how things turn out usually'.

Ārās ðā bī ronde rōf ōretta
heard under helme hiorosercean bǣr
under stāncleofu, strengo getrūwode
ānes mannes ...

For lesser mortals, the duel was essentially a single-combat fought between two opponents, each armed with sword and shield (although axes are also referred to in some Icelandic accounts). In Icelandic tradition this was known as *hólmganga* 'going to an island', which agrees with the evidence of the story of Offa above, and refers to the normal ritual site of such a contest away from interference or assistance by other parties. One Icelandic saga amplifies this by suggesting that *hólmganga* was limited by specific rules, as opposed to *einvígi* 'single-combat' where any weapon and tactic might be used, a less rigid format which was used to settle disputes informally. Nevertheless from the literature it seems that fair play and an exchange of strokes,[26] turn and turn about, was the order of the day even in *einvígi*.

A man could refuse to fight if challenged, but risked public ridicule and loss of credibility if he did so. In Iceland, such a man could have been the object of much moral opprobrium and his neighbours might raise a 'scorn-pole' against him, a device which publicly declared him outside the community, to be scorned and shunned by men and land-spirits alike. Once begun, the duel could not be stopped until either one man was dead, or so wounded that he could not hope to continue, or until the challenger declared himself satisfied and willing to make peace. It was the challenger's right to choose the spot for the duel, while the 'defendant' had the right to the first blow; the fighting could pause while the opponents refreshed themselves, or while they had new shields (to a maximum of three) and weapons brought to them. The fighting consisted of alternate strokes by each man, which the other could deflect or stop with his shield or sword. Later Norse evidence from the sagas shows the combat taking place on a mat (a substitute area of marked ground) that has been pegged down at its corners with hazel wands, so that if either man put a foot off the mat it counted as a fault, and if he put both feet off he was deemed to have given up.

Occasionally, whole groups of men were involved: Ólaf Tryggvason is reported to have taken part in such a contest as one of twelve warriors, and there are other, partly legendary stories of such competitions. Duelling to settle scores between individuals continued into modern times, though as a legal means of testing the validity of one's case it was already on the wane by the year 1000 even among the Icelanders. It was a form of 'trial by combat' and consequently open to all kinds of abuse, once the original religious idea of letting *wyrd* and the gods decide the matter had been abandoned under Christian influence.

The warrior's principal attributes were physical strength (OE *strengo*) and courage (OE *ellen*) and another quality, called *mægen* in the texts and perhaps best translated

---

[26] Terry Brown has suggested that the tit-for-tat exchange of blows is not due to any notion of 'fair play' but rather the knowledge that a warrior is at his most vulnerable when he has just delivered a blow, being partly off-balance and less well protected by weapon and shield.

'power' or 'latent ability'. The word is related to the verb *magan* 'be able to (do something), have the power to (do something)' and refers to potential for any kind of action or achievement. The warrior in combat summons his reserves of *mægen* and uses them to bring about his wish or intent. The concept of *mægen* is perhaps closest to the Roman idea of *augur* – a quality with which certain men could be imbued, usually temporarily, to bring success. Bēowulf has the quality in abundance, as well as strength and courage, until it finally runs out in his fight against the firedrake, when strength and courage alone are not enough.

Sword Rituals – The Oath and the Ring

As the warrior's most valued and most trusted weapon, the sword carried an unparalleled weight of symbolism in early Germanic culture. So much so, that warriors were occasionally obliged to swear mighty oaths on their swords, the implication being that if the oath should be broken then the weapon would fail the user at need, even turn against him. One such promise may have been the wedding vow, suggests Hilda Ellis Davidson, given that there is a memory in early German literature[27] of the tradition whereby the bride was handed her wedding ring on the hilt of her new husband's sword. Far from being an intimidating message of "stay true to your promise or it's the sword for you!", the real meaning seems to have been that the man staked his sword – symbol of his freedom and warrior reputation – on his loyalty to his word in this matter. The co-occurrence of sword-hilt, ring and oath is significant since the ring-hilted sword has elsewhere been linked to the practice of ritual oath-swearing, whereby the warrior laid his hand on the hilt of his lord's sword while swearing his loyalty.[28] Interestingly, the sword in the German wedding ritual had first to be rubbed against what is called in the Latin of the poem a *piramid* which may have been an earthen mound with kinship links – a family burial place, for example. A hereditary, family sword was customarily removed from the family grave-mound[29] to be offered to a new-born son who was to take the dead man's name and, in time, inherit his estates and 'luck'. These instances of the passing on of a family sword are mostly connected with the mother's line, and Tacitus's *Germania* refers to the fact that Germanic women were accustomed to receive arms from their husbands as a dowry, which they were expected to pass on to their children.

The wedding ritual described above has a possible parallel in the Frisian tradition whereby the husband's sword is used to block the bride's entrance through her new house's doorway – the weapon so used is then known as the *æftswird* 'wedding-sword' – while a variant custom has it carried, drawn from its sheath, in front of the bride to her new home. Here the symbolism is probably phallic, with no suggestion of implied

---

[27] The poem in Latin called *Ruodlieb* written by a German monk in 1023, according to Meyer, cited in Ellis Davidson's *The Sword at the Wedding*.

[28] See p.37 for more on the oath of loyalty.

[29] Ellis Davidson suggests that it may have been this desire on the part of descendants for ancient and 'magical' weapons which caused the disturbance of so many grave-mounds, rather than conventional tomb-robbers after plunder.

threat. In Sweden, at rural weddings the bridegroom would thrust his sword into the roof-beam, and the depth of the cut was an omen for the success of the marriage. One Norse saga (*Volsunga saga*) records an echo of this tradition, where at the marriage of King Volsung's daughter, the menacing figure of Óðinn appeared and stuck a sword up to the hilt into the stock of the tree which held up the king's hall, challenging any man there to draw it forth, then left. The bridegroom, King Siggeir, was unable to pull it out even though he coveted the weapon greatly, and was furious when Sigmund, the bride's brother, drew it forth with ease. Sigmund refused to sell or give the sword to Siggeir who eventually engineered the fall of Volsung's kindred over this incident (but, true to the conventions of heroic story, Sigmund escaped this fate). The parallel to the Arthurian tradition of 'the sword in the stone' is clear, but the association here is rather with kinship than with kingship: the tree supporting the hall (in Norse *barnstokkr* 'child-stock') is probably to be related to the inherent luck and well-being of the kindred inhabiting the building, which had been built round the tree. The sword, then, was an emblem of the continuing family and its prosperity; add to this the wedding associations and the inescapable conclusion seems to be that the sword stands for a new generation of healthy sons – hence the bridegroom's anger at his inability to acquire the weapon. Swords were certainly handed on within families for generation after generation – Æþelstān, brother of King Alfred gave away in his will a sword which had once belonged to King Offa of Mercia some two centuries before. The gift

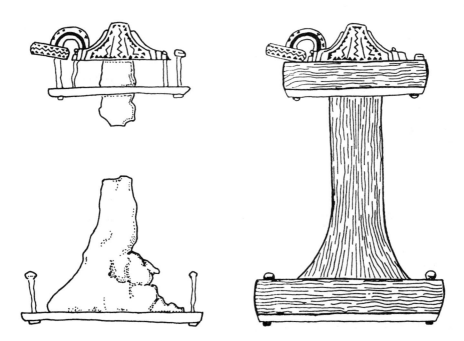

Figure 8 Ring-hilt from Bifrons, Kent as excavated (left) and with the perished wooden components restored (right).

of the sword was seemingly accompanied by a gift of land, marking the recipient young man's entry into adult society at the end of his period of teenage excess in the service of the king.[30] The inherited sword was associated with the 'luck' of the family, which was sometimes personified as a supernatural female being, called in Old Norse *fylgjukona* 'following-woman', whose favour and protection was passed on from generation to generation, with the family sword, as inherited possession (OE *lāf*). These supernatural women may be similar (or perhaps originally identical) to the *valkyrjar* 'valkyries' who distribute weapons to chosen heroes, along with Óðinn's favours. The heroes are said to enter into an ambivalent relationship with such women: partly filial, partly erotic, they become at once 'fostermothers' and sometimes bear the heroes' children. The women may appear as young and beautiful maidens, though they are evidently 'troll-wives' who can change their aspect at will. We have noted above that the passing on of weapons was the mother's responsibility in particular, parallel perhaps to the weapons a warrior could expect to receive from his lord: here we see a contrast between the protective, kindred set of arms and the offensive, Odinic one. It seems that the father's weapons, in turn, were often entrusted to the daughter so that she could pass them on to her children. In this way, the sword 'rested' between generations while in the safe-keeping of the woman, awaiting the maturity of the next generation's menfolk. It was thus fitting that, as a guardian of swords, the woman's marriage vow should be made before a drawn sword as a reminder of her family role.

Nevertheless, the warrior's oath was not invariably the sacrosanct expression of his honour that we might expect. We have the evidence of the viking *here* in the ASC for the year 867 who agreed to swear solemn oaths on their hallowed ring to leave King Alfred's kingdom, and handed over hostages from among their chief men as guarantors. Nevertheless, the *here* used the opportunity afforded by the oath-swearing to slip away from the English *fyrd* and occupy Exeter. It seems that this duplicitous element was not uncommon: the Norse myths show that the archetypal god of justice, *Týr*, swore a false oath. The story goes that the gods knew that the wolf *Fenrir* would be a threat to heaven and earth in years to come, but they did not wish to kill the beast outright; they hit upon the plan of binding it and after their various attempts to find a fetter strong enough had failed, they resorted to a magic chain made from invisible things (e.g. a woman's beard, a mountain's roots, etc.). Naturally, the wolf would not let the bindings anywhere near himself without some token of the gods' good faith, whereupon *Týr* put his hand in the wolf's mouth as a pledge; the collar held and the wolf was bound, but *Týr* lost his hand between its jaws. Evidently, with this model – and it is one of Indo-European antiquity with parallels in Roman and Celtic mythology – there was a clear precedent that a man could knowingly swear a false oath if the greater good of his community depended upon it. The vikings who swore great oaths to Alfred left their chiefs as hostages to the mercy of the English, but the chiefs themselves must have willingly offered their own honour and lives in order to safeguard the escape of their men.

---

[30] See p.113 for more on the 'family' sword.

Beasts of Battle, Gods of War

> ...the wolf belongs in the thicket,
> the sad lone-dweller, the boar belongs in the wood,
> firm in the strength of its tusks...
>
> (Exeter Book *Gnomic Verses*, lines 18–20)

> ... *wulf sceal on bearowe*
> *earm ānhaga, eofor sceal on holte*
> *tōðmægenes trum...*

Germanic poetic descriptions of battle and the artistic motifs on their leaders' equipment, consistently feature certain animals which must have epitomized the qualities of ferocity and cunning necessary for the warrior. These 'beasts of battle' are the wolf, the bear, the boar and the raven. Both wolf and bear held a special fascination for these early societies, and gave rise to special, exclusive clans of warriors.[31]

The raven was especially associated with the cult of the god *Wōdenaz*, whose Norse guise was *Óðinn* (Odin) and in England *Wōden*. The Norse tradition has it that Óðinn's two ravens flew forth each morning around the world, and reported to their lord what deeds were afoot among men at lunch-time. This, and other birds of prey, was regarded as a swift and deadly predator – a fitting symbol for men who practised fast raids against a foe who was unprepared for them.

Falconry (hunting with birds of prey who have been tamed) was introduced into northern Europe sometime in the Migration Age, before the fifth century AD. Gale Owen-Crocker has suggested that the sudden popularity of the bird-of-prey motif in Germanic art – as for example on the purse-lid from Sutton Hoo Mound I – may have been triggered by the introduction of the practice, although there are other possible explanations for this. Hunting with trained birds was an expensive business involving a considerable investment in time and patience, which made it attractive to the wealthy Germanic élite of England, Scandinavia and Continental Europe with the leisure to pursue it; the motif may therefore have been no more than a status badge for the upper echelons. The sport was popular with kings and nobles who retained special bird-trainers (OE *fuglere* 'fowler') for that purpose. The prey included ducks and waterfowl (it seems to be a duck that has been captured on the Sutton Hoo purse-lid) and especially cranes.

Trained birds were valuable enough to be used as diplomatic gifts. King Alfred of Wessex delighted in all forms of hunting, and had a staff of falconers, hawk-handlers and dog-handlers (the dogs to act as retrievers, presumably); even the ascetic and otherworldly Edward the Confessor did not stint himself this one form of pleasure and kept trained birds and hounds. The late Anglo-Saxon period homilists, Ælfric and Wulfstān, both denounced the sport when practised by clergymen, although this may

---

[31] See p.71 for more on the early wolf-brotherhoods, often known by their German name *Männerbund*.

have been part of their stock disagreement with worldly pleasures in general. The Bayeux tapestry shows Earl (later King) Harold mounted, with his hounds running in front of his horse and a bird of prey held aloft on his left wrist. Hunting was thus a popular royal and aristocratic pastime which allowed the exponents to get a lot of exercise and to sharpen those skills which they would have to use in battle: marksmanship, quick reactions, physical stamina, handling of weapons, pursuit of a quarry, defence against dangerous attack, planning and teamwork. The poet of *The Battle of Maldon* gives a vignette of a noble young warrior going to war:

> Then Offa's kinsman first found that out:
> that the earl would not endure faintheartedness;
> he then let his dear one fly from his hands –
> his hawk – to the wood, and strode to the battle;
> by means of that one could tell that the youth would not
> weaken in the fight when he took to his weapons.
>
> (lines 5–10)

> *Þā þæt Offan mæg ærest onfunde*
> *þæt se eorl nolde yrhðo geþolian*
> *hē lēt him þā of handon lēofne flēogan*
> *hafoc wið þæs holtes and tō þǣre hilde stōp;*
> *be þām man mihte oncnāwan þæt se cniht nolde*
> *wācian æt þām wīgge þā hē tō wǣpnum fēng.*

The young man evidently realized that the time for leisurely pleasures was past and that he should now put aside his pastimes and set his mind to fighting. Nevertheless, the bird was *lēof* 'dear' to him, not a mere plaything – hence his decision to release it. There are parallels to this scene – warriors taking their trained birds to the battlefield – in many Continental accounts, although this does not mean that the *Maldon* poet merely borrowed the idea.

Elsewhere in *The Battle of Maldon* the poet combines bird motifs for effect:

> A shout went up there, ravens circled,
> the eagle eager for carrion...
>
> (lines 106–7)

> *Þǣr wearð hrēam āhafen, hremmas wundon*
> *earn ǣses georn...*

That other frequenter of battlefields, the wolf, was of importance to the English warrior. Wolves had strongly negative connotations as fierce predators who would strike those least able to defend themselves; these associations could be turned to advantage by warriors wishing to set themselves off from the rest of society, using the normal human fear of the wolf to inspire fear of themselves. Notwithstanding this, many Englishmen had names with *wulf* 'wolf' as the second element, e.g. *Æþelwulf* king of Wessex.

The wolf seems to have been connected with *Wōðenaz* as much as the raven, particularly due to its strong link to violent death. 'Wolf-warriors' played a special part in northern ritual and mythology. Yet, while these two 'beasts of battle' are associated with Wōðenaz as god of death, he is equally strongly linked to the horse. In Norse tradition his mount *Sleipnir* 'slippery one' is an eight-legged horse which can convey him anywhere in the nine worlds he wishes to go, and he is depicted riding it on 8th century standing stones from Gotland. It may even be that the 'horse-and-rider' motif which turns up regularly in early Germanic art – on Danish bracteates and even the Sutton Hoo helmet – is actually a representation of the war god. He has passed into folklore, in connection with his steed and followers, as the leader of the Wild Hunt,[32] that nightly concourse of the souls of the dead across the sky. Rationalist modern explanations of the Wild Hunt dismiss it as the ferocious winter storm or the noise made by the passage of migrating geese, yet there is a strong case for accepting O. Hofler's[33] suggestion that the early accounts, which are often quite explicit about the nature of the phenomenon, refer actually to bands of warriors who formed cult groups for the worship of the god with nocturnal rituals and frenzied activity afterwards, giving rise to the reputation of one tribe, the *Harii*,[34] for unstoppable night attacks in which the men, their equipment, clothes and armour were all painted black so that their enemies were entirely unnerved by the sight of them. It may have been such a warrior band that was seen in England in 1127, according to the Laud Manuscript of the *Anglo-Saxon Chronicle* in a much-cited passage:

> Let no man think it strange which we truly tell, since it was well known through all the land that as soon as he [Abbot Henry] came there – that was the Sunday when one sings "Exurge quare O.D." – then soon thereafter many men saw and heard many hunters hunting. The hunters were black and large and ugly, and their hounds all black and big-eyed and ugly and they rode on black horses and on black goats. This was seen on the deer-park itself in the estate at Peterborough and in all the woods which extended from that same estate to Stamford, and the monks heard the horns blowing which they blew at night. Truthful men [who] kept watch at night said this: that it seemed to them that there might well be around twenty or thirty horn-blowers. This was seen and heard from the time he came there all through Lent, on up to Easter. This was his arrival; of his departure we cannot yet speak. May God provide!

> *Ne þince man nā sellice þ wē sōð seggen for hit wæs ful cūð ofer eall land þ swā rādlīce swā hē þær cōm þ wæs þes Sunendæies þ man singað "Exurge quare O.D." þā sōn þær æfter þā sægon ⁊ hērdon fela men feole huntes hunten. Ðā huntes wæron swarte ⁊ micele ⁊ lādlice ⁊ here hundes ealle swarte ⁊ brādēgede ⁊ lādlice ⁊ hī ridone on swarte hors ⁊ on swarte bucces. Þis wæs segon on þe selue*

---

[32] The identity of the leader of the Hunt is often changed to some figure from local legend: even Sir Walter Raleigh has been so dignified.

[33] Cited in Simek, R. *Dictionary of Northern Mythology*.

[34] Their name, if the same as the Germanic root of OE *here*, means 'raiders'.

derfald in þā tūne on Burch ⁊ on ealle þā wudes ðā wǣron fram þā selua tūne tō
Stānforde ⁊ þā muneces hērdon ðā horn blāwen þ hi blēwen on nihtes.
Sōðfæstemen heom kēpten on nihtes sǣiden þes þe heom þūhte þ þǣr mihte
wel bēn ābūton twenti oðer þritti horn blāweres. Þis wæs sægen ⁊ hērd fram þ
hē þider cōm eall þ lented tīd on an tō ēastron. Þis was his ingang; of his
ūtgang ne cunne wē iett nōht seggon. God scāwe fore.

The horse- and goat-riding huntsmen here are clearly practising some nightly activity designed to frighten and disquiet the local populace, aimed it seems against an unpopular Norman cleric. While the circumstances of their objection are possibly of no great significance, the form that their display of opposition took has strong overtones of Wōden-worship and the terrifying spectacle of the nocturnal attacks of the *Harii*.

The boar has a long history as a totem of procreation and masculinity, and is the special emblem of the Norse *Freyr*, whose name means 'lord' and whose memory may have survived into Christian times in the various references to 'our Lord' as *frēa* in Old English. Procreation and protection are definite 'third function' activities,[35] for which the boar is not an inappropriate symbol, and the use of boar figures is attested in various ways in the north. An early Anglian helmet from Benty Grange, Derbyshire, is surmounted by a small, gilded boar-figure which originally had tufts of hair clasped between the two parts of the casting to give the effect of the animal's bristling mane, and a helmet surmounted by a boar is depicted on the Gundestrup Cauldron, a large vessel of probably Thracian workmanship which ended up as a votive deposit in a Danish bog. In *Beowulf* such helmets are mentioned in connection with a group of splendidly-equipped warriors :

> ...Boar figures shone
> above cheek-protectors, adorned with gold,
> colourful and fire-hardened, [each] watched over life
> for the battle-brave man.
>
> (lines 303–6)

> ....*Eoforlīc scionon*
> *ofer hlēorbergan gehroden golde,*
> *fāh ond fȳrheard, ferhwearde hēold*
> *gūþmōdgum men.*

It seems from this reference in *Beowulf* that the boar emblem was supposed to keep watch over the warrior's welfare and to protect him – just what one would expect from the gods of wealth and well-being. (Because of the boar's duty to keep watch over the helmet's wearer, an initial blow to the boar figure to shear it away would leave the warrior unprotected by his 'spiritual helper' and so more vulnerable. A blow to the top or side of the helmet might well weaken the seams and weld-lines.) Freyr's own weapon was a sword of such virtue that it could fight of its own accord.

---

[35] See above, p.23, for the 'three functions' of early society.

The Germanic god whose remit included warfare as an extension of his role as sovereign ruler is believed to have been called *Tiwaz* (Old Norse *Týr*, Old English *Tiw*) although references to him and his myths do not form a coherent or easily comprehensible whole, even in the heavily rationalized Norse mythological scheme. There is a story about him binding the great wolf, and at the final battle he kills and is killed by Garm, the Hell Hound, who may be the wolf Fenrir by another name – Fenrir is said to swallow Óðinn and be torn apart by one of Óðinn's sons, a reworking of the same theme of two foes who can neither best one another nor be outfought, and who thus bring about each others' deaths. Óðinn has the great spear, *Gungnir* 'the waving (shimmering?) one', as his principal weapon with which he stirs up trouble in the world, while the rune which bears the name *Tȳ* or *Tir* is shaped like a spear (↑). Nevertheless, a Norse source suggests that to charm a sword *Týr* should be named on it twice – by marking with this rune – and one hilt which bears this very mark is known from an Anglo-Saxon context, that from Sarre, Kent, grave 91.

The Norse god *Þórr* (Thor) whom the early English called *Þunor* was the god of the rank and file warriors rather than their noble leaders, who worshipped Óðinn in the main. Þórr was the champion of mankind, a hard-fighting, but none-too-bright adversary for all the forces which threatened to destroy man's precarious existence – storm giants, ice giants, and the terrible serpent which dwelt beneath the seas. His habitual weapon was the hammer, *Mjolnir* 'crusher', which sums up his approach to warfare – the proverbial 'blunt instrument'. Yet his sacred animal was hardly an emblem of speed, stealth, cunning or pure, vicious power – the sign of the goat was unlikely to strike terror into the hearts of hardened vikings and berserks! It must, rather, show his association with food production, procreation and agricultural life generally – his supporters were farmers and smallholders in the main. Indeed, *Mjollnir* and *Gungnir* are the archetypal 'irresistible weapons' of mythology, with which the god cannot fail to overcome his foes, and the hammer has been seen as representing the summer lightning which is believed to be necessary for the ripening of crops in many farming communities. In Iceland, the symbol ⅍ which represents the sun is known as 'Thor's Hammer'.

The table below summarizes the chief attributes of the northern gods with regard to the themes discussed above:

social activity	god	weapon	emblematic animal	adversarial animal
1st function	Tiw	? spear, ? sword	? horse	wolf, dog
2nd function	Wōden	spear	wolf, raven	wolf
	Þunor	hammer	goat	serpent
3rd function	Frēa	sword	boar	–

Table 2 Main attributes of the northern gods

To what extent the early English were familiar with the warrior aspects of these gods in the way the Norse sources describe is a matter of conjecture, although the fact that many early place-names are derived from gods' names or titles does have weight. Many of the linear earthworks of Anglo-Saxon date bear names such as 'Grim's Ditches' or 'Grimsdyke', where *Grim* 'the hooded one' is a by-name for Wōden. Under his own name, he is commemorated in such places as Wednesbury and Wednesfield. The one-eyed war god also turns up on the Sutton Hoo helmet and his ritual dancing, or that of his worshippers, is portrayed on the Gilton, Kent, (Fig.10) belt buckle, where a warrior is shown running with a spear in each hand. This figure wears a distinctive kind of helmet surmounted by large animal-headed horns, rather like inverted drinking horns, and there are parallel depictions from Scandinavia; such helmets (or, better, forms of headgear, since they would be entirely impractical in warfare) were worn in the north in the Bronze Age and seem to have lingered in the artistic tradition as a means of showing divine possession of the human mind. The name 'Wōden' actually means 'master of inspiration, or mental excitement' (it is related to the OE word *wōð* 'poetic inspiration') and his particular gifts were associated with both inspiration and death – two forms of sending the soul forth from the body; the shamanic nature of his cult is obvious. His later association with warfare stems from the close connection between fighting and death, and the battle-fury (ON *berserkergang*) his followers could induce in themselves. It is possible, though not currently capable of proof, that the famous hill-figure at Wilmington, Sussex, called 'The Long Man' (Fig.9) who also holds two long staves in a pose reminiscent of the Gilton buckle figure, is actually a cult figure of Wōden.[36] It may then be that the characteristic 'horns' of the helmet are not a representation of anything physically present but, like a saint's halo, are no more than an artistic convention for the god's power, and so for a man inspired and possessed by the god. It is no coincidence that in later Norse mythology Wōden's counterpart, Óðinn, has the treasure called *Ægishjalmr* 'the helmet of terror'.

The worship of Þunor by the English is evidenced by the small hammer-amulets which occasionally occur as grave goods, while the hammer- and sun-symbol ⅚ occurs frequently on cremation urns and brooches. The place-names Thundersley and Thunderfield are among those commemorating him. Tīw is not so easy to pin down, apart from the odd rune on a weapon and such place-names as Tysoe.

There is a further piece of evidence relating to the pre-Christian priestly class of the English. Bede tells the story of the Northumbrian priest of the old gods, described as an *ealdorbiscop* 'elder-bishop' in the Old English version of the story, who recognized the futility of his office and the gods he served. He resolved to destroy his temple, and did so by first mounting a stallion and taking up arms – two things he was proscribed from doing in the ancient religion – then set fire to the building and threw

---

[36] The Long Man's head is somewhat elongated as currently marked, and has been shown to have once been distinctly illustrated as if helmeted: the overlong 'brow' can then be seen as the vestiges of the distinctive 'horns' of the helmet.

his spear into it. These actions are classic rites from the Wōden cult – death by burning and stabbing. Yet the title 'elder-bishop' is not credible as the native word for a priest, [37] and certainly reflects Bede's somewhat uncomprehending and dismissive Christian perspective on the religion. There is elsewhere a word for an official 'spokesman' which remained in use long enough to be recorded in *Beowulf*, which is *þyle*, the office which Unferð held at the court of King Hrōðgār. The word has a Norse equivalent *þulr* 'story-teller, spokesman, orator'[38] and there is a case for suggesting that the role of the *þyle* was that of an officiant at ritual occasions, making the proper declamations and dedications to win the favour of the gods.

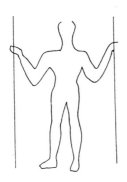

Figure 9   *Figure 10*

Figure 9 The Long Man of Wilmington, a hill-figure cut into the chalk of the Sussex Downs. Although undated, the figure bears a striking similarity to the pose of the dancing warrior on the Gilton belt buckle (Fig.10) and the slightly elongated deformation of the head may be a vestige of an eagle-crested helmet. The figure has been re-cut several times

Figure 10 Helmeted Warrior from a gilded belt buckle from Gilton, Kent. The warrior is naked apart from his eagle-crested helmet and belt, and brandishes a spear in each hand in a pose similar to that of the dancing warrior from Sutton Hoo (Fig.12, p.73)

The Warrior as Poet

> One must speak advice, write a secret,
> sing a ballad, earn words of praise,
> declare a judgement ...
>
> (*Maxims* I, lines 138–40)
>
> *Rǣd sceal mon secgan, rūne wrītan,*
> *lēoþ singan, lōfes gearnian,*
> *dōm āreccan ...*

---

[37] 'Bishop' is a clerical word taken over from the Greek. A native English word must have existed, even if it was not written down. See below for one possibility.

[38] This word has a distant and ancient relative in the Hittite root *talliya-* "propitiate the gods with formulaic speech", suggests Polomé.

Although the primary purpose of the warrior was to fight, it is no coincidence that the warrior who could use the harpstring as well as the bowstring was greatly admired. Poets fulfilled a useful, almost central, function in early societies in that they were jointly the 'collective memory' of their people. They knew the old stories which told of the origin of the people and how things in the world came to be as they are, tales of gods and heroes, battles won and lost and the vengeance taken for killings. They often record the laws and customs of the folk, especially in pre-literate societies – and even in proto-literate ones in which writing is reserved for certain well-defined purposes, much as the runes were among the early Germanic nations. Tacitus says of the *Germani* that their only records are *carmina*, 'songs' or 'verses'.

Poets are often also the voice of public opinion, responsible for airing grievances, scolding the blameworthy, supporting those in need of help. They may be ritual speakers (such as the OE *þyle*) whose task it is to utter the correct form of words on ritual occasions such as welcoming guests, honouring friends or singing the last words of farewell over a grave. In Christian contexts, they may deal in religious verse, while in heathen ones they may retell the stories of the gods and their doings, as cult narrators. In the lord's hall, the poet is the keeper of the tally of praise and shame for the warriors and it is his function to speak for those men who deserve the lord's favour, making poems of praise for their brave deeds and loyalty. Those who have failed, however, they may lampoon in satirical verses, while a lord who fails to reward his followers (and his poets!) may have had his niggardly name spread among his neighbours, to the delight of his rivals.

The Old English word for 'poet' is *scop* derived apparently from the verb *scieppan* 'create' with the meaning 'one who shapes or creates'; the Norse term corresponding is *skáld* apparently from the verb *skila* 'decide, expound' with the meaning 'he who knows and chooses [words]'.

While not central to his role, the poet was certainly an 'entertainer', though not in the modern sense of entertainment as something trivial or diverting, upon which to focus in order to become oblivious to the serious matters of life. One Old English term for 'poet' is *hleahtorsmiÐ* 'laughter-maker', suggesting that the poet could raise his hearers' spirits with his verse. Among the various forms of song and verse available to the Anglo-Saxon poet were the *giedd* 'song, lament', *lēoþ* 'lay, song, ballad', and *folcrǣden* 'rules of the folk', perhaps early laws and customs; *sang* seems to mean rather the 'act of singing, public performance' than the content of this.

Germanic poets were adventurers, travellers, wanderers; the archetypal English *scop* is called in the eponymous Exeter Book poem *Wīdsīð* 'Wide-farer'. This poem describes the journeyings of a Germanic poet throughout the known world (with Christian, biblical lands added in rather clumsily later in the light of an expanded world-view) visiting the courts and winning the favours of the great men of the Germanic world; it cannot be the record of a real journey since many of the kings named are known to have lived at different times, centuries apart. Nevertheless, a famed Icelandic poet such as Egil Skállagrímsson was welcomed at the English court of King Athelstan, who valued both his ready wit and skill with words, and his keen warrior instincts. Egil, if one believes his *saga*, was virtually alone responsible for Athelstan's victory over the Welsh, Scots and Danes from York in a terrible battle, called in Norse *Vínheiðr*, somewhere in northern England,[39] at which the power of an alliance between the foes of the English was broken. Egil was another great traveller, though his bad temper made him many enemies, and on one occasion he only escaped with his life from the clutches of King Eric Bloodaxe by composing a splendid poem about the king's victories and prowess, the *Hofuðslausn* 'head's ransom', which the king could not leave unrewarded without losing face among his men.

Poets were given their special gifts by the god of inspiration (OE *wōþ*, ON *óðr*) known as Woden or Odin (OE *Wōden,* ON *Óðinn*). There is some evidence to suggest that impromptu verse-making was not simply a social accomplishment, but was actually considered a message from the god himself. For example, *Egilssaga* relates an incident where Egil and his troop take themselves on a viking expedition and are divided as to whether they should attack the market town of Lund. The leaders and men express various opinions, then they ask Egil what he thinks, to which he replies:

> Out shall our swords [come] glittering, warrior, we have deeds to perform this summer; let each traveller [go] to Lund straightaway; let us there before sun's setting make a terrible battle.

> *Upp skulum órum sverðum,*
> *ulfs tannlituðr, glitra;*
> *eigum dáð at drýgja*
> *í dalmiskunn fiska:*
> *leiti upp til Lundar*
> *lýða hverr sem bráðast;*
> *gerum þár fyr setr sólar*
> *seið ófagann vigra.*

While this could be nothing more than a persuasive piece of verse rhetoric, the circumstances, the Óðinn-blessed poet and the verse form itself, combine to suggest that the one-eyed war-god is speaking here through his human proxy.

The special skills needed to construct the complicated verse forms – especially the very artificial vocabulary and metres of later Norse poetry – were such that one wonders at the audience's capacity to appreciate subtlety and word-play in something so transient as spoken verse. It may be that the poetry was not composed entirely off-the-cuff, but rather adapted from traditional and predictable stock phrases.[40] A knowledge of verse and a facility for expressing complex emotions while composing it

---

[39] There is reason to link this account with the English victory recorded in the *Chronicle*, s.a. 937, generally referred to as the battle of *Brunanburh*, and commemorated there in a short Old English poem. See Appendix I and p.180 below for the nature of the battleground.

[40] The formulaic nature of Old English and Old Norse verse has long been recognized. In this it resembles some of the traditional verse forms of eastern Europe, which are constructed largely from stock phrases varied to accommodate the metrical needs of the story.

was one of the great consolations of the Germanic warrior, hence the observation in the Exeter Book:

> He suffers that much less who knows a number of songs
>
> (*Maxims* I, line 169)
>
> *Longað þonne þy læs þe him con leoþa worn...*

Germanic warriors were not brutish louts; they respected skill with words as much as skill at arms, and they valued the good reputation and lasting memory the poet could confer. Their halls were the scene of merrymaking and laughter more often than of gloomy apprehension or artful menace. The life of a warrior could be short; while wine and women were among their transient pleasures, song had a place there too.

The Beginnings of English Warriorhood

> From there I travelled around the homeland of the Goths,
> I always looked for the best of comrades
> – that was the household troop of Earmanrīc...
>
> (*Widsith*, lines 109–11)
>
> *Đonan ic ealne geondhwearf ēþel Gotena,*
> *sōhte ic ā gesīþa þā sēlestan;*
> *þæt wæs innweorud Earmanrīces*

There can be little doubt that the twin influences of Rome and the Central European tribes (the Celts, Dacians and others) set off a change in the social systems of the Germanic north sometime in the later few centuries BC. What had been a relatively stable backwater of farming communities going about their daily business and seldom engaging in more strenuous military activity than cattle-raiding and occasional forays against suddenly-weakened neighbours, became very quickly a war-dominated society in which only the totally unimaginative were content to earn their living by the plough. The catalysts to this sudden explosion of military activity in the north were the introduction of iron weapons from Central Europe, and the opening up of cultural horizons through trade contacts with the Empire, which had taken the rule of neighbouring Gaul away from the native aristocracy in the first century BC. The *Galli* had been assisted by a Germanic tribe from across the Rhine, the *Suebi*.[41] It was the practice of this people, Caesar tells us in his *Gallic War*, to field a force of cavalry, each horseman in the force having selected an infantryman to fight with him, whose function it was to support the cavalry and to surround and protect any fallen rider. These infantry were extremely fast and agile, and could keep up with the horsemen, although over a longer advance or retreat they would hang on to the horses' manes and

---

[41] It was against this people that Offa fought his epoch-making duel; the OE source calls them *Swæfe*, the English dialectal form of the name.

hitch a ride to preserve their strength. These remarkable Germanic 'Panzergrenadiers' were used in support of the Gaulish leader, Ariovistus, in his bid to keep Roman power south of the Alps.

The Empire was, to some extent, the architect of its own final destruction by Germanic warbands. The threat posed by the peoples across the north-western boundary (the Rhine) to the prosperity of Gaul and Central Europe was such that the imperial powers had to strengthen their defences; this involved sending large numbers of men to the frontier, all of whom had to be paid from the imperial coffers and supplied with food and other essentials. This trend tended to move wealth from the centre of the Empire to its borders, which therefore made the borders that much more rewarding targets for the enemy. Furthermore, the legions' increased wealth and crucial importance put them in a position where they were effectively able to decide which of the various candidates should become emperor; where various legions backed different men, there would inevitably be rivalry, dissension and political manoeuvring, all of which distracted the leaders' attention from the real purpose of containing the enemy.

Figure 11 Carving from Repton, Derbyshire, 8th century. A warrior ceremonially laid out in his grave with his war-gear, which includes an axe, sword, shield , spear, seax (across his abdomen) and helmet.

In addition to these man-made problems, the Germanic folk living on the southern coastal regions of the North Sea had to contend with a rising sea-level, which caused widespread flooding and marine transgression. Naturally, the effect of this phenomenon was to drive families off the lowlands, which were rapidly becoming barren marshland; the Roman-held coast of Belgica was similarly affected. Where men had previously lived by agriculture, they now turned to their boats for a living, both as fishermen and as sea-borne raiders. The earliest Germanic naval activity consisted of attacks by small boats on the Rhineland bases of the Empire; some of these vessels were small, plank-built boats while others were large hollowed-out tree-trunks, capable of carrying about 30 men. Though these craft were no great threat to Imperial security, the Germans sometimes captured Roman galleys and were able to manoeuvre them with great skill.[42]

Much evidence about early Germanic warfare comes from the ritual deposits of Jutland and Fyn, and elsewhere in the Danish islands and southern Scandinavia. Briefly, there was among certain tribes a practice of sacrificing the men, war-gear and horses of a defeated foe to the god whose assistance had been sought to bring victory – be it Wōðenaz or Tīwaz or some other – by hanging the men from trees and depositing the weapons and armour in lakes held to be sacred. These lakes subsequently dried out, becoming peat bogs, and the artefacts were entombed in the earth awaiting discovery by peatcutters and, latterly, archaeologists. Exceptionally, the bogs have sometimes preserved the objects largely intact and it is possible to calculate from the quantities of various items present the minimum number of warriors who would have used them: e.g. if there are twenty shields, seven swords, thirteen spears and three mailcoats, then there should have been twenty men using the weapons found on the basis that each man would carry just one shield. Of course, what cannot always be determined is whether the twenty men all died in one battle or whether they represent the sacrifices from more than one campaign and their weapons were deposited over, say, a period of ten years. In this context, the finds from Ejsbol North are very obliging – archaeologists have reconstructed the recovered remains into sixty swords, sixty belt buckles and sixty two knives, all dating from the mid 4th century AD and clearly attesting to the sacrifice of about sixty sword belts (from sixty warriors?); there were also nine bridle-sets and nine sets of saddle fittings and (probably) nine sets of spurs, indicating nine horsemen. There were 123 complete shield bosses and fragments of about 50 more, indicating a force of about 200 men. 203 throwing-spear heads (i.e. with barbs) and 191 one 'lance' heads (i.e. for hand-held fighting) were found, which agrees with the shield-based figure on the assumption that each man had a throwing spear (OE *daroð*) and a hand-to-hand spear (OE *spere*). There were also about 30 quivers. Overall, the picture which emerges from this find is as follows:

---

[42] The first recorded voyage round the northern coast of Britain was undertaken by a runaway group of *Usipi* from the middle Rhine, who had seized some Roman galleys and were making their way back to their homeland. See *Dark Age Naval Power* by John Haywood for more on the beginnings of Germanic seafaring.

weapon sets	number of warriors
mounted warrior with sword, javelin, spear, shield	9
warrior with sword, javelin, spear, shield	51
warrior with javelin, spear, shield	131
warrior with bow	30
total force	221

Table 3 Estimate of minimum number of warriors represented
by weapons recovered from the Ejsbøl bog deposit

This does, of course, assume that those who were equipped with a high-status weapon (e.g. sword) also had the lower-status equipment as well. It also represents only the minimum number – there is no guarantee that the enemy's entire supply of battlefield equipment was recovered or transported for sacrifice. One could play devil's advocate and argue that the mounted men had no weapons, the swordsmen had no shields or spears, and so on, to give a very different picture (i.e. 9 + 60 + 173 + 203 + 191 = 636 men), though clearly this is based on very improbable assumptions!

It seems safe to assert that the weapons sacrificed in the bogs were offerings to the gods, and most probably they represent the captured equipment of a defeated enemy, which could not be used by men since they properly belonged to the deity who had brought victory, a thank offering. The weapons and other war-gear which were to be sent off into the next world were selected carefully, it seems, and transported back to the cult centre. It may be that only those who died in battle had their weapons sacrificed – the weapons had failed their users and were untrustworthy, possibly vengeful – while captives and men who surrendered had their finery, including their weapons, confiscated as a precaution against further resistance and as a mark of their worthless status. Unfortunately, it is very difficult to plot the incidence of specifics in the types of material found to determine whether the deposited material was made relatively locally (and represents the spoil of a battle between neighbours) or in more distant parts (and represents a long-range expedition); the quantities of goods which can be confidently allocated to any particular region are so small as to be statistically insignificant. Nevertheless, with the increasing development of local styles of arms manufacture, dress fastening, etc. in the later Germanic Iron Age, it is at least possible to say that none of the bog deposit sites seems to include material of that date (say, 400 AD) from mainland Scandinavia or western Europe. Similarly, where the weapons bear runic inscriptions (e.g. *ekerilaz* etc., from a Kragehul spear shaft) these are usually in the North Sea Germanic *koine* or 'literary dialect' without detectable regional features which could assist in establishing where the inscription (and, by extension, the spear itself) was made. Moreover, the geographical spread of Germanic dialect features at any period before the seventh century AD is only very imperfectly understood.

Some of the bogs allocated for ritual deposits came into use for this purpose back in Neolithic times and continued until possibly the Migration period (i.e. from say, 2500 BC to 500 AD) – a longer time span than any Christian religious site – with an upsurge in activity in many cases in the first centuries AD, the late Roman Iron Age, taking the form of weapons and war-gear replacing the more usual pottery of the previous era. Later, in the Germanic Iron Age (say, 2nd to 4th centuries AD) the range of artefacts widens to include such ancillary military material as horse furniture, and it is usual to find symbolic parts of weapons rather than whole ones, e.g. scabbard fittings instead of whole swords. In the 5th century, the character changes again to include fine gold work, including Germanic medallions (*bracteates*). This replacement of earthenware vessels containing animal bones by war-gear – which has generally seen active service and shows signs of hard use – almost certainly charts the growth of the cult of the war god (*Wōðenaz*) and its ousting of the fertility gods as the principal religious cult. Apparently the larger sites at least (Nydam, Kragehul, Vimose, Illerup, Ejsbøl, Torsbjerg) were the location for regular rituals over a period of time rather then one large votive offering, since some of the weapons found are not believed to be of contemporary types.[43] The conclusion is difficult to avoid that the handful of spectacular bog deposit sites discovered so far are linked to the political geography of the Germanic Iron Age, and that they each represent a tribal religious focus; the German scholar Jankuhn has argued that the ritual site at Torsbjerg served as the cult centre for the *Anglii,* as the English were then known. The territory of the *Anglii* is reconstructed as including modern Schleswig-Holstein, most of the island of Fyn and part of the Jutland peninsula south east of an earthwork called *Olgerdiget* which possibly represents the boundary with the Jutes of northern Jutland. The *Olgerdiget* is dated to the late 2nd century AD. This reconstructed area includes not only the large deposit site of Torsbjerg, but also those of Nydam (in Jutland) and Kragehul and Voldtofte (on Fyn). The other major finds are distributed in south and central Jutland and northern Fyn (Ejsbøl, Illerup and Vimose respectively). However, we know from Tacitus (*Germania,*ch.40) that the *Anglii* were one of a group of seven tribes (*Reudigni, Aviones, Anglii, Varini, Eudoses, Suarines, Nuitones*) who were characterized by the worship of the Earth Mother (*Tella mater*) under the name of *Nerthus,* and it may be more prudent to suggest that the site at Torsbjerg was held by the *Anglii* themselves – it lies in modern Angeln, which probably represents the heart of ancient *Anglia* fairly closely – with the other nearby major locations held by different members of this cult group. However, whether these sites can be regarded as 'national' cult centres is another matter – it is unclear to what extent pre-Christian northern Europe felt the need for dominant regional religious centres. Equally, if the sites are linked to 'tribal' patterning, they must in all probability represent successful

---

[43] Yet the possibility of men going into battle with old weapons has to be taken into account – see the remarks on the OE words *lāf* and *māððum* on p.35.

local defence against invasive warbands, since the bands of young warriors whose efforts created the Migration Age were by definition not affiliated to the previous religious system based round fertility and protection and the defence of the tribal lands, but were rather worshippers of new and aggressive gods whose agenda centred on power and fear. Moreover, if the *Anglii* had the political cohesion to build earthworks such as the Olmerdiget they would surely have had the means to drive off opportunist adventurers.

With the arrival in Britain, and the conversion of the southern and eastern areas of the island into a new Angeln, weapons burials take on a new importance perhaps as expressions of membership of a group which liked to present itself in a warlike manner and took pride in its military achievements. Many early Anglian and Saxon burial grounds are next to older similar sites, for example the early Saxon burials from Mucking occur in a large Neolithic and Bronze Age complex, and secondary inhumation[44] within barrows is fairly common where barrows occur. Even the famous Sutton Hoo graveyard overlapped to some extent an important Neolithic site. It seems that the newcomers were not going to begin afresh, but rather take over existing sites of cultic, religious or ritual importance[45] and 'bask in the reflected glory' of possessing and using them. Inhumation graves, where the corpse is buried in the ground (though seldom in a wooden coffin as far as we can tell), naturally present the clearest information about weapons, though there is a mere handful of cremations which contained war-gear: at Spong Hill, Norfolk, ten urns held parts of weapons (2 sword pommels, 4 scabbard mounts, 4 arrowheads) out of an estimated 2300 burials (i.e. 0·4%) as against an average of around 20% for inhumation cemeteries. This does not mean that those who practised cremation were Dark Age pacifists eschewing the use of weapons, but only that they did not habitually deposit weapons with the dead; equally, it is hardly safe to draw the conclusion that two in every ten people buried in inhumation cemeteries were warriors just because their families put a spear in the grave with them. Furthermore, in the very nature of things, substantial numbers of warriors must have died in battle some way from home and been disposed of in whatever way was customary in those circumstances; unless their bodies were recovered by their friends or families – which must have been physically impossible or just too dangerous in many cases – these men will not show up in the organized, local graveyards. Nevertheless, the fact that burial with weapons was to some extent limited – in England, it rarely exceeds 3 graves in 10 in any cemetery – can only point to the

---

[44] 'Secondary inhumation' is where an existing barrow has a further burial inserted at a later date – it may be within generation or two in some cases, or some centuries later. The practice confers the prestige benefits of 'mound burial' without the effort of building the tumulus.

[45] The attraction of pre-existent ritual sites for the early English has never been satisfactorily explained, but may be connected with the idea of 'power' (emotional and spiritual involvement) having been invested in such sites by the previous users; possession of the sites was therefore an expression of complete domination (mastery of the ancestors as well as of the living) as well as affording them the opportunity to subvert this 'power' for their own ends.

rite as an expression of membership of a group for whom the possession and use of weapons was very significant: probably therefore a warrior élite of some kind.

Heinrich Härke has examined the early weapon burials in (mainly southern) England, and determined that an average of 47% (say, 1 in 2) demonstrably male inhumation graves contained weapons of some sort, though this overall figure can only be an abstract statistical norm when local variation ranges between 11% to 90% from one cemetery to another – in the first case, 1 man in 10 had weapons in his grave and in the second case the same proportion did *not* have weapons. The mid-6th century was the peak of weapon burial activity, though the rite ended in the late 7th century in England, depriving us of a valuable source of information – enabling us to relate spearheads to the contemporary types of shield boss, and so on – yet the numbers of weapons found in each grave is fairly stable even as the custom was going out of fashion. This was partly under new and presumably Christian influence among leaders, though there was even in pagan times a trend that in times of greatest danger there would be greatest reluctance to part with valuable and useful weapons, while relatively peaceful and stable times saw a rise in the deposition of serviceable war-gear. By this logic, the grave-goods peak of the mid-sixth century should correspond to the relatively quiet period of consolidation after the military campaigns of the late 400s and early 500s which saw the greatest English advances and such events as the *obsessio montis badonici*.

Härke has determined that in English graves, the commonest form of weapon burial is the inclusion of just a spear (nearly half of all weapon graves) and the second commonest that of spear and shield. Virtually every other combination is uncommon or scarce, making the Anglo-Saxon weapon set very limited on this evidence. His figures, which are based on undisturbed male weapon burials from the early Saxon period, may be summarized in Table 4.

On the face of it and based on the evidence of this research, the English warrior appears to have been rather poorly supplied with armaments, nearly half having nothing but a spear to their names, and those with more than one weapon generally having only one other item additionally in their assemblages. There are chronological variations within the evidence, however, which show that axes became increasingly unpopular while seaxes, which are virtually absent from the very early graves, became more common in time.

It is, perhaps, worth stressing again that the combinations retrieved from graves do not necessarily correspond to those in use by the living: for instance, swords gradually stop being interred but there is no evidence to suggest that they stopped being made or wielded in warfare – probably practical priorities, and with them ritual fashions, changed in the course of time. The combination of spear and shield seems a logical set with which to be armed – and the table above suggests it was a popular one with which to be buried – but corpses accompanied by just a shield or just a throwing spear can hardly be reflecting battlefield practice.

weapon assemblage	number of burials	percentage
1 spear	237	44·4
2 spears	6	1·1
3 spears	2	0·4
1 shield	36	6·7
1 shield, 1 spear	139	26·0
1 shield, 2 spears	14	2·6
1 sword	9	1·7
1 sword, 1 spear	10	1·9
1 sword, 1 shield	11	2·1
1 sword, 1 shield, 1 spear	24	4·5
1 sword, 1 shield, 2 spears	4	0·7
1 sword, 1 spear, 1 axe	1	0·2
1 sword, 1 shield, 1 spear, 1 axe	1	0·2
1 sword, 1 shield, 1 spear, 1 seax	1	0·2
1 sword, 1 shield, 2 spears, 1 seax, 1 axe	1	0·2
1 seax	6	1·1
1 seax, 1 spear	9	1·7
1 seax, 1 shield, 1 spear	4	0·7
1 seax, 1 shield, 2 spears	2	0·4
1 axe	8	1·5
1 axe, 1 spear	2	0·4
1 axe, 1 shield, 1 spear	1	0·2
1 arrow	4	0·7
1 arrow, 1 spear	2	0·4
Total	534	

Table 4 Weapon sets and frequencies from early Anglo-Saxon weapon burials

The Warrior's Way

... A wise man must be patient
must not be too hot-headed nor too hasty in speech,
nor too bashful in battle nor too blindly reckless,
nor too craven nor too carefree nor too keen for wealth,
nor ever too fond of boasting before he fully understands.

(The Wanderer, lines 65–9)

... Wita sceal geþyldig,
ne sceal nō tō hātheort ne tō hrædwyrde
ne tō wāc wiga ne tō wanhydig
ne tō forht ne tō fægen ne tō feohgīfre
ne næfre gilpes tō georn ær hē geare cunne.

Warriors were not born with the skills they would need in later life: they had to set out to acquire dexterity with various weapons, fast reactions, a feeling for tactics; for some, strength, speed and weapon-skill were enough to enable them to earn a living; for others, a narrower outlook was needed – specializing in fighting on board ship, or in guarding bridges or doorways, or in attacking quickly on foot, or whatever. No doubt no matter what skills a man possessed there was an opportunity to deploy them somewhere. Moreover, many of the accomplishments which served the warrior could be acquired through hunting, and would serve equally well for that purpose: speed, accuracy, strength and agility were all essential to both pursuits.

Would-be warriors may also have identified with the powerful beasts of the forests in their hunting – the bear, boar, wolf and aurochs.[46] We have Caesar's testimony (*Gallic War*, chapter 6) that Germanic youths used to test their courage and skill at arms by capturing an aurochs and despatching it single-handed. Yet the constant reiteration of animal imagery in relation to warfare and warriors suggests some deep-seated thematic link in the imaginations of many northern European peoples – Germanic, Celtic and Slavonic. We shall look at the Norse *berserkir* shortly, but it is worth recording that tales of shape-shifting (werewolves and swan-maidens, to cite the commonest) are recorded independently from across Europe; not infrequently, they involve quasi-historical figures such as the grandfather of the (presumably historical) Icelandic warrior-poet Egil Skállagrímsson, named *Kveldulf* 'evening-wolf', whose strength and ferocity increased with the approaching darkness and abated in the morning.

More widely known is the *Volsunga Saga* incident where the heroes *Sigmund* and *Sinfjotli*[47] acquire wolf pelts which confer on them the savagery and nature of wolves, so that they are compelled to live as beasts for a while and are hunted by men. The

---

[46] The aurochs was a large species of bovine, a native North European buffalo.

[47] He occurs briefly in *Beowulf* under the English form of his name, *Fitela*.

youth *Sinfjotli* learns to hunt and think as a wolf, although his reckless courage almost gets him killed. Perhaps this narrative element is a reflection of a period of instruction which the trainee warrior had to undergo along with a more experienced older man – in this case, *Sigmund* is his mother's brother and this kinsman may have been the usual tutor for a youth. The relationship of mother's brother ~ sister's son was crucial in Germanic society and there are numerous examples of its influence in both legend and history – from Tacitus's statement that the Germans generally preferred to take nephews rather than sons as hostages since doing so gave them a wider hold on the family, to the close personal relationship between Bēowulf and his mother's brother Hygelāc.

Part of the importance of the bond between maternal uncle and nephew (*ēam* and *nefa* in Old English) was that in early Germanic society, on marriage the wife went to live with her husband and his family, leaving her kindred behind. This meant that she had no blood relations among her daily contacts, and was only a member of her husband's kinship-group by virtue of marriage, yet her children were full members of her husband's family, not hers. Nevertheless, the woman's own kindred-group maintained a strong interest in her and the children's well-being, and under the standard patriarchal family structure her brother (her nearest male relative) would represent her interests in dealings with her husband's kin (principally the husband's own father) and stood in the role of 'substitute father' to her children. The mother's brother was not subject to the strong disciplinary social power of the head of the paternal family, because he belonged to a different kinship-group, and so could deal with the husband's father on a more equal and business-like footing,[48] and apparently could act as a surrogate or foster-father to his sister's sons if need arose.

Military training of boys may have begun at the age of eight, since Bede records that St. Cuthbert at that age (the end of 'infancy' and the beginning of boyhood) was accustomed to play with other children at various contests; Cuthbert was lively, nimble, quick-thinking and had great stamina, and he would contend with others in wrestling, racing, jumping and other exercises and games involving twisting (perhaps running games where the person touched must chase the rest until he can touch one of them in turn). Bēowulf says:

> I was seven years old when the lord of treasures,
> the friend of nations, took me from my father …

> (lines 2428–9)

> *Ic wæs syfan wintre þā mec sinca baldor,*
> *frēawine folca, æt mīnum fæder genām…*

and goes on to describe his upbringing at the court of his *ēam*, King Hrēðel. Eddius Stephanus recounts the early life of St. Wilfrid in terms suggesting that, while

---

[48] The word *ēam* 'maternal uncle' is derived from a reconstructed Proto-Germanic form **awunhaimaz* '[he who has the] place of the grandfather' which makes this equality of status between the two male relatives explicit.

a boy, he had to wait on his father's guests in the hall, in place of his late mother, and that at the age of fourteen he decided to leave home and seek his fortune among the nobles he had entertained previously. He provided clothes, weapons and mounts for a small band and set off for the court of King Ōswiu of Northumbria. Likewise, the redoubtable St. Guthlac had a successful military career and, at the age of fifteen, had already been on raids with his band of youths, gained booty and slain foes. It seems likely, therefore, that at about fourteen years old the youngster had to determine if the military life was really for him, and if so to make his mark with a group of companions in the service of a king.

It may be that youths trained with mock weapons – staves, wooden swords, wicker shields – until they were physically strong enough to wield their full-size, 'active-service' equivalents. There are reference to wooden sticks among the Irish youths training for the *fiana*, and wooden weapons occasionally occur in archaeological sites in northern Europe (e.g. the rune-inscribed wooden sword from Arum, West Frisia). There are other traditions concerning the use of mock weapons against the warrior which we shall look at later.[49]

Later Norse stories provide further clues to the military initiation process as enacted in pre-Christian times, which apparently involved the prospective warrior being required to strike down a mock enemy, an effigy of a demonic foe which the youth was led to believe would attack him. This test of courage and willpower was intended to single out those with the nerve to face up to danger. It probably lies behind the story in which Þórr and his servant Þjalfi are ranged against the giant Hymir, armed with a hone, and his ally, a giant made of mud equipped with a mare's heart. The thunder-god attacks the giant while Þjalfi strikes down the mud-giant, which oozes and melts away, his heart having failed him at need. The meaning of the ceremonial combat may have been to show that even the most fierce-seeming opponent can be faced down, and it goes on to explain that Hymir's whetstone shattered against Þórr's hammer leaving a portion embedded in his skull – but that's another story.

There is also a tradition concerning the Danish hero Böðvarr Bjarki, who visited the court of King Hrólfr Kraki and found a wretched creature called Höttr skulking behind a wall of discarded bones which the king's champions had cast at him for sport. Bjarki takes the lad under his wing and that night he determines to destroy a fierce beast which has been ravaging the Danish countryside. He ventures out with Höttr and tackles the troll, slays it after some difficulties and then bids his companion drink its blood. Rather than taking the credit for the slaying himself, Böðvarr Bjarki props the carcass up in a field. The next day the sighting of the beast is reported to the king and none of the champions is willing to go out to face it, except Höttr who pretends to engage it in a fight and to fell it, whereupon Hrólfr is moved by the valour of the least-considered of his household and rewards the boy with a beautifully-hilted sword, whence he is later known as *Hjalti* ('hilt') and goes on to have an illustrious career as a warrior, due to the miraculous properties of the blood and heart of the troll

---

[49] See especially the ritual sacrifice of Baldr, p.67.

which have made him into a champion instantly. The parallel of the mock combat by a youth with a monster which is not what it seems is too strong to be coincidence and may reflect – if only dimly – an ancient test of courage.

The mediaeval Icelandic writer Snorri Sturluson also recorded the tradition of the god *Baldr* who was the brightest, fairest and most beloved of all the northern gods, and whose prophetic dreams of impending death so disturbed his mother, *Frigg*, that she secured promises from all things not to harm her son. Then the gods made a sport of Baldr's invulnerability, and took to standing him before them on the playing field so they could cast weapons at him without hurting him. At length the god *Loki* discovered that one small plant, the mistletoe, had not given any promise to Frigg and so he made a javelin from the wood of the plant and passed it to the blind god *Höðr* to throw at his brother. The stick pierced Baldr and he fell dead to the ground, so setting off a chain of events which were to bring the present cycle of the world to its end. The myth has been analysed and explained in many different ways, but there are certain elements in it which lead one to suspect that it is a late, tidied-up and rationalized version of something older and more powerful. The gods' names are interesting in themselves: *Baldr* may mean 'bright one', and has a parallel in the Old English poetic word *bealdor* which means 'warrior, lord, master', while *Höðr* is a Norse word for 'warrior': seemingly both gods are associated with aspects of warrior culture. Also the curious 'game' of throwing weapons at Baldr is nowhere clearly explained – it seems that the story here is an attempt to make narrative sense of something which the author did not understand fully. Polomé has suggested that Höðr is actually Óðinn (he is not blind, but one-eyed) and that a ritual drama is acted out in the myth as in real life: the warriors form a ring around the Baldr-figure (the candidate for initiation) and throw weapons at him until the half-blind(-folded ?) Höðr character enters and strikes him down with the mistletoe wand. The prospective member falls to the floor, to 'die' and rise up[50] – come back to life, no longer as an outsider, but as a member of the circle of sworn brothers.

In Irish tradition, the hero-to-be *Cú Chulainn* receives his warrior training from a druid called *Cathab* and from *Scáthach*, a supernatural female figure. The Norse tales of *Sigurðr Fáfnisbani* bear a strong resemblance to this situation, in that Sigurð is first trained by the smith *Reginn* who re-forges Sigurð's father's broken sword for his own purposes, and later by the *valkyrja Brynhild* from whom he learns runes, war-spells and counsel in when to act and when to refrain. In fact, Reginn's re-forging of the family sword is part of a long tradition whereby Germanic youths normally either received weapons as an heirloom (OE *lāf*) from an illustrious ancestor, or had to win them on the battlefield – taking them from a defeated enemy or receiving them as a gift from the *þeoden* they were serving. Even Bēowulf comes by his sword in that manner – in Denmark he had used no weapon against his first attacker, Grendel, and had borrowed a sword which proved useless in his second fight. On his return to

---

[50] The link with mummers' plays and the morris men is also suggestive – a masked figure of power strikes down one of the company, who is later revived.

Geatland, he hands over most of his winnings to his king and kinsman, Hygelāc, and is given land in return as well as a magnificent weapon:

> Then the protector of warriors had brought in
> – the battle-keen king – Hreðel's heirloom
> adorned with gold; among the Geats there was not at that time
> a worthier jewelled treasure in the form of a sword,
> he laid it in Bēowulf's lap
> and made over to him seven thousand [hides?],
> a dwelling and a high-seat.

(lines 2190–6)

> Hēt ðā eorla hlēo in gefetian,
> heaðorōf cyning Hrēðles lāfe
> golde gegyrede; næs mid Gēatum ðā
> sincmāðþum sēlra on sweordes hād
> þæt hē on Bīowulfes bearm ālegde
> ond him gesealde seofan þūsendo
> bold ond bregostōl.

Hreðel was his mother's father and so the sword has a strong family connection for the hero, especially as it was his *lāf* and had been owned and used by Hygelāc also. Their transfer to the young warrior mark his acceptance into the warrior society of the Geats. Quite often women, especially mothers, play an important role in the handing on of weapons on their sons' reaching the age at which they are entitled to bear them, i.e. about fourteen. Tacitus remarks on the Germanic custom of providing the new bride at her wedding not with fripperies for her adornment, but rather with weapons which she is duty bound to hand on to her sons,[51] and which the Roman writer considered altogether an admirable present.

At what point did a warrior cease to be required for active service? Was there a retirement age for military men? On the face of it, one would not expect men to be called on to fight once they began to grow stiff and weak with old age, when they would just be a danger to those around them in the *fyrd*. And there does seem to have been a general expectation that warriors whose careers began at around fourteen in the *geogoð* would have graduated to land-holding and the *duguð* by the age of about twenty five. Furthermore, we have the testimony of *Beowulf* that the aged king *Hrōþgār* was not expected to face his hall-invader personally, nor was the nearly-blind *Wǣrmund* supposed to meet the Myrcing champion. Therefore there was acknowledgement that past a certain point men were excused personally taking part in fighting. Yet we have contrary evidence that older men could take part in war, such as the case of the East Angles re-calling their king from his monastery to lead them against their Mercian invaders. We also have the testimony of *The Battle of Maldon* that an elderly *ealdormann* could take part personally in the fighting. At the time of

---

[51] See p.44 for more on the role of women as the custodians of family weapons.

the battle (991) Byrhtnōð must have been aged over sixty since he was already married in 951 when he was mentioned in his father-in-law's will. But that he was no armchair general is obvious from references like the following in the poem:

> Then the man hard in war strode, raised his weapon up
> – his shield as a defence – and stepped towards the warrior;
> with equal determination the *eorl* went to the *ceorl*
> – each intended evil to the other ...
>
> (lines 130–3)

> *Wōd þā wīges heard, wǣpen up āhōf*
> *bord tō gebeorge and wið þæs beornes stōp;*
> *ēode swā ānrǣd eorl tō þām ceorle,*
> *ǣgþer hyra ōðrum yfeles hogode.*

One could argue, of course, that Byrhtnōð is exceptional because he is the leader of the East Saxon troops there and consequently is obliged to be present despite his age, but later in the poem we read:

> Byrhtwold spoke, raised his shield,
> – he was an old retainer – brandished his spear,
> he boldly told the warriors ...
>
> "...I am old in life. From here I do not wish to go..."
>
> (lines 309–11 & 317)

> *Byrhtwold maþelode, bord hafenode,*
> *se wæs eald genēat, æsc ācwehte,*
> *he ful baldlīce beornas lǣrde...*
>
> *"...Ic eom frōd fēores. Fram ic ne wille..."*

This retainer Byrhtwold was seemingly one of Byrhtnōð's close friends, perhaps a member of his *heorðwerod*, and of much the same age as his leader whom he would not desert even in death.

Shield-maidens – Women at War

> ...Then the woman with braided hair took
> – the creator's maid – a sharp sword,
> hard in battle, and drew it from the sheath
> with her right hand ...
>
> (*Judith*, 77–80)

> ... *Genam ðā wundenlocc,*
> *scyppendes mægð, scearpne mēce,*
> *scūrum heardne, and of scēaðe ābrǣd*
> *swīðran folme...*

69

While warfare was generally regarded as men's work, there are enough allusions in the literatures of the northern peoples to suggest that women had a hand in the matter to some extent. The obvious candidates are the Norse *valkyrjar* – valkyries – who are women dedicated to Óðinn and sharing the military life of his devotees. While in the later Norse literature they are demure maidens who serve ale and welcome guests to Óðinn's halls, as good Germanic hostesses should, there are enough early references to suggest something grislier, possibly priestesses of the cult of Óðinn who sacrificed captives to their god. The Irish warbands (*fiana*) had female members who tended the wounds of the men and sometimes fought alongside, but nursing and cooking (amongst other things) are traditionally the roles of camp-followers, not shield-maidens.

Perhaps something closer to the English notion of the *wælcyrige*, the Old English word corresponding to *valkyrja*, is represented in the charm against a sudden stitch (*Wið Færsticce*) although here the supernatural nuances cluster closely together and do suggest something out of the ordinary – perhaps a troop of malevolent elf-women:

> "Loud were they, lo!, loud when they rode over the gravemound,
> they were bold when they rode through the land...
> [I] stood under lindenwood, under a light shield,
> where the powerful women readied their strength
> and, yelling, sent forth spears..."

(lines 3–4 and 7–9)

> *Hlūde wǣran hȳ lā hlūde ðā hȳ ofer þone hlǣw ridan*
> *wǣran ānmōde ðā hȳ ofer land ridan...*
> *stōd under linde, under lēohtum scylde,*
> *þǣr ðā mihtigan wīf hyra mægen berǣddon*
> *and hȳ gyllende gāras sǣndan...*

Saxo Grammaticus, describing the battle at Brávella, mentions a Slavic woman called Wisna and her band who took part in the fighting armed with long swords and shields, and wearing clothing covered with metal plates. The few Old English poems devoted to females (*Elene, Judith, Juliana*) all emphasize these women's strong, almost aggressive, characters and refer to them in terms not inappropriate for warriors (e.g. *ellenþriste* 'courageous', *collenferhðe* 'bold in spirit', *eadhrēðig* 'triumphant' used of Judith). Interestingly, there is some evidence to suggest that not all the graves containing weapons from Anglo-Saxon pagan cemeteries are necessarily those of men – there are some few with both spears and typically female goods such as weaving equipment.[52] Could these be the graves of shield-maidens? Or are the weapons perhaps those of a dead loved one, or restricted to one local kinship-group of which the buried woman was the last survivor? It is impossible to tell now.

---

[52] There is even a case of the weapon being recycled for another purpose: a grave at Shudy Camps, Cambs., contained a spearhead which had apparently been used as a weaving-slay.

Bearshirts and Wolfcoats

> Unhappy is he who must live alone,
> dwell without friends, his fate has been fixed
>
> (*Maxims* I, lines 172–3)
>
> *Earm biþ se þe sceal āna lifgan,*
> *winelēas wunian, hafað him wyrd getēod...*

English evidence for dedicated warrior bands is not as plentiful as the Norse, where saga literature in particular makes great play of the *berserkir* 'bear-shirts' and *ulfheðnr* 'wolf-coats', who are devotees of the war-god Óðinn. These warriors scorned the use of mail and other protection, and put their faith instead in their totemic garb (ON *vargstakkar*), made from the skins of bear and wolf respectively. In the sagas it is a literary convention that berserks are to some extent outside the normal laws of society, that they are impervious to both fire and iron due to the supernatural protective qualities of their ritual clothing, and that Óðinn is able to blunt the weapons of their foes. The distinction between the wolf as totem and the bear may be no more than that the wolf is closely linked to Óðinn in mythology and is a social animal attacking in packs, while the bear is a lone-fighter. Individual preference may have given rise to the slightly different emphasis in each case.[53]

Bear-slaying is a not uncommon theme in northern literature, attributed for example to Grettir in *Grettis saga* and even to Hereward the Wake (in *De Gestis Herwardi Saxonis*) and it is noteworthy that the word 'bear' is not the original, inherited name for the creature.[54] The most famous early English epic poem, *Beowulf* features the eponymous central character who is himself distinctly ursine – he crushes more than one foe to death – and whose name 'wolf of the bee' is a metaphor for 'bear' (honey-raider!). In Old English, as in Norse, the word 'bear' (*beorn, bjorn*) can be used in poetry for 'warrior'. *Bjorn* has remained a popular Scandinavian first name to this day, and was evidently so in Viking times: there are many references to men with names such as *Þórbjorn* (Thor – bear) or *Ingibjorn* (Ing – bear).

'Wolf' names are not uncommon, in the Scandinavian form *Ulf* (as a simplex) or in compounds such as *Þórolf, Ingolf*. English names often have the corresponding element *wulf* as in *Wulfstān* 'wolf – stone', *Æðelwulf* 'noble – wolf'. Lupine references are generally not flattering, for example in the poem *The Battle of Maldon* where the Vikings are called *wælwulfas* 'wolves of slaughter' or in the Exeter Book poem *Dēor* where it is said of a noted tyrant:

> "we have discovered the wolfish mind of Eormanric"   (line 22)
>
> *wē geascodon Eormanrīces wylfenne geþoht*

---

[53] Societies often characterise their warrior groups by the most impressive predators with which they are familiar – in Africa, it is often the leopard, in northern Europe and Asia the bear and wolf, in southern Asia the tiger.

[54] All the Germanic languages have substituted a word meaning 'the brown animal' (**bernuz*) for the root which produced Latin *ursus* and Greek *arctos*.

while the outlawed lover of the poem *Wulf and Eadwacer* is simply called *Wulf, mīn Wulf* (line 13) ('wolf, my wolf') with *Wulf* either a personal name, an epithet for an outlaw, or a pet name – the art of the poet lies in the multiple meanings of his verse, after all. The Old English word *wearg* means both 'wolf' and 'outlaw', like its Norse equivalent *vargr*. The outlaw associations of the word *wulf* are strengthened by one of the Old English words for 'bandit', *wulfesheafod* 'wolf's head' while the gallows where these individuals ended their days were known as *wulfesheafodtrēo* 'wolf's head tree'. Possibly the reference here is to the wild and unkempt appearance of the outlaw who is not bound by the normal dress code of society, and whose arduous lifestyle makes normal grooming impossible; outlaws may even have cultivated an unkempt appearance as a means of shocking and intimidating their victims. Indeed, Tacitus records in the *Germania* (Ch.31) that the Germanic people called the *Chatti* had the practice of letting the hair and beard of the young men grow untrimmed, and of only allowing them to shave off their beards once they had killed their first enemy – the less warlike had to remain unshaven, a mark of indignity. Their bravest also had the custom of wearing a neckring as a mark of servitude (a slave's collar shackle, in effect) until they had managed to kill a man, and Tacitus says that some chose to maintain the fashion, and to keep up the severe lifestyle they had chosen of possessing nothing themselves and roaming the land living off the hospitality of others. It is likely enough that these rough-living, fierce, unkempt and landless men were the forerunners of the later Scandinavian 'bearshirts' and 'wolfcoats' as well as the 'wolf's heads' of Christian England.

The *fiana* or roving groups of young men in pre-Christian Ireland may also be a reflex of a parallel concept among the Gael. In Irish tradition, the greatest warrior of them all, Cú Chulainn, was seized with a state called *ferg*, in which his body is contorted with battle-madness; a parallel tradition among the early Greeks called the state *lyssa*, derived apparently from *lykos* 'wolf' and meaning something like 'wolfhood', which is attributed to e.g. Achilles before the gates of Troy.

The particular quality of the 'bearshirt' which set him apart from other warriors was the state of mental ecstasy or exhilaration (ON *óðr*) he could enter, which allowed him to rush forward in battle without thought of danger, whooping like a beast and biting the rim of his shield. This power was the gift of Óðinn,[55] the god of inspiration, and allowed the warrior to operate without personal involvement – his body acted as a killing machine while his spirit was elsewhere, communing with the one-eyed war-god. This same sense of the separation of mind from body allowed the seer to foretell the future and experience past events at first hand, and the poet to weave his many-threaded word-webs.[56]

While direct English parallels to the *berserkir* are lacking – possibly suppressed under the influence of the church – there remains the evidence of early grave-goods

---

[55] *Óðinn* means 'lord of *óðr*'.

[56] It has been suggested that the sense of mental exhilaration the berserk experienced was due to certain psychotropic substances, particularly the fungus 'fly agaric', although its generally mellowing effect makes this unlikely.

from the pagan period, some of which feature wolves or 'werwolves'. The bronze die to make helmet plates found at Torslunda, Sweden, features two figures, one of whom is carrying sword and spear, and wearing what appears to be a wolfskin cloak complete with wolf-mask. This artistic tradition extended to eastern England (may even have originated here) and included the finest materials from cemeteries such as Sutton Hoo, Snape and Taplow. Curiously, the East Anglian royal family called itself *Wuffingas* 'descendants of Wulf'.

Figure 12 One of a pair of helmeted warriors from the Sutton Hoo helmet in a ritual 'dancing' pose. The confronted birds' heads surmounting it make an unlikely crest, and may be a graphic representation of mental possession by the god Wōden. The god's Norse equivalent, Óðinn, was associated with two ravens, Huginn and Muninn (Thought and Memory) who personify human mental acuity.

The English Military: from the Beginnings to the First Danish Wars

.... A greater slaughter was not
ever yet in this island
slain by an army before this
with sword's blades – as books tell us,
ancient scribes – since here from the east
the Angles and Saxons came over
across the broad sea – they sought Britain,
the proud war-makers overcame the Welsh,
the keen heroes won a homeland.

(Anglo-Saxon Chronicle 'A', s.a.937)

Ne wearð wæl māre
on þis eiglande æfre gieta
folces gefylled beforan þissum
sweordes ecgum þæs þe ūs secgaþ bēc,
ealde ūðwitan, siþþan ēastan hider
Engle and Seaxe ūp becōman
ofer brād brimu Brytene sōhtan,
wlance wīgsmiþas, Wealas ofercōman,
earlas ārhwate eard begēatan.

The Warband

The smallest military unit above the individual warrior was the 'warband', possibly represented in Old English by the term *werod*, derived from the verb *werian* 'defend, protect' and denoting a group of men which stands together for mutual protection. The usual number for such a group is between six and ten men (platoon strength, in modern terms) – any less and they are ineffective, any more and they will not cohere as a unit. It may be presumed that the men of the *werod* knew each other well, trained together, lived, ate and slept together when on campaign and were sworn to mutual protection. Such a group would naturally have a leader whose responsibility it was to take the necessary decisions for the common good – both policy decisions and tactical ones, according to circumstances.

There is, unfortunately, no real evidence to show that the *werod* had anything approaching a uniform – be it a common shield design, clothes made from the same bolt of cloth, the same shape of spearhead, or whatever. This is a pity, since we would expect a close-knit band to develop a group identity and express this in some form of heraldic display. Later mediaeval armies sometimes used sprigs of flowering plant, such as broom, for this purpose, and this practice may well date back to Anglo-Saxon times or before, but there is sadly no real evidence to support the idea. Men operating in groups of a dozen or two would quickly come to know and recognize each other, of course, but in the larger groupings – the multiple shiploads of the early chronicle entries, or the regional armies of Ælfred's day – the need for a clear and unmistakable badge marking a man out as 'friend' or 'foe' would be paramount if unnecessary injuries were to be avoided.

Leaders may have been singled out on the battlefield primarily by the quality of their equipment – the wearing of a helmet or mailcoat, the wielding of a golden-hilted sword, the decorated plates on the shield – although here again if a particular group marched behind, say, the emblem of the boar then the leader might well have worn this device prominently in his equipment, as on the Benty Grange helmet. One further piece of evidence for a mark of leadership from late in the period – the battle fought in 991 at Maldon, Essex – is the fact that when the English thane Godric decides to flee and seizes his lord's horse for his getaway, the English troops automatically presume that the escaping horseman must have been their *ealdormann*, Byrhtnōð, who had previously instructed his men to drive off their own mounts:

> "He then bade each of the warriors to let go of his horse,
> to drive it far off and to march forwards"
>
> (*The Battle of Maldon*, lines 2–3)

> *Hēt þā hyssa hwǣne hors forlǣtan*
> *fēor āfȳsan and forð gangan*

In the poem *Beowulf*, one of the treasures with which the hero is rewarded by the Danish king Hrōðgār is:

> "a saddle, skilfully ornamented, made precious with decoration
> – it was the seat in battle of the high king"
>
> (*Beowulf*, lines 1039–40)

> *sadol searwum fāh since gewurþad*
> *þæt wæs hildesetl hēahcyninges*

hence it may be that remaining mounted was the privilege of men of royal or similar status, although both Hrōðgār and Byrhtnōð are elderly men at the time of the action of their respective poems, and it may equally be that those advanced in years were accorded the concession of sitting down as much as possible. Nonetheless, Byrhtnōð was in the thick of it at Maldon, trading spear thrusts and sword blows with the Norsemen along with his companions, and his horse was possibly kept by as a precaution in case the day were lost (and ironically, as Byrhtnōð falls dead, one of the thanes decides to take the only horse left on the field).

A physical symbol of the *werod* group would be expected – a totem or, in our terms, a 'mascot' – which might have been what the Anglo-Saxons called a *gūðfana* 'war-flag' or *segen* 'standard' or *cumbol* 'banner' – a flag round which the troops would rally, and which held a special significance as the emblem of their group identity, their warrior status and their luck: it is in effect a group 'soul' which cannot be allowed to fall into the hands of the enemy while the group still exists (consider also the lengths some men have gone to in modern times to recover the regimental colours). A spearhead recovered from a grave at Welbeck Hill, Lincs., was both very large in the blade (nearly 20ins – 50cm) and had the lower corners pierced with holes as if some decorative streamer or flag were meant to be attached there. It is certainly recorded of the Norsemen that they had the famed 'Raven Banner'.

> "...Now accept a banner, for I have made (it) with all my magical skill, and I forsee that he before whom it is borne must be victorious, but he must die who bears it." The banner was made with much fine work and resplendent craftsmanship. It was made in the form of a raven, and whenever the wind blew the banner it was as if the raven stretched its wings for flight.
>
> (*Flateyjarbók* – Ólafssaga Tryggvasons Ch.186)

> "... Tak þú hér við merki því er ek hefir gört af allri minni kunnáttu ok vænti ek at sigrsælt mun verða þeim er fyrir er borit, en banvænt þeim er berr." Merkit var gört af miklum hannyrðum ok ágætligum hagleik. Þat var gört í hrafns mynd ok þá er vindr blés í merkit þá var sem hrafn beindi fluginn.

Evidently this banner was something more than just a badge, since the Norsemen believed that the banner itself could bring victory and death. That it bore the raven – symbol of Óðinn, god of war, god of victory, god of violent death – is hardly surprising. In *Beowulf* it is recorded that the hero's people, the *Wederas*, received *wīgspēd* 'success in war' from a similar gift:

> ... But the lord gave them
> weavings of war-might, to the Weders' folk
> benefit and assistance ...
>
> (lines 696–8)

> ... Ac him dryhten forgeāf
> wīgspēda gewiofu, Wedera lēodum
> frōfor ond fultum ...

although the nature of the *gewiofu* 'weavings, webs, woven things' is not made more explicit, the likelihood is that an Anglo-Saxon audience would have understood the implicit reference to a 'magical' banner. However, the Raven's magic did not always work, as we read in the *Anglo-Saxon Chronicle* for the year 878:

> "There that banner was taken which they called 'Raven'."
>
> Þār wæs se gūðfana genumen þe hī ræfen hēton.

The *werod* was centred on an individual, and in later times every political leader or *æðeling* seems to have had his own *werod*, the men owing personal allegiance to him even before their own families. We read in the *Anglo-Saxon Chronicle* for the year 755 of a situation where a king has been slain by a rival whilst paying a visit to his mistress, and the king's *werod* have arrived to avenge his murder only to find that some in their group have kinsmen among the enemy force. Offered their freedom in exchange for changing sides and leaving their colleagues, the record says:

"...And then they said that no kinsman was dearer to them than their lord, and they would never follow his killer; and then they offered their kinsmen that they might leave unharmed, and they said that the same [terms] should be offered to their companions who had previously been with the king. Then they said that they could not accept that..."

(lines 32–7)

... Ond þā cuǣdon hīe þæt him nǣnig mǣg lēofra nǣre þonne hiera hlāford, ond hīe nǣfre his banan folgian noldon; ond þā budon hīe hiera mǣgum þæt hīe gesunde from ēodon; ond hīe cuǣdon þæt tæt ilce hiera gefērum geboden wǣre þe ǣr mid þām cyninge wǣrun. Þā cuǣdon hīe þæt hīe hīe þæs ne onmunden...

Loyalty to *gefēran* 'companions, men with whom one travels' claimed first place for warriors, beyond the calls of family duty, even though for kinship's sake the offer of safe passage had been made.

An alternative term for *gefēra* is *secg*[57] which, with its Norse counterpart *seggr*, remains a slightly poetic word for a warrior, and in *Beowulf* it occurs in apposition to *þegn*:

'...so should a *secg* be,
a thane in time of need...'

(lines 2708–9)

*... swā sceolde secg wesan,
þegn æt ðearfe...*

pointing to an approximately equivalent relationship of loyalty to sworn brothers and service to the leader.

The *werod*, though, for all its close-knit companionship and *ésprit de corps*, was only capable of so much. While the early English mercenaries had carved out kingdoms with a couple of shiploads of men, even the *heorðwerod*[58] was not really intended to do more than protect the king's person in battle, and act as escort and bodyguard in peace. It was fine for cattle-raiding, for intimidating recalcitrant farmers and opportunist robbers, for quelling any local unpleasantness: all largely symbolic roles, and not at all the proper use of all the training and equipment tied up in the *gedriht*. Larger operations, especially in settled kingdoms, called for larger forces; it is to these that we will now turn.

---

[57] OE *secg* has been convincingly derived by Eric Hamp from an original Proto-Indo-European root *sokwoHi-* with the meaning 'loyal comrade', which also gives rise to the Latin *socius* 'member of a brotherhood' and Greek *aosseō* help, assistance', with the underlying concept of loyalty and mutual support.

[58] See p.31 for more on this institution.

The Fyrd and its Leadership

The armed forces as a whole were known as the *fyrd*[59] service in which constituted the military duty of the free adult male landowners; it may be thought of as a mobilized force of yeomen, probably numerous and keen to protect their holdings, but in the earlier period quite unwieldy and ill-equipped compared with the *werod*. It is unlikely that the full *fyrd* would have been summoned to war except under serious threat of conquest, however; for local and small-scale matters such as raids the *gesīþas* would have sufficed. The immediate leaders of the local *fyrd* were the *gesīþas* or *þegnas*, who were the king's own personal followers, his retinue, or men who had sworn to serve him even though they were themselves lords of other lands with their own followers – often, such men were members of dynasties which had been overcome and their lands absorbed into the larger kingdoms, or were disaffected members of rival royal houses who had fled to serve their former foes. Such men may attest royal charters (land-grants) where they have the title *minister* equating roughly to the English 'thane', or *dux* 'ealdormann' – for example, one *Sigered dux* attests several Mercian charters of King Coenwulf from c. 811 to c. 836, and he may be the last survivor of the East Saxon royal family, reduced in status to provincial governor before the Danish wars swept away the royal dynasties of both Essex and Mercia.

Service in the army was to some extent a requirement on all free men, but the actual front-line fighting was generally confined to the biggest and the bravest, the professional warriors. 'Military service' for the bulk of the population meant various kinds of support, or even in later times simply financial payment towards the expenses of the warrior class. The modern word 'army' is Latin-based (*armata* '[that which is] provided with weapons, armed') and translates two Old English words, *fyrd* and *here*. The *fyrd* was the local English military force, and in the context of the Danish wars it is the military body charged with the responsibility of carrying out the king's will in offensive and defensive operations. Its name is related to the verb *faran* 'travel' with the sense 'excursion, campaign, time spent away travelling'. The other 'army' term, *here*, in Old English has generally a negative sense 'raiding force, enemy army' and gives rise to the verb *hergian* 'harry, raid, plunder'.[60] A *here* is generally the enemy in Old English, a raiding force bent on rapine and slaughter; Ine's law code specifies that a *here* numbers more than 35 men, to distinguish it from a *hlōþ*, a smaller band of outlaws or robbers.

Military service, then, was a matter of duty for the free, land-owning populace even if seldom a matter of physical presence at battles except for the leaders and those chosen for their retinues. There is a strong likelihood that for every professional warrior out on active service, there was at least one servant in attendance to look after his equipment and manage his affairs (somewhat like a 'batman' in more recent times).

---

[59] Also spelt *fierd*.

[60] Its origin lies in a series of ancient terms for warfare, such as Lithuanian *karas* 'battle' and Old Persian *kāra-* 'army, troop'.

In the ASC annal for 893, King Alfred is said to have divided the army (*fyrd, fierd*) into two parts so that while the one was out campaigning the other would be available at home:

"the king then had divided his army into two, so that they were always half at home, half away, except for the men who had to keep the strongholds"

(lines 28–31)).

hæfde se cyning his fierd on tū tōnumen swā þæt hīe wǣron simle healfe æt hām, healfe ūte, būtan þǣm monnum þe þā burga healdan scolden

Isn't this evidence that the English army consisted at least in part of farmworkers? Actually, no – a more natural reading of the text is that the *fierd* was split up (*tōnumen* 'taken apart') so that Alfred could take one section off with him (*healfe ūte*) while the other remained in the English-held lands to protect the harvest from raiding by the Danes, with the fortress garrisons constituting a third element outside this arrangement. In effect, then Alfred had at his disposal a strong, offensive, proactive force, presumably faster moving due to the smaller numbers involved; an equally strong, reactive, defensive force; and a further static group of garrison troops, providing defence in depth. Under those circumstances, it would make sense for the defensive part of the *fierd* also to be mounted and mobile, as the strongholds were themselves able to provide fixed points of defence throughout the landscape and the 'missing' element was that of non-static protection. Alfred's arrangements were very successful and the principle of 'split service' remained in force up to the Norman Conquest,[61] although the fortresses proved too expensive in the long run and were generally converted to other uses.

The men who served in the *fierd* would no doubt have become progressively uneasier the further they had to travel from their homeland – leaving their loved ones, homes and chattels open to attack – and Alfred's measure may have been designed to offset this tendency, given that with the increase in English territory, the warriors from his powerbase in the southwest would have had ever further to travel in order to confront the enemy. Nevertheless, military service certainly did involve time away for all those eligible to perform it, since that same year (893) things went wrong for Alfred :

"Then the army besieged them [the Danes] there [on an island in the Colne] from outside for as long as they had food there; but then they had completed their term of duty, and used up their food; and the king was [still] on his way to that place, with the division which was serving with him" (*ASC* lines 39–42)

---

[61] Nicholas Hooper suggests that Harold had kept his troops out on watch against the expected Norman attack from early May to 8th September, a period of four months; since Domesday evidence tells us that men out on military service took payment for two months, the logical conclusion is that the army was called out in two stages. The fateful decision to disband must have been based on Harold's belief that October was too late in the year for the invasion to take place.

Þā besæt sīo fierd hīe þærūtan þā hwīle þe hīe þær lengest mete hæfdon; ac hīe hæfdon þā heora stemn gesetenne ond hiora mete genotudne; ond wæs se cyning þā þiderweardes on fære, mid þære scīre þe mid him fierdedon.

The outgoing campaigning force had used up all its food and was preparing to return home before the fresh troops (presumably those previously watching over the English homeland) had arrived to replace them, when other elements of the Danish army mounted a seaborne raid into Wessex. The word translated as 'division' above is *scīr*, which elsewhere denotes a political division of a kingdom – it is our word 'shire' – and may mean that mobilization was handled on a territorial basis. There are certain good psychological advantages to be gained from raising armies among neighbours and men who know each other well – they tend to cohere better and to operate in units the more readily – but it then has to be assumed that the protection of the shire land they left behind was then the responsibility of the troops of neighbouring shires. Nevertheless, Alfred's system remained in place under his son, Edward, and grandson, Athelstan, but proved too expensive during the peaceful hiatus of Edgar's reign. It had been partly dismantled by the time of Ethelred, and the fortifications which had withstood Viking assaults and housed English warriors in the 9th and 10th centuries were in disrepair or converted to commercial purposes by the early 11th.

The accent on defence noticeable in the military innovations of Alfred's day was understandable in the light of the fact that generally the initiative rested with the vikings, who tended to mount attacks which the English had then to fend off or counter. The vikings were able to move very quickly by land or sea, and this alone threatened disaster for the English – until the last remaining kingdom, having had time to study their tactics and re-think its own, devised the notion of defence in depth to counter the Danes' advantage. Nonetheless, no other English kingdom was able to withstand the twin advantages of speed and superior strength of the Vikings. It no doubt helped Alfred that the Danish leader who opposed him, Guðrum, was aiming to gain political control of English territory, and therefore could not indulge in the excesses enjoyed by raiders with only short-term aims.

In the time of Athelstan, Alfred's grandson, the English were able to take the fight to the Scandinavians, who by then were more-or-less firmly settled in Britain; they had forced a treaty on Alfred whereby they held the northern and eastern parts of the country in their own right. The reliance on a heavily defensive strategy was not abandoned, however, since with each success the construction of English-held *burh* fortifications across the newly-acquired northern regions consolidated the territorial gains and enabled them to be held against counter-attack.

The Call to Arms

How were English armies mustered? Direct evidence is lacking, unfortunately, for the actual mechanisms involved, but the apparent speed with which kingdoms were mobilized, especially in the days of the Heptarchy when armies were presumably smaller and more dependent on chiefs and warbands, suggests that there were ways of relaying the call to arms quickly[62] which allowed the men involved to foregather in places from which they could move on in strength to meet the foe. After his ignominious flight from Chippenham and retreat into the marshes, Alfred sent out word to his men to meet him after Easter at 'Ecgbert's stone':

> ... Then in the seventh week after Easter he rode to Ecgbert's stone on the eastern side of Selwood, and to him there came all the men of Somerset and Wiltshire and from that part of Hampshire on this side of the sea, and they were glad of him...
>
> *(ASC 'A' s.a.878)*

> ... *Þā on þǣre seofeðan wiecan ofer ēastron hē gerād tō Ecgbryhtes stāne be ēastan Sealwyda ⁊ him cōm þǣr ongēn Sumorsǣte alle ⁊ Wilsǣtan ⁊ Hāmtūnscīr se dǣl se hīere behinon sǣ wæs ⁊ his gefǣgene wǣrun*...

We can imagine a romantic scene of English messengers disguised as peasants moving through the Danish-occupied areas under cover of darkness, but in fact if Alfred was able to muster his men at the site we presume to be Ecgberht's stone today (where the three county boundaries meet) then he was within a few hours ride of the Danes in their base at Chippenham, and the occupying force's hold on the surrounding area must have been non-existent.

Figure 13 English warrior with drawn sword and baldric-slung scabbard, based on a detail from an Anglo-Saxon manuscript illustration

---

[62] A network of manned vantage points is evidenced, sited along main roads – see p.198.

There is suggestive (rather than conclusive) evidence for a device possibly used for mustering troops in the form of the wooden sword,[63] its tip burnt, found at Arum, West Frisia. The blade bears a short inscription in runes 'edœ : boda' which has been interpreted as 'one who carries a message back, return messenger', and may have been a token used as a summons to war – if a symbolic sword is indeed a 'messenger' then it can betoken nothing but fighting. Other wooden swords have been found in Denmark and the Low Countries, where waterlogged soil conditions have preserved them. Furthermore, Saxo Grammaticus mentions that the practice (presumably of his day) was to summon troops by sending round a wooden arrow (another symbolic weapon) while there was a parallel Scandinavian custom using a piece of burnt timber, perhaps explaining the burnt tip of the Arum sword.

Nicholas Hooper points out that in 1004 Earl Ulfcetel of East Anglia found it expedient to pay a substantial Danegeld to the viking force attacking Norwich, and though he subsequently raised an army, it was not his entire force even though it had taken him some three weeks to gather it. The situation necessarily called for secrecy if the Danes were not to get wind of the army being mustered against them, but even so three weeks is an unreasonable period in which to raise only part of a defensive force. Likewise Harold Godwineson, having disbanded his forces for the winter of 1066, had considerable difficulty calling them out again, though he had to do so twice within a matter of a few days, once to meet the Norsemen in Yorkshire and then again to meet the Normans in Sussex.

The Ceorl as Warrior

I have suggested above that military service was confined to a limited and specially-selected section of society, who earnt the right to accompany the king on his expeditions by their loyalty and talent for violence. However, this view does not agree very well with the 'traditional' historians' image of the Anglo-Saxon army as consisting of the nation's freemen, each exercising his traditional right to bear arms. So prevalent has this view been that it has seldom been discussed, although at the beginning of the century the renowned historian H. M. Chadwick expressed doubts about the idea of Anglo-Saxon peasant levies, on the evidence of Domesday Book. A compromise solution to the riddle of the composition of the *fyrd* is that there were different types of army: the *'select fyrd'* (nobles and mounted thanes), and the *'great fyrd'* (peasant levies), with the latter taking the blame for the defeat of Harold at Hastings. Elsewhere, up to three different types of army have been identified: the *regional*, the *shire* and the *royal*. Regional forces were composed of professional warriors backed up by mounted thanes and landholders, led by ealdormen; royal forces were the sum of the regional forces available to the king, while shire forces were peasant levies called out for local defence, led by thanes.

There is evidence showing that military service was not always confined to the very highest social strata and their cohorts of bodyguards. In 991, during Ethelred's

---

[63] Terry Brown suggests a possible link with the Roman custom of presenting a retiring gladiator with a wooden copy of his sword.

reign, a viking fleet sacked Ipswich and then set up base outside the *burh* of Maldon in Essex, probably on what is now called Northey Island a mile or two downstream of the town. The raiders were brought to battle there, and a fragment of an English poem[64] commemorating the event has survived; the text offers the nearest thing we now have to a contemporary eyewitness report of an English military engagement of that period. We will be examining aspects of the poem later, but it will suffice for now to note that one of the men on the English side, among thanes and other nobles, is called *Dunnere* and is described as a 'humble yeoman' (*unorne ceorl*). The circumstances surrounding the battle were perhaps to some extent extraordinary, and it may be that Dunnere was present at the encounter to supply local topographical knowledge or to act as a guide to the English forces; yet the fact remains that he was armed for fighting and had the authority to call out encouragement to his comrades:

> Then Dunnere spoke, shook his throwing-spear
> (the) humble yeoman called out over all
> bade that each of (the) warriors should avenge Byrhtnōð...
> > (*The Battle of Maldon*, lines 255–7)
>
> *Dunnere þā cwæð, daroð ācwehte*
> *unorne ceorl ofer eall clypode*
> *bæd þæt beorna gehwylc Byrhtnōð wræce ...*

Unfortunately, nothing more is known of Dunnere or his background; it would certainly be instructive to discover whether he was a regular member of the armed forces, a member of the English leader's personal following or simply a local farmer conscripted to help defend his land and home against a numerically vastly superior foe. It has been proposed that he may have been a member of a family working the estates at Hatfield, Hertfordshire, though the evidence for this is at best no more than suggestive; if so, his status would have been closer to that of free peasant than gentleman-farmer.

The much earlier law-code of King Ine of Wessex, which is a status-symbol[65] for the king rather than a law-code in any modern sense, sets out a penalty of 30 shillings for any *cierlisc mann* (man of *ceorl* status) who does not perform his military duty (OE *tō fierdwīte* 'as army-fine'). Yet it is not clear whether this means that all men of *cierlisc* rank had such obligations, or whether perhaps the king could require military service from individuals on an *ad hoc* basis and if they failed him they had to pay the fine. However, Anglo-Saxon laws generally do not attempt to legislate for situations upon which common custom agrees; they are more naturally read as documents designed to enhance the king's legal powers. Therefore, we would not really expect the law-codes to tell us what the military service requirements were for every rank, when everybody knew them, but rather only to specify what the king's expectations were in

---

[64] See Appendix III for the text.

[65] Like many of his royal contemporaries, Ine was aware that issuing a law-code was one of the things that respectable Christian kings were supposed to do; it was good for Ine's 'image' but is so brief and concerned with such a small range of topics that it can have had very little practical application.

certain grey areas (such as failure to perform). Richard Abels has suggested in explanation that, within any Anglo-Saxon state, there were various landholdings which passed down in families of *cierlisc* status. However, these were grouped together into tenurial holdings under 'lords',[66] and control ('lordship') of the various groups was handed out to the king's *gesīðas*, particularly the *duguþ* or veteran warriors, as rewards for past support and incentives for future service. These 'manors' were not inherited by retainers but remained in the king's gift, however, and could be taken back if the *gesīþ* failed to support him; they reverted to the crown on the individual's death so each succeeding generation of warriors had to win their holdings anew. However, the king retained direct lordship over some estates himself, the food-rents and dues from which went to support his household; these may be the origin of the various places called 'Charlton'[67] from OE *ceorla tūn* 'estate of the *ceorlas*' which occur regularly next to known royal estates. It is probable, according to Abels, that the reference to *cierlisc* men in Ine's law is to the king's own *ceorlas* (that is, men whose tenurial lord was the king), and who were bound to follow him in times of war. From this it is obvious that the 'free men' of Anglo-Saxon times were not free of all duties and obligations, and that each class had its own share of the common burdens to bear. Only the *æðelingas* or nobles were free in anything like the modern sense, and even they held their *regiones* from the king with his consent rather than by right. The yeomen were thus the retainers of lords who were themselves the retainers of kings, and we may imagine a structure like this:

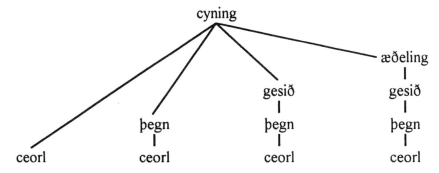

cyning – the king;
æðeling – any other adult male in the king's kindred, any tributary king or any other hereditary nobleman;

gesīð – any member of the warband;
þegn – a thane or any other non-hereditary royal official;
ceorl – yeoman or any other land-owning freeman.

Figure 14 Schematic representation of military obligation within the social hierarchy

---

[66] The *ceorlas* on the estates forming the lord's holding owed service to the lord, just as the lord did to the king. This system gave the lord rights over his holdings which were a subrogation of the king's own rights. The similarity to the later feudal system (often alleged to be a Norman introduction) is striking.

[67] Or variously 'Chorlton' or 'Carlton'.

There is an interesting story told by Bede about a Northumbrian thane called Imma, a member of the *geoguþ* who was stunned in battle and woke to find himself heaped among the corpses for burial. Knowing that if his thanely status were to be revealed there would be problems (at best, punitive ransom demands, but more probably death in vengeance for blood-feud) he tried to pass himself off as a lowly, married and penniless *ceorl* who had been working in the supply train. His strategy could be read as showing that *ceorlas* were fit only for non-combatant work, but it is likelier that he was relying on the suggestion that he was both poor and married for his release: professional warriors of whatever status were always young and unmarried, and his claim to poverty explains his lack of war-gear and having been put to work as a quartermaster. (Nevertheless, his captors saw through his disguise, suspecting him to be a nobleman by his looks, clothes and speech. This suggests a class hierarchy in which warfare is the proper business of nobles, even though it involves these nobles' supporters as well.)

Perhaps a further piece in the jigsaw of determining whether the lowly were 'constitutionally' required to fight is the Bayeux tapestry, which shows Englishmen using spades and clubs as weapons to defend themselves.[68] There is little doubt that these men were not regular troops but hapless victims of an attack; if they were actually engaged on military service (which is not certain – they could have been working in their fields) then the likelihood is that they were engaged in *burhbōt*, fortress maintenance – digging ditches, raising mounds, repairing walls. If these men were *ceorlas* rather than unfree *þēowas* 'servants' then, like Imma's assumed identity, they were men too poor to equip themselves for war.

Taken as a whole, the evidence for the 'nation in arms' is unconvincing; freemen seem actually to have been obliged to fulfil their duties to their lords and while this was sometimes a matter of military service, it was not necessarily so. We can imagine that a *gesīð* with lordship of a dozen or more estates might want a handful of followers to enforce his will and support him in war; being owed service by his *cierlisc* tenants, he might choose some of the more promising youths to assist him, to enter his household and enjoy his hospitality. Nevertheless, such military involvement did not impinge on the other members of these men's families, nor on neighbours whose duties were fulfilled in other ways.

The Exiled Warrior

Probably the worst fate that could befall a warrior was that his lord should fall in battle and he survive. The death of the leader almost inevitably meant defeat, even at so late a date as 991, the year of the battle at Maldon, Essex, where Byrhtnōð's death sealed the issue. For those who outlived their lord, this could literally be a fate worse than death, since it meant that the survivor's entire livelihood – dependent as it was on the favours of the leader – was taken away, so personal were the ties of loyalty. Yet, although there is repetition of this theme in Old English verse, it seems that the true

---

[68] Special Forces in the modern era are sometimes issued with a sharpened spade which doubles as a close-combat weapon and an entrenching tool.

shame attached to surviving one's lord lay in having failed to protect him – which the *þegn* should do even at the cost of his own life. Perhaps equally pressing, given that no-one can guard against every eventuality and battlefields are inherently dangerous places, was the duty to avenge the fallen lord, by slaying his *bana* 'killer'. The *bana* could be the actual warrior who delivered the death-blow, the *handbana* 'hand-slayer', but more usually would be the opponent who bore the moral responsibility for his death, the leader of the enemy force.

It is evident that if all warriors were obliged to die with a fallen leader, the chances of any folk recovering from the loss of both the lord and the bravest warriors would be minimal. Yet the duty of 'revenge or death' is a recurrent theme in early English verse and other literature, including the (quasi-historical) *Chronicle*, as for example the entry for 755.[69]

The classic expression of the fate of the exiled warrior is in the Old English poem now called *The Wanderer* in the Exeter Book, which is cast as the reflection upon his fate of a warrior whose lord and comrades have fallen. It is worth quoting sections of this poem to show the frame of mind an Anglo-Saxon audience would expect from such a man:

> I had often alone at each dawning
> to mourn my cares. There is none among the living now
> to whom my heart's thoughts I dare
> to declare openly. I know for sure
> that for the hero there is a noble custom
> that he close tight his breast,
> hold fast his heart, no matter what he feels…

(lines 8–14)

> *Oft ic sceolde āna ūhtna gehwylce*
> *mīne ceare cwīþan. Nis nū cwicra nān*
> *þe ic him mōdsefan mīnne durre*
> *sweotule āsecgan. Ic tō sōþe wāt*
> *þæt biþ in eorle indryhten þēaw*
> *þæt hē his ferðlocan fæste binde,*
> *healde his hordcofan hycge swā hē wille….*

Yet while he regretted the loss of his lord, he could hope still for another such close relationship:

> thus my heart I must
> – often sorrowing, parted from my homeland,
> far from kinsmen – hold back with fetters
> since long ago my gold-giving friend
> the earth's darkness enclosed, and downcast from there I

---

[69] See p.207 for part of this entry.

strode with the worries of winter across the boundary of the waves,
homesick I sought a hall, a giver of gems,
somewhere, far or near, I could find
him who knew my mind in the mead-hall
or wished to comfort me, friendless as I was ...

(lines 19–28)

"swā ic mōdsefan mīnne sceolde
oft earmcearig, ēðle bidǣled,
frēomǣgum feor, feterum sǣlan
siþþan geāra īu goldwine mīnne
hrusan heolster biwrāh ond ic hēan þonan
wōd wintercearig ofer waþema gebind,
sōhte sele drēorig sinces bryttan
hwǣr ic feor oþþe nēah findan meahte
þone þe in meoduhealle mīn mine wisse
oþþe mec frēondlēasne frēfran wolde... "

But it seems that generally such lordless men were regarded with extreme suspicion. For one thing, if they had managed to outlive their lord, there was at least a suggestion that they had not fought in a manner befitting true warrior-retainers, but had perhaps fled the field of battle, or worst of all betrayed their lord to his enemies. Moreover, there was also the consideration that such men might have powerful enemies among the kin of those they had slain, who would expect vengeance by *wergild*, and the new lord would take on any existing feuds himself if he took the man into his retinue. Small wonder, then, that the speaker of this poem concludes that all human affairs are precarious and transitory:

Where is the horse? Where is the comrade? Where is the giver of *māþmas*?
Where is the seat at the *symbel*? Where are the joys of the hall?
Lo, bright cup! lo, armoured warrior!
Lo, lord's glory! How that time has gone by,
grown dark beneath the cover of night as if it had never been.

(lines 91–6)

Hwǣr cwōm mearg? Hwǣr cwōm mago? Hwǣr cwōm māþþumgyfa?
Hwǣr cwōm symbla gesetu? Hwǣr sindon seledrēamas?
ēalā beorht būne, ēalā byrnwiga,
ēalā þeodnes þrym. Hū sēo þrāg gewāt,
genāp under nihthelm swā hēo nō wǣre

Yet it was not only the survivors of a fallen lord who travelled in exile.[70] Disaffected relatives of the current dynasty and especially younger sons with no prospect of

---

[70] See below, p.204, for the *Beowulf* poet's conception of the fate of the folk when the lord falls and their military strength is dissipated.

inheriting anything worth having would often turn their backs on their kindred and set off in search of a new lord from whom they might expect to receive greater benefits; they would then bind themselves to this new relationship, forsaking the duties and obligations as well as the privileges of their previous situations.[71] Such men were called *wreccea* in Old English, from a root which gives rise to the German *Recke* 'adventurer' as well as the English word 'wretch' for an unhappy, friendless person.

Later Anglo-Saxon Military Organization

...They were attacked as they fled
– that mighty army – until the greater part
of the raiders lay felled by war
on the plain of victory, hewn by swords
as an enjoyment to wolves, as to flesh-hungry
birds a joy ...

(*Judith*, lines 292–7)

.... *Him mon feaht on lāst,*
mægenēacen folc, oð se mæsta dæl
þæs heriges læg hilde gesæged
on ðām sigewonge, sweordum gehēawen
wulfum tō willan and ēac wælgīfrum
fuglum tō frōfre...

Some time between the first Danish wars, culminating in Alfred's peace treaty, and the later period of viking activity beginning in the 990s, the character of English military service changed. The *werod* had always been principally composed of young men whose aim was to receive treasure, led by older men whose aim was to receive lordship of estates and land on which to settle down and raise the next generation of king's retainers. Bede and other early witnesses certainly suggest that the *werod* system flourished in his day, but it was even then threatened and by the time of the later viking attacks, warrior service had become a matter of landed men leading troops of armed and armoured professionals.

The first nail in the coffin of the early English military system was the church. In order to win lordship over a group of yeomen in later life, the noble warriors had to serve the king well. The church introduced a new concept into the equation: *bōcland* 'bookland', which is to say, land held in perpetuity by royal charter. The church wanted the security of permanent and inalienable land-holdings, and early Anglo-

---

[71] This *lord:retainer* bond was central to close male relationships in Anglo-Saxon England; when Bishop Wilfred quarrelled with his king, Aldfrið of Northumbria, and was driven into exile, it was considered remarkable behaviour that his monastic colleagues and dependants did *not* choose to follow him. The cleric, Aldhelm of Sherborne, sent them a letter reproaching them for their lack of personal loyalty to their 'lord'.

Saxon kings were glad to exchange a few farms for a seat at Christ's right hand. Unfortunately, because the land so donated did not revert to the king ever, this had two unforeseen results. The first was that there was less advantage in risking one's life in the military, and leading men began to establish their own religious houses – with land-grants from the king – as a means of securing permanent rights to land without the corresponding duties of military service. These spurious monasteries were roundly condemned by Bede's contemporaries as they did not further the church's cause with prayer, but rather offered an attractive tax haven for the unscrupulous. The second result was to reduce the amount of land the king had at his disposal with which to reward those who did serve him; the more able warriors were able to choose between potential lords in order to find the most generous terms. Naturally, for any state involved in large-scale endowment of the church, the first effect was to weaken the military base of the kingdom, while the second was to strengthen those of potential rivals through the leakage of the most promising men.

The second 'nail' was a direct reaction to the weakening effect of tenure by bookland. To counteract the trends discussed above, the Mercian kings devised a revision whereby the owners of all landed estates, whether religious or secular, had three 'common burdens' from which they could not be granted exemption: *burhbōt*, maintenance of fortifications; *brycgegeweorc*, work on bridges; *fyrdfæreld*, army service. Men holding land by charter had to obey the call to war, to serve personally and to bring with them a specified number of armed men (depending on the value of the estate). However, while combating the immediate problem of maintaining a credible military potential, the move away from the notion of earning lordship through support and service actually served to weaken the ties of loyalty between leaders and their followers at all levels.

The final 'nail' was the Danish wars, which effectively wiped out the smaller and weaker kingdoms, ultimately leaving only the West Saxon royal line. Military service was on a threefold basis: national (the king's *fyrd*), regional (the *scīr*) and personal (the *werod*); it was then organized at two levels: 'local' and 'national'. After the later Danish incursions, by King Ethelred's time, the standing armies which had enabled Alfred, Edward and Athelstan to fight off and defeat wave after wave of viking attacks had been replaced by a looser, levy-based system, whereby men served under a provincial leader called an *ealdormann*; each province was known as an *ealdordōm*, and could be called out to fight off local attacks, assist neighbouring shires, etc. The king also had the right to call out the national force, consisting of the sum of the forces available to the *ealdormen* plus his own personal retinue (*werod*). Naturally, where the military leaders were lords of (and resident in) separate estates dispersed in the countryside, the time it took to gather them and organize a defence strategy was much increased. Alfred's answer to this problem had been the permanent garrisons and the bipartite standing army, which left a sizeable force ready to take the field at any time, but by Æþelred's day the *burh* had become an administrative centre more than a fort and the *fyrd* had changed from 'standing army' to 'fire-brigade' – only called out in emergencies.

Whereas, under the earlier system, military service was largely a matter for men of wealth and status – the king's companions – and their chosen followers, the demands of the situation were such that the burden had to be more evenly spread. Thus it came about that relatively modestly endowed freemen, who had previously largely escaped military 'active service', were now expected to join together into groups to provide equipment for an armed man between them – according to the *Chronicle* (s.a. 1008), every eight hides had to provide a helmet and byrnie. This meant an additional tax burden for the relatively non-affluent – they were not expected to make the war-gear themselves, only to contribute sufficient money to pay for it. The mobile coastal defence called the *scipfyrd* was paid for in a similar way. The system could only be operated in a kingdom where there was a strong and well-organized controlling body which could refer to records of assessment and establish any man's 'worth' (i.e. liability) from the value of his landholdings. In other words, what was needed was a chancery and the bureaucratic personnel and processes which go with it. England, having been such a well-ordered and thoroughly governed society for so long, was easily capable of supporting the administration of such taxation, even when the money itself was not forthcoming.

The forces of the *ealdordōm* were organized by shires, shires by hundreds, and hundreds by tithings and private holdings (sokes). This pyramidal structure was based on the notion of *hlāforddōm* 'lordship', whereby every free landowner owed a duty of service to his immediate superior and, where he was himself a 'lord', was owed a similar duty by his inferiors. Men fought alongside their lords, and the network of loyalties thus created allowed the English *fyrd* to cohere remarkably well. Where a leader of national importance also held a great deal of land, as in the case of Ealdorman Byrhtnōð, he was the personal superior of many of the men whom he summoned to his banner to fight the vikings, both on behalf of King Æðelred and as his own supporters. Ealdormen at this time exercised what Richard Abels calls 'delegated regalian powers' – the oaths of support for the king which were required of all men liable for military service, were put into effect through support for the delegated leader of the mustered forces.

Against the re-organized Anglo-Saxon *fyrd* was the later type of viking *here* – no longer a mere opportunist raiding party or *ad hoc* band of freebooters. These new viking forces were larger and better organized, as we would expect given that within Scandinavia itself many of the smaller kingdoms had been completely supplanted and absorbed by new, modern nation-states each with a single dynasty: it was to escape this centralizing process that many Norwegians fled to the newly-discovered Atlantic territory of Iceland, where they would be able to continue with their cherished lifestyle of independence and self-reliance. Denmark had undergone this process for the longest time, and had begun to accept the Christian church and other Western European ideas, due to close diplomatic and trading contacts. The Danes constructed large, circular military bases (e.g. Trelleborg, Fyrkat, etc.) although these have now been dated to the reign of Harald Bluetooth in the ninth century – one of the first of the kings to try to found a 'new order' and establish his central authority widely in the southern Baltic.[72] The new armies were larger and better led, the English opposition not so well led as previously – the *Chronicle* attributes most of the spectacular failures of the reign of Ethelred to poor leadership and some plain bad luck.

The Danish forces had also re-organized with the move towards a central state, and the system called *leiðangr* was instituted whereby recruitment to the king's banner was based on the landed wealth of freemen – the greater the landholding, the greater the number of armoured followers the freeman had to field.

With the victory of Cnut Svensson and his accession to the English throne, a new element was added to the multi-layered body which was the late Anglo-Saxon *fyrd*. English kings – even the later ones who ruled virtually all lowland Britain – had at their disposal a force of men who were their own followers (*gesīðas*, to use the anachronistic term from the period of early English emergence in Britain) independent of any other nobles, and probably hand-picked for their skill, loyalty and aggressive qualities. But Cnut was not English, he was Danish; and he already had sterling supporters who would serve and follow him, his own 'household men', his 'huscarls'. The traditional view of this body is that they represent the cream of the viking invasion force whom Cnut would not pay off, but kept about him in case his new English subjects proved reluctant to co-operate. They were professional soldiers, whose job was as much to overawe the English military as to enforce the king's will, with Cnut insisting that they bore the most resplendent mailshirts, two-edged swords with gold-inlaid hilts, and the two-handed axe which was their trade-mark. They did not submit to the king's justice but organized their own affairs (courts martial, in effect) and formed a closed society of sworn-brothers with strict rules of conduct to preserve order among such blood-thirsty individuals.

Sadly, the 'traditional view' has proven to be greatly overstated, and there is little that was once accepted as fact about the huscarls that would now go unchallenged. Much of the substance of the *huscarl* concept is derived from later Scandinavian accounts about another warrior-society from the Baltic, the *Jómsvíkingar*, allegedly based around Wollin in Poland. Much that was taken on trust about these Jómsvikings has since been shown to be both specious and spurious, and the source document *Jómsvíkingarsaga* is now largely discredited; with the fall of the Jómsvikings from history into romance, the only real parallel[73] to the huscarls is no longer of service.[74] Therefore, while the huscarls doubtless existed as the king's personal following, they

---

[72] These forts were previously thought to date from the reign of his son, Swein Forkbeard, and so be the mustering points and training grounds for Swein's armies which supported his successful bid for (and short occupancy of) the throne of England.

[73] Unless one sees the Byzantine Varangian Guard, composed largely of Scandinavians (and, after the Conquest, of disinherited Englishmen) as relevant to Northern European society.

[74] A document called *Lex castrensis sive curie,* purporting to be the rules of Cnut's household, was used to contrast the tight discipline of Cnut's men with the Danish royal retainers of the twelfth century. Yet there is every likelihood that it was actually composed in the twelfth century, albeit possibly on the model of an earlier regulation, to support moves by the clergy to limit the rowdy behaviour of the contemporary king's retainers.

were probably in fact 'stipendiary troops' (i.e. men paid a wage to fight), and so closer to our idea of 'professional soldier'[75] than anything else.

As a postscript to this section on the later Anglo-Saxon military, it is worth noting that the Norman élite virtually replaced the native English nobility after the Conquest. Most of the titles of the aristocracy came from their Norman French dialect (*baron, count, marquis, duke*) but certain English forms lived on, notably those of the highest grade (*king, queen*) as well as *earl* and the more general *lord, lady*. But the typical mounted warrior of mediaeval times was known by the name 'knight', an English word (OE *cniht*). Yet *cniht* does not usually mean 'warrior' in Old English texts, having the more general sense 'boy, youth, young man'. However, in the later period (say, the 11th century, for convenience) the word already had developed the secondary meaning 'young man in service, household retainer' with, admittedly, wider implications than just the military ones. However, the 'new' brand of warfare imported with the Norman expropriators – lance-brandishing cavalry supported by archers – seems to have been immediately identified in the English mind with the kind of military service performed by *cnihtas* so that there was never any question of the Norman-French name for these men (*chevalier*) becoming the common term.

---

[75] Richard Abels points out that stipendiary troops differ from mercenaries in that the former serve their lord and receive a wage in return, whereas mercenaries will fight for anyone as long as the price is right.

II. Weaponry

...bear shields forward,
boards before your chests and mailshirts,
steep helmets in the press of enemies,
with ornate swords slay chieftains
doomed leaders...

(*Judith*, lines 191–5)

... berað linde forð,
bord for breostum and byrnhomas,
scīre helmas in sceaðena gemong,
fyllað folctogan fāgum sweordum,
fǣge frumgāras ...

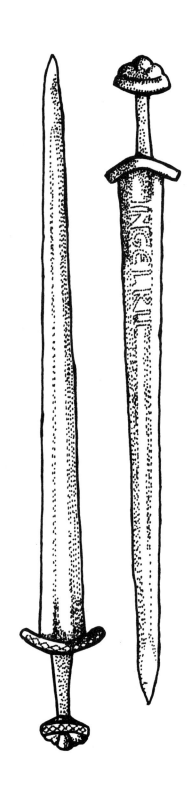

II. Weaponry

If the purpose of battle is to overcome the foe, then all hinges on the troop's effectiveness in attack, since the only decisive kind of defence is that which annihilates the foe, a result dependent on the ability to mount a counter-attack. Effectiveness in attack is conventionally achieved by one of two means: the weapons available and the ability to out-manoeuvre the foe through mobility.[1] The normal, and often the most efficient, combination of weapons is the long-range offensive, the short-range offensive and the defensive. This means, in terms of the early English warriors, the combination of a missile (bow-and-arrows, hammer, francisca, dart), a hand-held weapon (spear, sword, axe, seax) and a protective weapon (shield, mailshirt, helmet). The need for mobility dictates that a warrior should not carry more than one weapon of each type, although in the nature of the case men often did carry several missile weapons which were going to be used before the others would be deployed, and not infrequently had a second, smaller short-range weapon as a fall-back device. Those who could afford a mailshirt and helmet would hardly leave them at home when war threatened.

Although weapons themselves received much attention from their makers and users, the manufactured quality of individual items is not so important as the way in which they are used. This comes down to training and practice with the weapons, as well as organization and leadership which puts the right men armed with the right weapons into the field in the right places, and ensures as far as possible that they are in the right frame of mind for the task.

In the following section, I shall be dealing with the warrior's normal equipment rather than with the exceptionally rich or prestigious, as far as possible. Certain items, such as the helmet, were seemingly never common (until the very end of the period, at least) while the ubiquity of the spear and knife suggest that these were almost 'everyday' items of which many examples might be owned.

---

[1] Mobility in defence is something of a drawback, since it assists and invites a strong attacker to dislodge the defensive force. The ultimate piece of defensive equipment is not the hand-held shield but the castle wall!

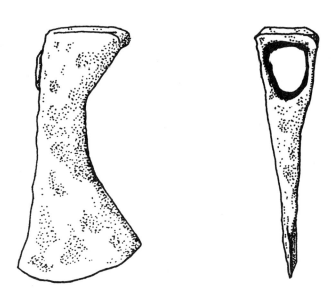

Figure 15 An early Anglo-Saxon axe-head from Morningthorpe, Norfolk.
6in (15cm) from blade to back

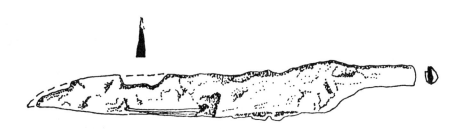

Figure 16 An Anglo-Saxon seax, originally with a hilt made of horn, from Morningthorpe,
Norfolk. 9½in (24cm) long

Weapon Vocabulary

The Germanic peoples took a great pride in their weapons and lavished much attention on them, in their appearance and in their effectiveness. A man's weapons marked him out, defined to some extent his status and *weorþ*. As the paradigm of a *māððum*, the sword held a special place in the Germanic arsenal for both what it could do now and what it had done before. This attitude, whereby each weapon has an identity, is entirely alien to the Roman idea of weapons as something issued by the authorities, to be returned after use.

Germanic languages use a variety of vocabulary for weapons, many terms being common to all the separate tongues of the group but not shared by other related language groups, such as Greek, Celtic or Slavonic. Germanic verse also made use of a specialized vocabulary which may have been specifically poetic in many cases – there is no obvious reason to have several words for 'sword' unless it is to meet different metrical requirements.

In a pioneering study by Caroline Brady, the vocabulary of Old English verse (specifically *Beowulf*) dealing with military equipment has been examined to determine what the associations are for the various terms. It is obvious that the fact that the poet uses half a dozen or more words for 'spear' must mean that there are shades of meaning or technical differences between these terms. This may be partly 'poetic' versus 'prosaic' vocabulary, of course – just as we today will recognize *ere* for 'before' and *brook* for 'stream' if we meet them in verse, even though we would never use these words in normal conversation or correspondence. This is not the place to present the semantic fields of all the OE military vocabulary, but it may be useful to offer a short summary of the main findings of Brady's study.[2]

Many poetic names for weapons consist of the simple name with another word prefixed to it, so that *wīgbill* is a compound of *wīg* 'war' and *bill* 'sword'; but how does 'war-sword' differ from the simple word *bill*? What does the word *wīg* add to the meaning of 'sword' and what are its associations? It is to answer this fundamental question about the poetic military vocabulary that Brady made the necessary contextual comparisons to arrive at the conclusions tabulated below. There are distinctions to be made between at least three different types of compound, however: the explicit type, e.g. *wīgbill* 'sword for warfare'; the circumlocution, e.g. *beaduleoma* 'battle-light, thing which shines /glistens /flashes in battle=sword'; the metaphoric type, e.g. *wælsteng* 'dead body-pole, staff for carrying dead bodies=spear'. Assignment of words to such rigid classes is not always possible, of course, since we no longer have the opportunity to understand at first hand what these terms really mean. In the following tables the literal meanings are shown in quotes.

term	meaning	association
beadu-, beado-	'warfare', realistic fighting	grim and bloody but not frightening
heaðo-	'battle', destructive force	the frightening aspects of war
here-, hild-, gūð-, wīg-	'war', glorious deeds of arms	the fame and glory of war

Table 5 The commonest prefixes of Old English military vocabulary

---

[2] The study is confines to *Beowulf*, however, and excludes words not found in that poem, such as *þeox* and *gafeluc* for 'spear' etc.

term	meaning	association
helm	helmet	neutral, generic term
grīmhelm	helmet with face-plate	awe-inspiring, attention-grabbing headgear
heregrima	'mask for raiding', helmet with face-plate	awe-inspiring, attention-grabbing headgear
hlēorberg	side-piece of helmet, 'cheek-protector'	protective function of helmet
hrōf	'roof', skull of helmet	protective function of helmet
beadugrima	helmet with face-plate, 'battle-mask'	ornamented helmet
gūþhelm	helmet for war	glorious, adorned helmet
wīgheafola	'war-head'	helmet with ornamental facial features (like that from Sutton Hoo?)

Table 6 The principal Old English poetic terms for 'helmet'

term	meaning	association
gūþgewǣdo	'war-clothing'	defensive clothing for deeds of arms (helmet and byrnie)
hildewǣpnu	'war-weapons'	offensive weapons for deeds of arms
-geatwe, -getawa	equipment	things made for use in war
rēaf	'plunder', armour	things taken from the dead

Table 7 The principal Old English poetic terms for 'wargear'

term	meaning	association
sweord	sword	neutral, generic term
heoru	sword	neutral but rare (poetic?)
bil, bill	'cleaver', sword	long, thin, two-edged weapon (also the name for sickle, hoe, and other cutting tools)
mece	sword	long, two-edged, pointed weapon
hæftmece	'hilt-sword'	as *mece* but with longer hilt
seax	'cutter', knife	shorter, single-edged, thrusting weapon
secg	'blade', sword	(? one-edged) sword
brond	'brand, flame', sword	short sword
wægsweord	'wave-sword'	rippling-patterned (= pattern-welded) sword
māþþumsweord	'treasure-sword'	sword which is a costly thing
gūþsweord	'war-sword'	sword which is used for *gūþ*, glorious deeds of arms
gūþbil, wīgbil, hildebil	'war-sword'	*bil* which is used for glorious deeds of arms, *bil* as weapon rather than as tool
wællseax	'slaughter-knife'	honed and razor-sharp *seax*
hildelēoma	'battle-light'	thing that flashes in *hild*, glorious warfare
hildegicel	'battle-point'	pointed thing for *hild*
gūþwine	'battle-friend'	thing that supports and assists the warrior
lāf	'leavings, remnant'	sword as legacy, heirloom from glorious ancestors

Table 8 The principal Old English poetic terms for 'sword'

term	meaning	association
byrne	mailshirt	neutral, generic term
syrce	'shirt'	mailshirt as garment
searo, searu	'weaving, linking' mailshirt	mailshirt as item made up from metal links, always with heroic associations
searwa	arms and armour, war-gear	plural of *searo*, war-gear with heroic associations
-hrægl, -pād, -scearp	'garment'	clothing for war (only the first element shows the military meaning, e.g. *herepād*)
hringīren	'ring-tool', mailcoat	item made from metal rings
hringnet, brēostnet, herenet, searonet	'ring-net', 'breast-net', 'raiding-net', 'linking-net', mailcoat	network (item made up from linked components) made of iron, worn on the chest, worn in glorious deeds of arms, made by linking respectively
līcsyrce	'body-shirt', mailcoat	mailcoat as garment
leoðosyrce	'limb-shirt', mailcoat	mailcoat with sleeves
fyrdhom	'army-shirt', military dress	garment worn on campaign
scrūd	apparel, covering	garment with special purpose

Table 9 The principal Old English poetic terms for 'armour'

term	meaning	association
bord	'board', shield	thing made of thin planks (boards)
hildebord, wīgbord	'battle-board', shield	board used in deeds of arms (as distinct from any other kind of board, e.g. plank, deck of a ship, table)
rand	'rim', shield	flanged boss, also the whole shield (by metonymy)

Table 10 The principal Old English poetic terms for 'shield'

term	meaning	association
gār	'rod, stick', spear	neutral term for thrusting spear with triangular head
daroð	'dart', spear	light throwing spear
wudu	'tree', spear	thing made of wood
æsc	'ash tree', spear	thing made of ash wood
eoforsprēot	'boar-sprout', boar-hunting spear	long hunting spear with barbs
bongār	'killer-spear'	stout hand-held spear, perhaps associated with Óðinn's weapon *Gungnir*
æscholt, gārholt	'ash-copse', 'spear-copse'	group of spears held by a tight-knit formation of men
heresceaft, wælsceaft	'raiding-shaft, slaughter-shaft'	metal-tipped length of wood
wælsteng	'dead-body pole', spear	pole from which a corpse is suspended as an emblem of victory
mægenwudu	'might-wood'	shaft of wood for use with all one's strength
þrecwudu	'thrust-wood'	shaft of wood for thrusting, pressing, piercing

Table 11 The principal Old English poetic terms for 'spear'

The Weapon Folk of Northern Europe

Many of the northern tribes have folk names which are derived from words for types of weapon. This fact has been commented on by many, but so far defies any explanation other than a desire to characterize the group by its use of a particular weapon, even though the basic Germanic set of armaments seems to have been common to most if not all. Just what was remarkable about the handling of spear or sword by this or that tribe is difficult to say at this remove.

Among such folk we may include the English themselves *Engle, Angle* (OE *angul* 'barb, hook, ?spearhead with barbs'), the Franks, *Froncas* (OE *franca* 'axe?, spear') and the Saxons, *Seaxe* (OE *seax* 'sax, knife'), as well as the *Secgan* (OE *secg* 'sword, blade'), *Rondingas* (OE *rond* 'shield'), *Sweordweras* (OE *sweord, weras* 'sword, men'). Similarly military in theme are such others as *Gār Dene* 'spear Danes', *Herefaran* 'raid-farers' and *Swæfe* 'killers?' (OE *swebban* 'kill').

The Sword

> ... A sword belongs on the lap,
> the noble weapon
>
> (Exeter Book Gnomic Verses, lines 25–6)
>
> ... *Sweord sceal on bearme,*
> *drihtlic īsern*

The sword[3] was the most symbolically important weapon of the Anglo-Saxon period. Though the spear was more popular and so more numerous, the sword held a glamour greater than any other piece of offensive equipment.

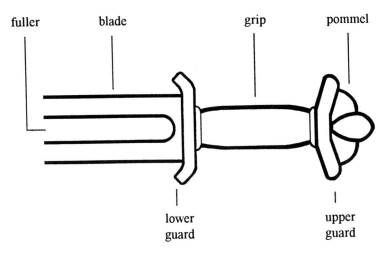

Figure 17 Schematic diagram of sword hilt

---

3 The actual word 'sword' is directly descended from the Old English *sweord*, with related forms in many other Germanic languages. *Sweord* was not the only word for the weapon, however: Old English prose and more so the verse records a handful of other terms which were to some extent interchangeable with *sweord* (just as we have words such as glaive, rapier, cutlass, dagger, sabre, falchion, etc. which are partial synonyms for 'sword'). An ancient word with wide application is *heoru, heru* also found in Old Icelandic as *hjorr*, in Gothic as *haírus* with the same meaning; more distant related forms are Russian *cherv'* 'sickle' and Sanskrit *caru* 'spear, missile'. Similarly, *bill, bile* has an Old High German cognate *billi* 'sword, blade' and derives from the same Proto-Germanic root **biþl-* as Old Icelandic *bildr* 'cutting tool, scythe' and related more widely to such words as Old Irish *biāil* 'hatchet' and Russian *boj* 'warfare'. Another word confined to Germanic and of unknown derivation is Old English *mēce, mǣce* which appears in Old Saxon as *māki*, Old Icelandic as *mǣkir* and Gothic as *mēki*.

Origins and Typology of the Sword

A sword is essentially a combination of a blade and a hilt (a part for cutting and a part for holding, in effect) and traces its ancestry back to the Mesolithic period in some form or other. The Middle Stone Age peoples combined razor-sharp flint shards called *microliths* with wooden or bone handles which enabled them to wield these rather clumsy but certainly effective instruments for both hunting and, probably, some form of self-defence or warfare. These early implements would not be recognizable to us as swords, but they stand in direct line of ancestry to the more recent artefacts bearing the name. Swords of the modern type really only became possible with the development of metallurgy giving rise to the Bronze Age in Europe, when bronze billets were worked into long, slender weapons suitable for use as slashing swords, known to archaeologists today as *rapiers,* and into stubbier, heavily-ridged daggers.

The early sword's blade is conventionally flat, straight and two-edged, often with a fuller (a hammered or ground groove running the length of the blade which makes it lighter without reducing strength). The upper portion of the blade, above the sharpened portions or 'edges', tapers into a narrow tongue of iron, the 'tang', to which the fitments are attached which form the hilt. This normally takes the form of a lower crossguard or 'quillons' below the 'grip' where the hand holds the hilt, which is surmounted in turn by an upper crossguard and the final section, the 'pommel' which secures the hilt in place (the tang is fitted into it) and acts as a counterweight to the blade. Sword blades can be on average between 25 and 31in (65 and 80cm) in length and 2 to 2½in (5 to 6·5cm) in width; the grip is invariably designed for one-handed use, with a length of about 4in (10cm).

By the time of the Iron Age in Northern Europe, there is already a strong local tradition of metallurgy. Fine, imported swords of La Tène type from Central Europe form part of the weapon set of the Germanic warrior; later, in the pre-Roman Iron Age, locally produced variants are common in the Danish marshland weapon-deposits of Hjortspring and Krogsbølle. These so-called bog-finds have been associated with the rise of a 'warrior cult' from the common Neolithic tribal structure of farmers, priests, warriors and slaves;[4] they certainly indicate an increase in regard for the technology of arms and warfare. The rapid development of the Germanic sword as both practical weapon and ritual implement goes hand-in-hand with the increase in prestige of the warrior at the expense of the priest-king.

In Germanic hands, the sword was always a hacking and thrusting weapon – long and narrow in the blade, sharply pointed and with a fuller. The blade, which is generally quite flat, with a shallow fuller, varies little during the entire Anglo-Saxon period, so typological studies focus on the hilt which can be richly ornamented, and thus offers much more material for analysis. Indeed, the form of the hilt can be used to ascertain the approximate date and region of manufacture of the weapon, and the status of the commissioning warrior or target purchaser. The weakness in this reliance

---

4 See also p.23 and Fig.2.

on the hilt for study is that the sword may consist of an old blade with a new hilt (or vice versa) or an imported blade to which a local craftsman has added his own design of hilt. The Rhineland was a thriving export centre with access to good quality raw materials and expertise, from which blades were despatched all over the Germanic north in the post-Roman period. There is considerable regional variation in both the overall form and the smaller details of sword design which greatly assists in determining where new discoveries fit into the overall picture.

The hilt has to provide a convenient handle for the user while protecting his hand from the metal spike which is the tang. It has to be sturdy enough to withstand the rough use it will receive in battle, but also an attractive object in its own right to complement the workmanship of the blade. A poorly made hilt might break in combat, leaving the swordsman with no control over his weapon.

The earliest Anglo-Saxon swords are, not surprisingly, indistinguishable from those found in their Continental homelands. Typically they feature hilts of organic material (wood, bone or horn) and have virtually no pommel, just a metal ring through which the tip of the tang passes and is hammered back down. The most famous example is that from Feltwell, Norfolk, found in a disused Roman bath house. The form is usually attributed to the fifth century. In the sixth and seventh centuries, Anglo-Saxon sword hilt design parallels Continental developments quite closely, to the extent that there must have been strong cultural links across Germanic Europe from Scotland to Hungary: both the guards are generally still of organic material but metal plates are fitted to the top and bottom of each with rivets, and there is a distinct metal pommel of roughly pyramidal shape. Later examples acquire all-metal hilts but the decoration is executed in such a way as to reproduce the layered construction of the earlier examples, even down to dummy rivet heads. Gilding and ornate decoration are increasingly common in this period.

Dating typologies rely heavily on the form of the pommel, since it shows the greatest variation within close limits of any of the hilt's constituents. The earliest examples are merely knobs of metal where the tang protrudes from the grip and is hammered down flat on a washer. Variation into many distinct shapes took place quite quickly in England, and some of these have been given descriptive names, such as 'boat', 'cocked hat', 'tea cosy' 'lobed', 'brazil nut' and so on. Two of these are illustrated below. (Fig.19, p.112)

It is in the sixth century that the phenomenon known as the 'ring-sword' (Fig.8, p.45) emerges: the upper guard or pommel[5] has a staple riveted on to its leading edge, by which a decorated metal ring is held; later examples have the staple and ring cast in one piece, and some swords appear to have had the ring removed at a later date. The obvious use for a free-running ring on the top of a sword hilt is for the attachment of a cord or thong which could be looped round the wrist so that the weapon would not be lost if the warrior's grip slackened, and just this practice is mentioned in later Icelandic writings (e.g. *Gunnlaugssaga*). However, a solid, cast ring-and-staple

---

[5] Some rare and early examples have the staple attached to the underside of the lower guard.

fitment cannot be used for this purpose – there is no hole through which to pass the thong – and there is every likelihood that the object has ritual meaning. Rings (OE *bēagas*) were of great symbolic importance in the north, strongly associated with the honour and dignity of the warrior, and with the performance of promises for which they were the proper reward.[6] The lord distributed rings to his followers, and was known for this function as *sinces brytta* 'treasure's sharer', *bēahgiefa* 'ring-giver' and so on. Furthermore, the ring was the token of truth upon which oaths were sworn – acted as the symbol of the promise, somewhat like a wedding ring does in our culture – and therefore probably symbolized the warrior's oath of support, service and fellowship to his lord; the absence of any such ring on putative kingly swords suggests that whatever it symbolized, the king was not expected to display such a badge, which was therefore presumably a mark of *ðegnung* 'thanely service'. It may be, then, that the ring was removed when the warrior failed his lord, or fell in war and the sword passed to a successor who perhaps had won no such distinction. There was a similar dummy ring on the face of the shield recovered from the Sutton Hoo ship burial (Mound 1). The present evidence suggests that ring-swords were an English device – the earliest examples occur in Britain and southern Scandinavia – which caught on in Germanic Europe, so that they even occur in Lombardic Italy.

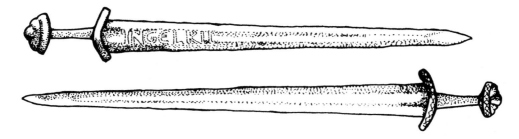

Figure 18 Two late Anglo-Saxon swords with lobed pommels, from which the wood and leather grips have perished. The 'trade-mark' INGELRII marks out one blade as of Rhenish workmanship, though its hilt has been added in England

With the rise of Christian influence and the virtual abandonment of overtly pagan practices such as weapon burial – the church taught that the matter of this world and all forms of social status display were illusory, not important and so should be despised – there is a dearth of evidence for English sword hilts from the 700s. An important find usually ascribed to the eighth century on art-historical grounds is the 'pommel' from Fetter Lane, London, comprising a lobed pommel and guard and the upper half of the grip itself, of all-metal construction. The features are paralleled from Continental hilts known to be of eighth century date. The triangular lobes flanking the pronounced central rib are also paralleled across much of the northern world.

---

[6] As Vera Evison remarked, the interlinking of two rings can surely only represent some sort of bonding.

Late Saxon swords become relatively abundant after the scarcity of the 700s, and many examples having been found in riverside sites. This may mark a return to the practice of deposition in sacred waters – to which the bog finds of southern Scandinavia testify – or perhaps reflect the many battles at fords recorded in the *Anglo-Saxon Chronicle* and elsewhere. Ninth century hilts begin to show a characteristic English development: the crossguards are no longer thick and straight, but now stubbier and curved away from the hand. This fashion later spread to the Viking lands and was widely adopted. The hilts of these swords are almost exclusively of all-metal construction, decoration taking the form of silver inlay or gilding. The earliest examples retain the strong central pommel rib with its flanks, while later ones have a more rounded contour.

The Danish influence of the protracted Viking campaigns produced the so-called 'tea-cosy' pommel, shaped like a capital 'D', which is a direct copy of Scandinavian patterns, as is the use of a series of up to five radiating fullers on the blade.

There are a few finds of crystal, amber, glass and meerschaum (clay) beads with swords, suggesting that they were used for decoration, perhaps being attached to the scabbard with twine or leather threads – a common Germanic fashion copied from the Huns during their 5th century overlordship. These may be the 'peace-thongs' of later Norse literature which were used to secure the weapon in its scabbard on religious occasions, when to draw it would be sacrilege. Some Continental examples of similar beads on leather straps seem to have served no practical purpose, though there is one intriguing possibility: in some later Icelandic sagas there are references to swords (e.g. *Sköfnung*) which had a 'healing-stone' attached, the virtue of which was that it alone could heal wounds given with that sword. Materials such as crystal and meerschaum are not durable enough to make useful scabbard fittings, but they are elsewhere apparently imbued with magical powers of healing.

When not in use, the sword was worn in a scabbard consisting of two lathes between which the blade fits snugly. The resulting slot was often lined with wool, from which the lanolin would help to prevent rusting of the iron. The exposed areas for wear and tear are the mouth, where the crossguard rests, and the tip which will tend to be abraded in use. To combat these tendencies, and also to provide opportunities for further decoration, metal parts were often added – a chape at the end and a frog or locket at the mouth. The whole was then attached to a shoulder strap or 'baldric' which passed over the right shoulder and held the weapon quite high on the left lower chest, a convenient place which does not interfere with walking or running and stops the chape from dragging on the ground. The method of attachment varied but was often by means of metal bars on the reverse side of the scabbard behind which the baldric is passed; less often and only in the earliest period, hooks attached to a metal band are affixed to the ends of the baldric. Later in the period, the practice of mounting the scabbard from the waist belt gained in popularity – it is the only method of wearing the sword shown in the Bayeux tapestry.

The metal belt fittings from Sutton Hoo Mound 1 included a gold strap distributor which may have helped to keep the scabbard angled mouth-forward, which makes it easier to draw the sword and more comfortable to wear. As illustrations frequently show swords worn in this way, it seems likely enough that there were other means of balancing the sword and scabbard to achieve the effect. There are also examples of small, decorated metal pyramids which occur in relation to the scabbard but which have never been properly explained. They are virtually unique to England and may have served as some kind of strap-end or tag, but were evidently not required after the 7th century. Here one can only suppose that some local fashion for carrying the sword in a particular way flourished and died.

The word 'scabbard' is derived through Frankish,[7] the common Old English word being *scēap* 'sheath'. However, Hilda Ellis Davidson discusses another word which is found in connection with swords, *fœtels*, which normally has the meaning 'bag, pouch, pot, vessel' and which looks as if it should have the same meaning (a scabbard is a sword's 'container'). However, if *fœtels* means 'that which holds things together, binding' then it may refer to a sword-belt with its buckle and fittings. One Anglo-Saxon sword had 4 pounds of silver on its *fœtels*, so it must have been a substantial piece of equipment.

pommel type	period	description
washer	Continental Germanic	flat lozengiform washer through which tang passes and is hammered flat
boat-shaped	early Anglo-Saxon	long, rounded billet, thickened centrally to accommodate the hole for the tang
cocked hat	early Anglo-Saxon	a triangular-sectioned block, in which the upper sides are s-profiled to give a shape like an admiral's hat
animal-headed	early Anglo-Saxon	two animal heads face outwards from a central thickening in which the hole for the tang is found
triangular	early Viking	as 'cocked hat' but with more regular sides
lobed / lobiate	middle Anglo-Saxon (9th C)	similar to 'triangular' but with the upper part divided into 3 or 5 rounded areas or lobes
tea cosy	middle to late Anglo-Saxon (10th C)	similar to lobed, but upper part only has dividing lines marked in, no separate lobes
brazil nut	middle to late Anglo-Saxon (10th C)	similar to 'tea cosy' but with shallower curvature to lower edge
wheel/disc	post Anglo-Saxon (11th C)	flat disc of metal pierced across the diameter edge to edge to accommodate the tang

Table 12 Summary tabulation of sword pommel types

---

[7] It is from a presumed original *skaraburg* 'protection against shearing'.

Making the Sword

A term one meets frequently in discussions of Anglo-Saxon sword blades is 'pattern-welding', a technique for their manufacture which dates back to the 3rd century AD at least. In essence, the idea is to twist together iron rods, and then to weld these rods together into a blade-shaped blank which is then further treated to produce the finished piece. Its derivation is from an earlier process whereby alternating qualities of iron sheet or strip were forge-welded together then beaten into the final shape. Aside from swords, pattern-welding has been found on spearheads and seaxes. It is a time-consuming and labour-intensive technique which would hardly have been used at all, except for the fact that the blades produced by this method are quite durable and robust, and strikingly beautiful. They were also quite exceptionally supple, which would make them difficult to break in normal use; springy blades were much prized for this reason.

The 'pattern' in pattern-welding is the surface effect caused by the welding together of rods of slightly varying quality (higher or lower carbon and phosphorus content being the most obvious factors), and the twisting of these rods so that the final blade bears a characteristic herringbone patterning. A comparable effect was achieved in the Near East by damascening, whereby differing grades of iron are folded in on each other to produce a wavy effect, though the techniques are quite different in execution. The intention in both cases is to distribute the carbon (which hardens the metal) evenly throughout the blade, since this element strengthens the sword if it is evenly dispersed, but causes brittle flaws if it is concentrated in one part. The twisting action used on the rods would tend to remove a lot of the slag adhering to the metal (where the carbon would be in dangerously large clumps) and would further spread out the remaining small particles. Generally speaking, the higher the carbon content, the harder the metal will be, and so the better its cutting power and ability to retain its edge. The pattern-welding technique was used only for the 'core' of the blade, which might also bear inlaid decoration or an inscription, while a steel[8] shoe was added to the sides and tip which would be honed to form the cutting edges and point. In constructing a seax by this method, only one side would be filed to an edge, the other forming the reinforcing back of the blade.

Whether the technique was primarily decorative or functional is a difficult question to answer, since a production method with a functional purpose which incidentally provides a decorative result may have been preferred over one which does not. Given that swords were generally regarded as expensive and precious items, possession of which conveyed prestige and social status, there must be a case for assuming that the decorative effect was every bit as important as the technical benefits, the more so in a culture like that of the early English which delighted in robust yet delicate artistry.

---

[8] Anglo-Saxon steel of the 5th to 10th centuries was of a superior quality to that produced in Roman times, or later in the Norman and medieval periods, according to Dr. G. McDonell (quoted by Philip Dixon). Only modern scientific production techniques have succeeded in equalling the remarkable products of the Anglo-Saxon steel-makers.

Moreover, we may suspect that the standing of the smith in Germanic culture – he was a figure of power and mystery with arcane knowledge which enabled him to turn basic materials into objects of beautiful craftsmanship – depended to some extent on producing fine workmanship, and it may have been beneath his dignity to hammer out swords which were little more than iron clubs. Nonetheless, later blades found in English cemeteries and rivers were not pattern-welded, but they sometimes feature inlaid inscriptions, the individual letters and shapes being made up by a pattern-welding process – a rather down-market weapon using the prestigious technique in a very limited way, which would do nothing to enhance the practical effectiveness of the blade, but which may have enabled the owner to show his friends the characteristic stratified markings on part of his weapon at least.

Furthermore, we should bear in mind the fact that the Germanic notion of time remained very much intact in the early English mind. In this model, time exists only as 'past' and 'non-past' (what we would call both 'present' and 'future') and these two interact constantly throughout creation. Therefore, the pattern produced by welding the blade together was in a sense a piece of 'frozen time', a replication in metal of the constant ebb and flow of the processes of past and present. The Germanic smith may well have deliberately used techniques which would produce a 'flowing' pattern in which there was an infinity of convolutions, mirroring the way present events are moulded by past ones.[9]

Attempts at classification by visible patterning have been made, though not generally accepted. These include Neumann's romantically named 'stripe-pattern' / 'chevron-pattern' / 'rose-pattern' taxonomy, and the more prosaic 'V-forming' / 'N-forming' / 'M-' or 'W-forming', all referring to the characteristic herringbone effect on the blade's surface. An alternative classification describes the number of rods (most often three per side, less often two, four or six) and the pattern of twisting, since the swords have alternate right- and left-hand twists along their length, but in some cases individual rods feature straight sections between the twisted ones. None of these systems is particularly useful, often due to the condition of the blades – generally recovered from graves or rivers and subject to extensive corrosion – which can only be examined by radiograph photography. Contiguous layering does not always show up at all clearly on the photographs, making determination of the exact number of rods virtually impossible, while other radiographic results are so confused as to be impossible to use. Some (probably most) swords consisted of two or three layers of rod sections, but examples of single-layered weapons are known; not infrequently, the middle layer of a three-layered blade was of plain iron.

Pattern-welding as a manufacturing technique in England for swords began in the fifth century, reached its peak in the 600s, judging by available finds, and virtually died out in the following century, probably due to an improvement in the quality of ore available to English and Frankish smithies, which allowed for the production of good quality steel without the lengthy pattern-welding process. The greatest known

---

[9] See p.35 above for more on the relevance of past time to the present in this system.

occurrence of pattern-welding on swords is in the Kentish cemeteries, which is predictable given the general richness of grave-goods from that area in the early Anglo-Saxon period. Continental, possibly Rhineland, workshops began producing plain steel blades with a pattern-welded surface veneer in the 9th century, and a few have been found in England. By the end of that century, plain steel blades with inlaid pattern-welded iron inscriptions are common – it has been suggested that the metal used for the inscriptions had a higher phosphorus content, which would make the letters noticeably shinier than the rest of the blade. These inscriptions often give a maker's name on one side, in the fuller and towards the hilt, often with a design on the other side in the same position. The inscriptions are most often in large and inexpert Roman capitals, and the names 'ULFBERHT' and 'INGELRII' are the commonest, suggesting that these were the names of two master smiths with workshops turning out quantities of weapons. In fact, even into the eleventh century these names still recur, probably used by less competent workmen on 'pirate' copies of 'trademarked' goods. Indeed, it seems likely that from the ninth century onwards the economics of weapon production were changing, the increasing standardization suggesting that it was no longer viable for a smith to spend days or weeks on a blade and that individual smiths serving local communities probably gave way to large-scale workshop manufacture with early mass-production techniques.[10]

Swords occasionally bear inscriptions other than personal names in Roman letters: a very few have short runic texts, virtually always on the hilt rather than the blade. Probably the best known is the Gilton, Kent, pommel which features a short and unfortunately badly-cut inscription on the inner face which has been partly worn off. Scholars differ as to the meaning of the text, although the word *sigi* 'victory' can be discerned, probably as part of a personal name *Sigimǣr*. This may in itself support the view that sword blades were made by central workshops and that the hilts and other fittings were added locally to suit regional or provincial taste. The modern popular fancy for runic inscriptions on swords is derived in part at least from the passage in *Beowulf* in which King Hrōþgār surveys the giants' sword which Bēowulf used to kill Grendel's Mother, of which only the hilt survives after the monster's blood melts the blade:

> It was so on the hilt-plates[11] of bright gold
> truly marked out through rune-staves
> set down and stated for whom the sword,

---

[10] It is perhaps no coincidence that many rich Kentish cemeteries lie within striking distance of Faversham, which has been thought to mean 'smith's village', OE *fæferes hām*, with the unique word *fæfer* derived from Latin *faber* 'smith, maker'.

[11] So the word *scennum* is usually translated, although it occurs nowhere else. A possible Norse equivalent is *skán* 'crust', both from Germanic **skanjō* 'membrane' referring to the usually organic covering of the hilt. If the *scenna* in question were of gold, then either the word has been transferred to another part of the hilt, or the poet envisaged an all-metal hilt without organic components.

choicest of weapons, was first made
with interlaced hilt and serpent decoration.

(*Beowulf*, lines 1694–8)

Swā wæs on ðǣm scennum scīran goldes
þurh rūnstafas rihte gemearcod
geseted ond gesǣd hwǣm þæt sweord geworht,
īrena cyst, ǣrest wǣre,
wreoþenhilt ond wyrmfāh.

Using the Sword

While Anglo-Saxon swords can be used for hacking, slashing and thrusting quite effectively, the balance of the blade generally favours the slash as the preferred stroke. Indeed, devastating blows can be delivered which in combat would doubtless have finished off an opponent caught off guard. We have the testimony of *The Battle of Maldon* that a sword blow could be deadly:

I heard that Edward struck one
mightily with his sword – he did not withhold the blow
– so that the doomed warrior fell at his feet...

(lines 117–9)

gehȳrde ic þ Ēadweard ānne slōge
swīðe mid his swurde – swenges ne wyrnde
– þ him æt fōtum fēoll fǣge cempa ...

The combination of sword and shield would provide an excellent combination of offensive force and protection, suitable for close-in fighting and the strenuous hacking-match which much early warfare seems to have been. Indeed, even without a shield, the warrior could defend himself against sword or spear thrusts by holding his own weapon with the hilt at head height, the blade slanting down and back towards his body, enabling him to protect it by parrying with relatively small movements of the hand.

Analysis of sword cuts from skeletal remains clearly shows that it was possible for a well-placed blow to shear through an opponent's skull (with or without headgear we cannot say). An opponent who protects himself with a shield is still vulnerable in the areas of the head, chest and lower leg, and these must have been the weak spots at which sword blows were aimed. A blow landing in any one of these places, even if not at full force, would probably still have enough impact to stun and disable the victim.

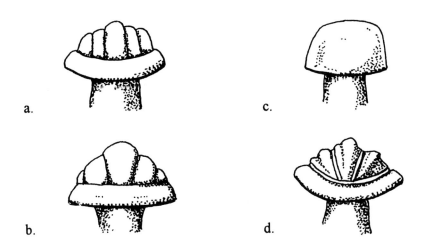

Figure 19 a: Pommel of the Witham sword of lobed type; b: Pommel of the Battersea sword of teacosy type; c: Pommel of the Shifford sword of lobed type; d: Pommel of the Westminster sword of lobed type

The Warrior with Two Swords

There are enough references to warriors with two swords in Northern European literature for there to be a good case for assuming that some men habitually wielded two swords in battle. One notable example is the fighter *Grim* in the Icelandic *Droplaugarsona Saga* who believed his foe was capable of blunting weapons (a typical Odinic trick) and carried two swords when he had to meet him in combat, one in each hand, as a means of countering such treacherous magic. As he showed one sword – which became bewitched – and hid the other, it seems likely that this latter was a shorter and smaller weapon, perhaps a seax. Other sagas mention men going to fight duels (ON *hólmganga*) armed with two swords as a precaution in case the opponent knew how to charm the cutting power out of a sword by looking at it.

There are other Icelandic and Norse references to warriors switching their swords from hand to hand in battle, though this comes down to individual skill-at-arms rather than any particular predisposition to using two swords. Two-handed swords were virtually unknown in the north at this time – the normal two-handed weapon was the axe – although there is one early English seax from Shudy Camps, Cambs. (Fig.30a, p.148), with a hilt so long that it could have been grasped by both hands easily; references to men holding their swords with both hands are mainly those acting in desperation.

What, then, of men who are known to have used two swords? Although the hero Grettir the Strong of *Grettissaga* had an heirloom sword (OE *lāf*) from his mother he also took a *heptisax* 'long-handled seax' from a Norwegian grave-mound. Likewise Egil Skállagrímsson inherited the sword *Dragvendil* from his father but acquired another, *Naður* 'adder', while abroad. The legendary Danish champion Böðvarr

Bjarki is credited with two weapons – *Laufr* and *Snirtir* – one of which he inherited, and the other he won.

From the Norse evidence, it seems that sometimes a warrior would inherit an 'heirloom' blade and also come by another (often a short-sword or seax) by robbing the dead, either in battle or from a grave-mound, as for example the Icelandic hero Skeggi:

> Skeggi was a great warrior and duel-fighter. He went a-viking for a long time. At one time he came to Denmark and travelled to Leire where the mound of King Hrólfr Kraki stood, and broke into the mound and took out through the breach King Hrólfr's sword, *Sköfnung*, which is the best of swords and axes to come to Iceland, which Hjalti the Stalwart had owned … (*The Saga of Þórðr Hreða*, Chapter 3)

> *Skeggi var garpr mikill ok einvígsmaðr. Hann var lengi í víkingu. Ok eitthvert sinn kom hann við Danmörk ok fór til Hleiðrar þangat sem haugr Hrólfs kunungs kraka var, ok braut hauginn ok tók á braut sverðit Hrolfs konungs Sköfnung, er bezt sverð hefir komit til Íslands ok öxina, er Hjalti hafði átt hinn hugprúði…*

A warrior with two swords had a choice of which weapon to use, and the decision was not without significance, since it would to some extent determine other aspects of his career. The heirloom, family blade set him on a course of 'socially responsible' fighting and marked him out as a worshipper of *Þórr* (Thor), a god whose responsibilities ranged between protection, procreation and production (second and third functions, in Dumézilian terms). Such a man would be concerned with the defence of the folk and their output. Choosing the blade tinged with death, however, marked the warrior as a worshipper of *Óðinn* (a first and second function god), more likely to be involved in aggressive wars of conquest, following a warlord and interested primarily in the acquisition of fame and booty. Such a sword would be the legendary *Sköfnung* which Hrólfr Kraki bore, and which must never be drawn in the presence of a woman (perhaps she could inadvertently blunt it or take away its particular power), and the sun must never shine on its hilt (it must always be gripped when worn) – a sinister blade indeed. It came with its own healing-stone.[12]

The *Þórr* sword was generally held to be effective against human foes, but of limited use against any form of sorcery or charm, hence Grim's resorting to the Odinic seax when he must fight a warrior capable of sorcery. Even Bēowulf found the heirloom sword *Hrunting* lent to him by Unferþ of no use against the supernatural giant woman, and had to resort to using one of her own weapons to bring her down. Nevertheless, the *Þórr* sword was considered part of the kindred's 'luck' and handing it on meant passing on the protection of the family's spirit guardians, while *Óðinn* swords were generally bringers of bad luck (they were taken from *dead* men, after all!). Some swords, presumably of the *Þórr* type, were formally cursed by their owners knowing that such weapons would be passed on in the family, in order to bring

---

[12] See above, p.106 for more on healing-stones.

down the kindred of the men who took them – they become 'anti-family' weapons of destruction, not protection. The *Þórr* sword was the normal, two-edged sword wielded by warriors for slashing and cutting at the head and upper body of their adversaries in the traditional Germanic 'heroic' manner of fighting and duelling. The warrior using it was, by this reasoning, very much within the mainstream of society, standing ready to defend land and loved ones, or king and country. By contrast, the *Óðinn* sword – the short, heavy-backed seax – is a weapon for stabbing, for dealing deep-thrust wounds to the abdomen and vital organs. It is also a hidden, personal weapon (rather than a public, family one) and its use requires carefully calculated strokes; it is the weapon of a man who fights for his own account, his own fame and profit, and who fights to win.

Perhaps the most famous two-sworded warrior was *Starkaðr* of Norse mythology, whose exploits are recorded separately by both Snorri Sturluson and Saxo Grammaticus. A warrior who bore two swords would symbolically represent both aspects of warriorhood (overlapping with the first and the third functions). Starkaðr is both an *Óðinn* warrior and a *Þórr* warrior, with many brave personal achievements to his name, yet also given to inducing young nobles into the arts of war so that they may protect their lands and peoples. The young Starkaðr was trained by a warrior named *Hrosshárs Grani* 'Grani Horsehair' who turned out to be *Óðinn*, and who supported his protégé in debate with Þórr over the hero's future:

> Odin said "I shape it for him that he shall live for three men's lifespans", Thor declared "He shall do a disgraceful deed in each lifespan" ... Odin said "I give him victory and strength in every battle", Thor said "I lay it on him that he shall receive a deadly wound in each battle".   (*Gautrekssaga*)

> *Óðinn svaraði "Þat skapa ek honum at hann skal lifa mannsaldra þrjá", Þórr mælti "Hann skal vinna níðingsverk á hverjum mannsaldri"....Óðinn svaraði "Ek gef honum sigr ok snild at hverju vígi", Þórr svaraði "Þat legg ek á hann at hann fái í hverju vígi meiðslasár".*

The support of *Óðinn* and the enmity of *Þórr* are used to explain the conflicting aspects of the hero, whose greatest achievements he is doomed never to enjoy, and whose long and violent life provides the northern myths with one of their more useful and memorable characters. Wherever strife is, Starkaðr is there.

In English tradition, warriors with two swords are not commonplace but one reference does make it clear that the practice was familiar to the English. This is the story of *Waldere* (Walter of Aquitaine), who had angered Attila, his Hunnish captor, by stealing both a beautiful, noble female hostage and a large quantity of treasure before escaping from his clutches; Attila's men set off in pursuit and trap the hero in the mountains, where he takes up his famous defensive position between two walls of rock so that they can only attack him one-by-one. With the literary convention of Germanic bravado, Waldere calls out words of exultation to his opponents. Unfortunately, the poem is a fragment only – two sides of a single written sheet – so it is not possible to be entirely sure what precedes the beginning of our visible text:

a better .....
except that one only which I also have
hidden fast in the jewelled case.

(Waldere II, lines 1–3)

... *ce bæteran*
būton ðæm ānum ðe ic ēac hafa
on stānfate stille gehīded.

The conjecture is that the first, partly missing word is [*beadume*]*ce* 'battle-sword' and that Waldere is boasting that there is no better sword in the world than the one he is using, except his other one which is still in its sheath!

Aside from the literary evidence, is there any proof that English warriors ever used two swords? Härke's examination of weapon distribution (Table 4 above) shows that out of 534 inhumations reported, only one had the weapon set 'sword, spear, shield, seax' while one other had the set 'sword, spear, shield, seax, axe' (virtually a 'full house' by early English standards!). Therefore, going by the grave-goods and with all the customary reservations about what such evidence can imply, warriors with two swords were distinctly rare.

There is one interesting further piece of evidence, however: the chance discovery during ditch-digging of a set of swords[13] in an inhumation cemetery at Prittlewell, Essex, which was in use from the sixth to seventh centuries. Regrettably the details of the excavations were not recorded very clearly at the time, but one particular grave-group (no.17) yielded two sword blades (one with a separate, broken tip). The weapons have been subjected to radiographic analysis which confirms that they are both of the highly-prized pattern-welded construction. The larger of the two weapons survived as just the blade, of which the remainder was 21½in (54·5cm) long and 2in (5cm) wide – the tang and a length of blade are missing, as is the hilt. It was deposited in a leather-on-wood scabbard, probably because it had been shattered in two during use, and there was a small buckle near the top which would have fixed it to the wearer's belt or baldric. Each face of the blade had been welded up from three bars of five, six or seven rods each, with alternate straight and twisted sections. The other sword, also just a blade fragment, was 12½in (32cm) long and 1½in (4cm) wide, although this time the tang and about half the blade remained and had been put in its scabbard before burial. This weapon was also pattern-welded, but from two sets of three bars, and it seems likely that the 3½in (9cm) point from the same grave-group belonged to this weapon. Both were of very good quality, the larger rivalling the sword blade from Sutton Hoo Mound I for the number of elements used in its construction, and both seem to have been broken when buried. The shorter of the two (although in

---

[13] There were five, or possibly six, in all from this site. All were of pattern-welded construction and had seen hard use during their employment. Other swords of a similar type have been found elsewhere in southern Essex, suggesting that there was a single smith or workshop producing these weapons.

two parts with a length missing) has a distinct taper and is probably an early example of a 'long seax', while the other, straighter blade is from a conventional sword. Here we have a good case for suggesting that the buried warrior owned and used two swords – a long sword and a shorter seax – during his lifetime; or, rather, we would have such a case if only it were clear beyond dispute that these two weapons did actually come from a single grave, and were not just found within a few inches of each other by accident.

It is not intrinsically unlikely that some men would fight using two edged weapons at once rather than the more traditional combination of spear or sword and shield. There are parallels from Japan, where swordsmen often used both a larger and a smaller sword, as well as from later European tradition such as that of fighting with rapier and dagger.

The Spear

> ... A dart belongs in the hand,
> a spear adorned with gold ...
>
> (Exeter Book Gnomic Verses, lines 21–2)
>
> *... Daroð sceal on handa,*
> *gār golde fāh...*

The spear was the symbolic weapon of the Germanic foot-soldier, as against the more lordly sword. Indeed, the right to carry a spear was part of the status of the 'freeman' in many early northern societies, and a slave found with a spear could be punished by having the weapon struck across his back until it broke, under a Carolingian law code. When the spear forms part of the grave-goods, which is not infrequently in the pagan period, it seems likely from the slender evidence that survives that the buried warrior was made to grasp the shaft of the weapon in death.[14] Indeed, male children could be buried with symbolic spears which they would hardly have been able to wield in life. It seems that the relatively common and inexpensive spear seldom became a *lāf*, much less a *māþþum*, and was personal enough to go to the grave with its owner. Yet the great, archetypal spear *Gungnir* was the special weapon of Óðinn, the Norse war god which he used to stir up strife in the world.

One OE word for 'leader' or 'prominent warrior, champion' is *frumgār* 'first spear', which quite clearly designates a warrior who stands in the front line in battle, whether in the shieldwall or acting independently, while the conventional term for the 'vanguard' or front-line troops is *ord* 'point [of a spear]', presumably mimicking the spearhead's triangular shape.

---

[14] Strangely, where a grave contains more than one spear, they are more often pairs of the same type of weapon than of different types.

blade   rib   shank   socket   languet   shaft

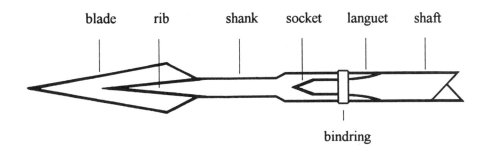

bindring

Figure 20   Schematic representation of a spear

The commoner names for the spear in Old English are *gār* and *spere*.[15] The throwing-spear is specifically called *daroþ* (our word 'dart'), based on the same root as Old English *daru* 'hurt, harm' and refers to the ability of the missile weapon to wound. There are, nevertheless, many poetic words for the spear, such as *æsc* '[item made of]ash wood', *ord* 'point' *þrecwudu* '[thing of] wood for harming' which refer to some particular aspect of its use or manufacture (see p.101, Table 11). Ash wood has been detected in the sockets of some English spearheads, confirming the linguistic evidence of its use for the shaft. At the point of balance, about one third down the shaft from the blade, a cord or thong was wound tight round the wood to serve as a convenient grip and to mark the proper place to hold the spear for one-handed use. A single loop of this material was left loose and, when the spear was not in use, it could be suspended from this. A warrior who needed to keep his right arm free for, say, throwing his *daroð*, could put his left forefinger through this small loop without letting go of his shield. Decorated shafts are not well attested archaeologically, but some of the early Danish bog-finds featured pigmented areas, and occasionally a short runic text. Presumably these were for identification purposes as well as showing off the Germanic love of decoration.

The traditional Germanic weapon set, as reconstructed on the basis of grave finds, included a throwing-spear and a hand-held 'lance', less often two lances. This combination arose in the late Roman Iron Age and seems to have been fairly consistent with Germanic troops throughout the Migration period. Nevertheless, as mentioned elsewhere, the military items placed in a grave or cremation urn need not represent those taken onto the battlefield. Would a warrior armed with a close-in weapon such as a sword also need a spear? Or would he be more effective if armed with a throwing spear (javelin) to soften up his target from a distance, and then close to use the sword to despatch him?

---

[15] The first of these has its equivalent in Norse *geir* and German *Ger*, from an original **gaisaz* to which are related such other 'spear' words as Greek *gaison* and Old Irish *gae*. *Spere* is related to Norse *sporr* and German *Speer*, as well as Latin *sparus* 'spike' and originally meant 'beam, rafter, item made of wood'.

Typology of the Spear

The classic text for the morphology and typology of the earlier English spearheads and their Germanic antecedents is Swanton's study. Most of the evidence for variation in the shape of spears, as studied by Swanton and later by Nicholas Brooks, comes from spearheads found in pagan period cemeteries as grave-goods. This evidence has limitations, as often noted, in that the weapons buried with the dead are not necessarily those used by them in life, as well as the fact that the surviving iron tips tell us little about the dimensions and possible decoration of the shaft. Nevertheless, the range of spearheads which has survived shows a huge variety in shape and size: first in popularity are broad, leaf-shaped blades which would be suitable for thrusting as well as for hacking: these are probably the Germanic infantryman's all-purpose weapon. Many have a pronounced central rib, some others a corrugated profile, to strengthen the cutting edge.

Second to these are long, barbed spikes with a solid shank, of the type generally called 'angon' (OE *ong* 'ballista dart' *angul* 'barbed fishhook'); these are presumed to have been used as missile weapons, since their design (perhaps based on the Roman *pilum*) allows the head to penetrate a shield and then bend down at the neck under the weight of the shaft – one example from the Prittlewell cemetery survives with its head bent over at right-angles in just this manner. The third set of spearheads are straight-sided with a thick, square cross-section. These may be the ones referred to as *ord* 'point' in the verse, and would be especially suited to piercing mail or plate armour.

As Brooks points out, there is no reason to suppose that this early range of basic spear types was not still in use at the time of the battle at Maldon (991), and all seem to be identifiable on the Bayeux tapestry. However, Swanton contends that later spearheads are comparatively longer than earlier ones, as well as stronger, more likely to be of welded construction and reinforced with a tang or lugs: this change in manufacture indicates that the later spear was intended to be used for parrying blows and striking laterally, whereas the earlier one could only really be used for thrusting. Common in manuscript illustrations, as also on the tapestry, are small projecting 'wings' behind the spearhead, apparently fixed to the socket – an actual example of a spearhead with this feature was found in the Thames at Twickenham, although it remains remarkably rare in archaeological evidence considering how often it is illustrated. This kind of device is well-known from hunting spears, where it serves to prevent the weapon penetrating too deeply into the flesh: this would make it impossible to remove quickly in the heat of battle, leaving the spearman defenceless.

The spear's shaft, usually of ash wood which grows tall and straight, could be of a length between 6 and 11 feet, and again manuscript illustrations suggest that something nearer 8 feet was normal – somewhat over man-height. Actual examples found in the Nydam bog deposit were 8 to 11½ feet long, up to twice man-height, which feature is also illustrated in later Anglo-Saxon drawings. The shaft is sometimes shoed with a metal ferrule, to protect the wood from splitting, and occasionally decorated with small metal plates. Swanton suggests that the very lightest Anglo-Saxon

Series	Swanton's Type	average size range	distinctive features
A			barbed blades
	A1	9¾ – 21½in 25 – 55cm	long, slender shank topped with short, flat, barbed head; all from Germanic Roman contexts (Hadrian's Wall, etc.)
	A2	20½ – 45½in 52 – 116cm	with longer blades than Type A1, and with lozengiform section
B			spiked forms
	B1	11¾ –24in 30 – 61cm	narrow, long head in which the blade has dwindled to produce a square-sectioned iron spike
	B2		as for Type B1, but with the spike forming the midrib of a small leaf-blade; sometimes decorated with pointwork along the midrib and at the base of the blade
C			leaf-shaped blades with longer blade than socket
	C1	4 – 7¾in 10 – 20cm	small, simple, cheap forms, lentoid in section, with crude sockets, perhaps Frankish imports
	C2	7¾ – 13¾in 20 – 35cm	as C1 but longer, slimmer forms with a short, solid neck; remained in use throughout A-S period
	C3	11¾ – 19¾in 30 – 50cm	as C2 but very long and slim, with a short neck and the widest part of the blade nearer the socket
	C4	13¾ – 19¾in 35 – 50cm	as C3 but with no real neck, the blade merging smoothly into the socket
	C5	6¼ – 10¼in 16 – 26cm	a shorter version of C4 found mostly in Kent, with a narrow split in the socket rather than a true cleft
D			leaf-shaped blades with longer socket than blade
	D1	6¼ – 11in 16 – 28cm	small, simple, lentoid-sectioned blade with a narrow split rather than a cleft
	D2	7¾ – 15¾in 20 – 40cm	as D1 but with a short, round-sectioned shank; cleft socket often with a binding-ring
	D3	7 – 21¾in 18 – 55cm	as D2 but longer overall with a shorter blade; perhaps mimicking the Roman *pilum*
E			angular blades with longer blade than socket
	E1	5 – 7½in 13 – 19cm	small, simple blade with sharp taper from angle to tip; sometimes tanged
	E2	7¾ – 13¾in 20 – 35cm	as E1 but longer, slimmer, with cleft socket

Table 13 Summary of Anglo-Saxon spearhead types based on Swanton's classifications

Series	Swanton's Type	average size range	distinctive features
E (cont)	E3	13¾ – 17¾in 35 – 45cm	as E2 but longer, with a shallower taper; some later examples are of pattern-welded construction
	E4	11¾ – 19¾in 30 – 50cm	as E3 with a shallower taper and a very small socket – weak construction
F			angular blades with longer socket than blade
	F1	7 – 9¾in 18 – 25cm	small with sharp taper, cleft socket and slight shank
	F2	11¾ – 15¾in 30 – 40cm	as F1 but with longer shank and late examples with broader blade
	F3	13 – 13¾in 33 – 35cm	as F2 but extended shank, a delicate construction; shallower taper to the longer blade
G			parallel-sided blades with rounded tip ("sword-shaped blades") and longer blade than socket
	G1	8¾ – 11¾in 22 – 30cm	smallest examples with small, cleft socket
	G2	13¾ – 23½in 35 – 60cm	as G1 but longer, cleft socket sometimes with binding-ring
H			angular blade with concave curve between angle and tip, sometimes decorated
	H1	6¼ – 8¾in 16 – 22cm	early type with long, broad cleft
	H2	7¾ – 13¾in 20 – 35cm	longer, slimmer blade with shallower curve
	H3	13¾ – 19¾in 35 – 50cm	longer blade with solid shank and large socket
I			corrugated leaf-shaped blades
	I1	9¾ – 13¾in 25 – 35cm	early, broad-bladed form with a welded socket
	I2	9¾ – 13¾in 25 – 35cm	as I1 but slimmer with a fuller on each face of the blade
J		6 – 15¾in 15 – 40cm	as Series H but with a fuller on the wing of the blade
K			step-sectioned leaf-shaped blades
	K1	6¼ – 14¼in 16 – 36cm	as I1 but with cleft socket and stepped section
	K2	6¼ – 11¾in 16 – 30cm	as I2 but narrower, with smoother curves and narrow cleft socket, sometimes languets; a few have a smoothed step-section and a tang
L		7¾ – 13¾in 20 – 35cm	concave step-sectioned blades sometimes with languets and a binding ring, often decorated with inlay and balustering

Table 13 Summary of Anglo-Saxon spearhead types based on Swanton's classifications

spearheads may have been loosely attached to withes as an inexpensive throwing weapon, possibly that called *wīgār* in Old English, *vīgr* in Old Norse, and that the references to OE *flān* which are usually translated 'arrow' should refer to this type of light spear instead, or a combination of these and arrows as missile weapons. Of course, the staff of the spear can be used in both offensive and defensive roles quite separately from the use of the spearhead.

The small size and inexpensive nature of the spearhead meant that it could be made in quantity by local workshops, and so would not normally pass out of the purchaser's region except on campaign. Yet the fact that each one had to be made individually by forging and welding means that no two are exactly alike, in the way that, say, cast decorative plaques from the same mould will be almost identical. English smiths seem to have experimented with the various traditional forms – perhaps to save time or materials – by introducing the corrugated section (which saves having to weld a midrib onto the blank, then grind it down) and the cleft socket (which is easier to make and to fit, but only suitable when the spear will not be used for lateral blows).

The details of the spearhead's typology are discussed at length by Swanton, but his classification system may be summarized in a table (see p.119–20, Table 13).

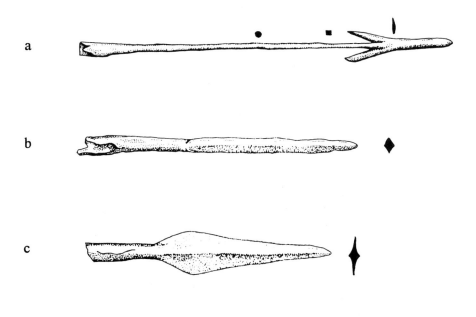

Figure 21 Spearhead classification system (after Swanton)
a: Type A. from Carvoran, Northumberland 25¼in (64cm) long;
b: Type B1 from Kingston, Kent 10½in (27cm) long;
c: Type B2 from Brentford, Middlesex 11¾in (30cm) long;

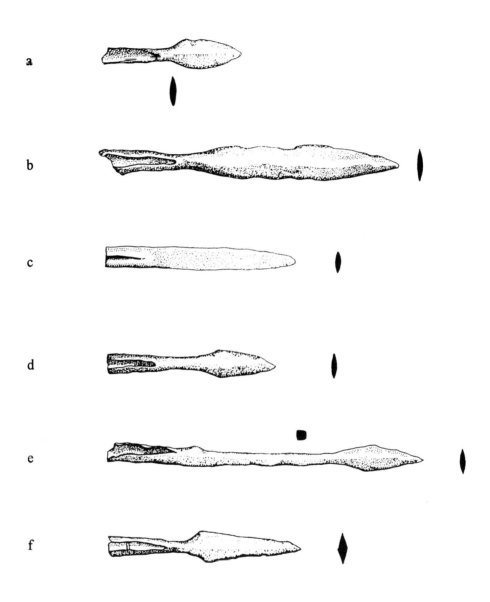

Figure 22 Spearhead classification system (after Swanton)
a: Type C1 from Bulford, Wiltshire 5in (13cm) long;
b: Type C2 from Beddington, Surrey 11½in (29cm) long.
c: Type C5 from Polhill, Kent 9½in (24cm) long;
d: Type D1 from Little Wilbraham, Cambridgeshire 6¾in (17cm) long;
e: Type D3 from Stratford, Warwickshire 12¼in (31cm) long;
f: Type E1 from Long Wittenham, Berkshire 7½in (19cm) long;

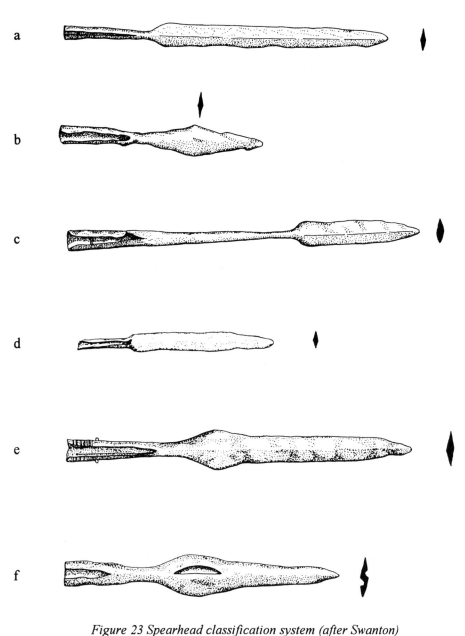

Figure 23 Spearhead classification system (after Swanton)
a: Type E3 from Barham, Kent 17in (43cm) long;
bf: Type F1 from Woodstone, Huntingdonshire 7¾in (20cm) long.
c: Type F3 from Prittlewell, Essex 13½in (34cm) long;
d: Type G from East Shefford, Berkshire 11in (28cm) long;
e: Type H2 from Salisbury, Wiltshire 13in (33cm) long;
f: Type I1 from Guildown, Surrey 10½in (27cm) long;

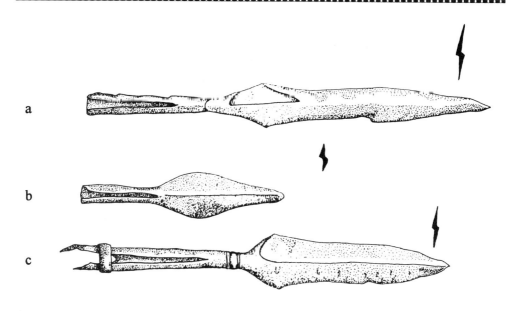

Figure 24 Spearhead classification system (after Swanton)
a: Type J from Brentford, Middlesex 12¼in (31cm) long.
b: Type K1 from Frilford, Berkshire 7¾in (20cm) long;
c: Type L featuring balustering and with languets and a binding-ring,
from Nassington, Northamptonshire 15in (38cm) long;

To summarize, the early Germanic range of spearhead types used by the mercenaries serving on Hadrian's Wall in the Roman period were later introduced into the British Isles as the weapons of immigrant *foederati*. These traditional forms began to disintegrate in the latter part of the 5th century as the autonomous settlements developed their own distinctive culture, and the ready availability of iron across lowland Britain made local workshops viable and so encouraged the resultant experimentation and formal diversity. Local trends emerged, perhaps because individual smiths handed on their own particular skills and practices, so generating unevenness of supply. Nevertheless, a wide range of forms was available across the country even though, as Swanton remarks, the South Saxons for example preferred their leaf-shaped blades as narrow as possible and their angular blades as wide as possible.

Evidence for spearhead types becomes severely limited with the adoption of Christian burial and the corresponding decline in grave-goods. Yet there was already towards the end of the pagan period a general trend towards simplification and production of less extreme forms. The style of fighting evidently changed little as the thrusting weapon remained the principal type even to the end of grave-goods deposition in the late 600s, but the trend towards ever larger blades throughout the 6th century may reflect nothing more than increased availability of iron (or security of supply), an incipient 'arms-race' and a desire to impress. The very largest blades such as Type H3 often had to be reinforced with a metal ring round the base of the socket which was under increasing strain in combat.

The effect of the Danish wars on English weaponry is hard to estimate, but there seems to be a marked increased in standardization, possibly due to the centralization of production and linked to the Alfredian *burh* system whereby labour-intensive smithing on a village or estate scale was no longer economic. However, the evidence from these Christian times is so scant that it may not be safe to press this line of argument very far. Certainly from the later Anglo-Saxon period, the only well-attested forms are the stoutest types of leaf-shaped and angular blades.

Using the Spear

To use a spear effectively one would expect warriors to grip its shaft in both hands and put the full force of their bodyweight behind the thrust; however, to do this is to dispense with the protection afforded by the shield, which must be dropped or slung behind the back, and it is fairly clear that the Germanic manner of fighting involved the one-handed manipulation of the spear while keeping the shield close to the body with the left hand. This arrangement is characteristic of the shieldwall, where men stand in line abreast with clearly defined territory to defend (the line of shields forms the boundary of the protected zone) and it has been suggested that for warriors stationed behind the shieldwall – positioned to deal with any foes who manage to break through the boundary – sword, shield and javelin would be the optimal weapon set, roughly equivalent to the Roman soldier's equipment.

Specific references to the spear in use are often quite general and uninformative, although the use of spear and shield together seems to be taken for granted. In *The Battle of Maldon* the English leader Byrhtnōþ gives his answer to the vikings' demand for tribute, as the poet says:

> Byrhtnōð spoke out, he raised his shield
> brandished his slender spear, uttered words
> angry and resolute, gave them an answer…

(lines 42–22)

> *Byrhtnōð maþelode, bord hafenode,*
> *wand wācne æsc, wordum mælde*
> *yrre and ānrōd, āgēaf him andsware…*

The associative link between spear and shield is too great for the poet to ignore even in so formulaic a set-piece.

The purpose of the spear is to keep the enemy at a distance, outside the range of hand-held weapons such as sword and axe. This helps to minimize the risk to the warrior, since generally the further back the adversary is, the easier it is to dodge his blows. The longer the spear is, the greater the reach, but conversely the harder the spear will be to manage, and some of the 11 feet long examples must have been heavy and unwieldy.[16] The Bayeux tapestry and other illustrations show spears being used overarm, which would enable greater weight to be put behind a one-handed thrust, but this method of fighting would make parrying blows almost impossible. Spears, of whatever type, were used by all ranks at Maldon, according to the poet, which bears out what had been deduced from grave assemblages, that the spear was the universal weapon of the fighting man.

Throwing spears, and presumably other missiles such as arrows as well, could be re-used by being launched back at the men who had hurled them. This is shown in *The Battle of Maldon* where the young Wulfmær removed the bloody spear from his lord's body and "let the hardened [weapon] fly back again" (*forlēt forheardne faran eft ongēan*, line 156).

The Axe

> axe-age, sword-age, shields [are] cloven
>
> (*Snorra Edda*)
>
> *skeggǫld, skálmǫld, skildir klofnir*

The word 'axe' is found in Old English (*æcse*) and the related Germanic languages.[17] The axe is not a weapon commonly associated with the early English, although there have been finds of axe-heads from pagan warrior-graves from the earliest Anglo-Saxon times. These are mostly small with straight or only slightly curving blades – that from Lyminge II, grave 1, for example, was an estimated 4¾in (12cm) along the cutting edge. Weapons such as these are best regarded as for personal defence or perhaps for throwing: some Frankish examples have an upwardly curving blade which has been thought to assist their efficiency as missile weapons, and these types occur sporadically in early England. As already noted, axes seem to occur in inverse proportion to seaxes, perhaps having declined in popularity as a close-in weapon once the larger-scale manufacture of seaxes began.

A remarkable example of a more substantial kind of axe is that from Sutton Hoo Mound 1, which is made entirely of iron (shaft and head). It featured a slightly downward curving profile on the blade side, with a heavy, square, hammer-like extension on the other. The 31in (78cm) shaft is much longer than would have been expected, and it ends in a swivelled ring to which its strap would have been attached. With so long a shaft, it would have been perfectly feasible to swing this weapon two-

---

[16] Nevertheless, pikemen in the English Civil War used broadly similar weapons to good effect, for protecting the other ranks from cavalry. Ideally, such weapons should be used in large numbers, since they are somewhat vulnerable if not drawn up together for defence. It may have been no more than a matter of training which determined how effective the weapon would be.

[17] It derives from a presumed original *akuzjō, meaning 'the sharp thing' and is distantly related to Latin *acies* 'sharpness'.

handed, although the all-iron shaft would surely have conducted the force of the connecting blow back up the holder's arms! This unique piece rather resembles the later mediaeval 'war-hammer', which was used effectively as a cavalry weapon.

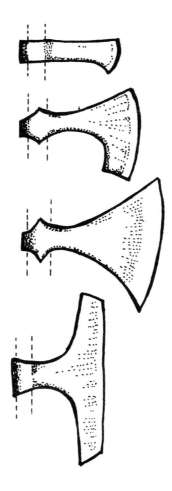

Figure 25 Four later viking axehead types

The two-handed axe is more characteristic of the very late Anglo-Saxon period when Danish influence was making itself felt. With Cnut's accession to the English throne in 1016, the Scandinavian *húskarl* 'household man' became part of the entourage of the English monarch, and with him the fearsome bearded axe. The 'bearded' form, called in Norse *skeggøx*, occurs from the later ninth century in Scandinavia, with a progressively more elongated extension from the bottom of the

127

blade; from the later tenth century it was gradually supplanted by a more balanced blade in which the neck flares into a broad, gracefully curved edge. The origins of the bearded axe lie in the similarly shaped woodworker's tool, no doubt. The Norsemen also used axe-blades of other kinds, including the *breiðøx* or 'broad-axe' – probably the 'flared' form derived from the bearded axe – and the *handox* or 'hand-axe', suggestive of a smaller, slighter weapon. Viking axes are characterized by their sumptuous decoration, including elaborate inlays in precious metals, which indicate the relatively greater interest in this weapon in Scandinavia than elsewhere.

The Shield

> I am a loner, wounded by iron,
> bitten by a blade, sated with war-work,
> weary with swords. Often I see battle,
> a fierce one fighting, yet I expect no consolation
> that from the battle-strife help shall come to me
> before I am destroyed among the warriors,
> but the hammers' leavings beat against me,
> the hard-edged, the blade-sharp, the handiwork of smiths
> bite in strongholds, I must endure
> a more hateful meeting; never a kind of healer
> could I find in the folkland
> among those who healed wounds with herbs,
> rather on me the scars of swords grow greater
> day and night with death-blows.
>
> (Exeter Book *Riddle 5* – 'shield')

> *Ic eom ānhaga īserne wund,*
> *bille gebennad, beadoweorca sæd,*
> *ecgum wērig, oft ic wīg sēo,*
> *frecne feohtan, frōfre ne wēne*
> *þ mē gēoc cyme gūðgewinnes*
> *ær ic mid ældum eal forwurde,*
> *ac mec hnossiað homera lāfe*
> *heardecg, hearoscearp, hondweorc smiþa*
> *bītað in burgum; ic ābīdan sceal*
> *lāþran gemōtes, næfre læcecynn*
> *on folcstede findan meahte,*
> *þāra þe mid wyrtum wunde gehǣlde,*
> *ac mē ecga dolg ēacen worðað*
> *þurh dēaðslege dagum ꝺ nihtum*

Old English literature commonly calls the shield by the name *bord* which can also mean 'board' and 'table'. Other names are *lind* 'linden-wood' (from which it is made), *rand* and *scyld*.

The shield is perhaps the most culturally significant piece of defensive equipment. Once the shieldwall is drawn up, by implication all those on the same side of the wall are classified as 'us', and all those beyond it are 'them'; we shall see the importance of this attitude when we look at the structure of warfare in Section III.[18] The advancing shieldwall marks the boundary where the incorporation of acquired ground takes place; the retreating shieldwall, in contrast, marks off the stragglers, dead and wounded who have to be abandoned to maintain the group's integrity and chances of survival. In cases of total defeat, a group may have been able to indicate surrender by dropping their shields – abandoning their collective boundary and preparing to be absorbed by the victors.

In the *Germania*, Tacitus mentions that the Germanic warrior's worst disgrace was to lose his shield in battle, but common sense suggests that for many men a hard-fought battle would have left them with little or no board, and all that would remain would be the metal boss. Nevertheless, re-fitting a new board to an existing boss would not be difficult and it may therefore be that the boss itself held the symbolic significance. The aggressive spikes of the early Saxon shield bosses mark off the boundary effectively, in that those on the outside (*fiend*, the foes) are faced with the shield as weapon, while those behind (*friend*, the friends) see it as a means of protection. The spike and studs also serve to intimidate the foe by declaring the bearer's force and preparedness to harm others.

Forming and holding a shieldwall are not as easy as they may appear if there is to be enough room to wield weapons effectively. It seems certain that the English practised the manoeuvre – it may have formed part of the regular induction process for warriors – and that when the poet of the *The Battle of Maldon* says:

> Then Byrhtnōð began to draw up the troops,
> [he] rode and advised [them], taught the warriors
> how they should stand and hold their ground
> and bade that they should their shields correctly,
> firmly in the fist, and that they should not be afraid.

(lines 17–21)

> *Ðā þǣr Byrhtnōð ongan beornas trymian,*
> *rād ⁊ rǣdde, rincum tǣhte*
> *hū hī scoldon standan ⁊ þone stede healdan*
> *⁊ bǣd þ hyra randan rihte heoldon,*
> *fǣste mid folman ⁊ ne forhtedon nā*

this does not mean that the men are raw recruits who do not even know how to stand in a line or hold their weapons, but rather that the elderly commander is passing

---

[18] For more on this, see below, p.182.

among the men, offering words of advice and encouragement as a psychological means of quelling anxiety during the wait for the viking attack, reminding them of the way they have been taught to act at a time when their practice is about to be put to the test. The lives of the men present would depend in large part on their ability to hold their shieldwall intact while breaking up the enemy onrush with their spears.

The *Maldon* poet's repeated use of the shieldwall imagery probably reflects battlefield practice in which, for the greater part of the army, successful maintenance of the defensive line was their best hope of survival. Of course, the breaking of the shieldwall by so many men in the panicked flight is the crucial factor which leaves the East Saxon forces without effective defences.

There are references throughout Old English heroic literature to kings and leaders as 'protectors' (OE *hlēo*) which supports the view of the higher-status men as responsible for the protection and well-being of those below them, in terms of both good tactical deployment (not exposing the men to unnecessary danger) and good political manoeuvring (not exposing the polity to aggression). Elsewhere in the Germanic north, new kings were sometimes raised on a platform of shields by their supporters, although this is not recorded among the English.

Typology of the Shield

Early English shields have received surprisingly little attention from archaeologists although they are among the commonest grave-goods from the pagan period. The most comprehensive study to date is that by Tania Dickinson and Heinrich Härke, based on the burial material of the Upper Thames region, who bring together data from much of the available excavated material. According to these writers, shields occur in almost half the inhumation burials containing weapons, though never with cremations, but the rite seems to have declined towards the end of the seventh century and at a greater rate than weapon burials in general declined. When a shield is included with an inhumed body, it normally occurs on the stomach, less often covering the chest, upper legs or head, and seldom over either arm or elsewhere in the grave. Shield burial was favoured in Anglian regions, less popular among Saxons and in Kent. They point out the varying (and therefore imprecise) terminology of the subject and offer a set of fixed terms for use in descriptions of shields, which it is worth recording here. (Table 14)

The shield was conventionally made from lathes of hard wood, to which a metal rim (OE *lǣrig*) was attached and through which a central, circular (less often D-shaped or 8-shaped) hole was cut. This hole was covered with the boss, serving both as handle and as protective covering for the hand. The shield was normally circular in shape, though some later depictions (from the Bayeux tapestry and other 11th century sources) are square with rounded corners, or kite-shaped and identical to those borne by their Norman foes. In use, it was held by the grip, with the hand passing inside the conical boss where it was held quite tightly (probably very tightly if there were padding inside the boss); when not in use – or when the warrior needed both hands to wield his weapon – it was slung over his shoulder or back. Evidence for the attachment of straps to the inside of the board is lacking, but one example (from grave

Härke/ Dickinson term	alternative terms	meaning
apex	*neck, spike*	projection surmounting the cone
board	-	wooden disc surrounding the boss
boss	*umbo*	central circular projection which covers the grip and so protects the hand
cone	*dome*	conical part of the boss atop the wall and surmounted by the apex
convex board	*curved, hollow board*	board which is 'dished', curved back from the boss towards the user
edge bands	*rim fittings*	metal edge binding strip
flange	*rim, brim*	outer, flattened area of the boss by means of rivets passing through which it is attached to the board
flanged grip	–	grip in which the sides are turned up
flat board	–	board which is not convex
flat grip	*strap grip*	grip with flat section
grip	*brace*	metal strut attached to the reverse of the board often by the rivets of the flange
handle	*grip*	wooden bar with cloth bindings attached to the grip to make it easier to hold
laminated	*plywood, composite*	board construction method whereby several pieces of wood are laid over each other in layers
long grip	*stringer, strut*	grip which extends beyond the immediate reverse of the boss
plank construction	*solid wood, single-layer wood, composite*	board construction method whereby several pieces of wood form a single layer
wall	*collar, waist*	part of the boss, the truncated tube between the flange and the cone

Table 14 Summary of shield components and terminology

94 at Pewsey) showed traces of a leather thong bound round the metal grip, and there are a few small, unaccounted-for buckles which may also have belonged to such straps. A long, leather loop attached to the grip would have been the simplest and safest means of carrying the shield without special fittings.

Devising a typology of the surviving shields is really only possible with regard to the metal shield fittings, especially the boss, as the board hardly ever survives even vestigially and there are only very infrequently any other fittings present, such as edge-bindings, rivets or decorative plaques. Nevertheless, there is enough variation within the features studied for a typology to be erected against which future finds may be compared and evaluated. The variable features include the overall height of the boss, and the presence on some examples of an apex terminating in a point, a flat flange or a separate decorative disc.

Based on clusters of features, Härke posits a typology of which Table 14 is a brief summary.

Härke suggests a further classification of the shield grip into short (4-6in, 11-16cm), medium (8-10in, 20-25cm) and long (12-16in, 30-40cm) each with 'flat' and 'flanged' forms. The short, flat type is the commonest, being nothing more than a strip of iron with rivet holes punched through. Other metal fittings on the shield which may survive archaeologically are: circular studs or discs, commonly iron or bronze; lozengiform plates; 'shaped' plates (e.g. animal-shaped appliqué fittings); geometric-shaped mounts; iron bands, often radiating from the boss; edge-bindings, commonly of bronze. All these may be considered 'decorative' although they may equally be practical (strengthening the shield) or particularly in the case of the animal-shaped mounts they may have had some heraldic or religious significance.

Shield bosses from Anglo-Saxon graves are always of iron, though the possibility of all-wooden shields cannot be entirely discounted (and wicker may have been used in some cases). The formal development seems to have been largely due to increased confidence in iron-working, probably backed up by more reliable access to the raw materials for smithing. The early, carinated, low types are assumed to have been made by shaping a single iron billet into a cone, then thinning this while drawing and flattening out the wall and flange; the taller types were probably made in two pieces – a cone section and a wall-flange section, welded together; the exaggerated 'sugar-loaf' bosses were seemingly made up from iron bands filled in with plates, much like the construction method for helmets. The apex, especially if a rod, button or disc type, could be inserted from inside the completed cone and welded into place, strengthening a weak point in the construction. The number of rivets on pagan period shields is consistently four or five, evenly spaced around the flange; a single, early type from Mucking, Essex, had only three rivets, while the later 'sugar-loaf' types could have more. The rivets themselves are usually iron shanks with a broad head, each shank being bent over at right-angles through a washer on the underside of the board. The flange is usually convex, angled back towards the rear of the shield, which may suggest a convex shield surface. The function of the angled flange may have been to preserve tension on the rivets and prevent them from working loose. Whether the interior of the boss was padded or not is unknown – there are sometimes organic remains inside recovered Anglo-Saxon shield bosses, but this may be due to settling of the grave contents.

Group 1	most popular in Wessex, Essex, Kent, the Upper Thames and Sussex
1·1	wide and low overall with large flange, straight carinated cone, more often 4 than 5 rivets on the flange
1·2	as above but smaller, more often concave cone and rod apex
Group 2	most popular in East Anglia and the West Midlands; similar in size and shape to Group 1 but straight walls, 5 rivets on the flange
Group 3	commonest form in Kent, Essex, Sussex, East Anglia; slightly narrower and taller than Groups 1 and 2, carinated with convex cone, 5 rivets on the flange, often a disc on the apex; associated with the long grip in Kent
Group 4	distributed mainly in Wessex and the West Midlands; high and narrow with medium to high, straight walls, concave or straight, uncarinated cone, usually 4 rivets on the flange and spike apex; grip is short, flat, with expanded terminals
Group 5	minor group in the Upper Thames; as Group 4 but with a wider flange and broad apex disc-heads
Group 6	a south-eastern form; low with a shallow, convex cone with narrow flange bearing knobbed rivets, small disc-headed or rod apex
Group 7	common in the south and east; a distended form of Group 6, tall, wide-flanged and often without any discernible wall, the so-called 'sugar-loaf' boss
Group 8	not a well-defined type, a straight-to-convex cone with low walls

Table 15 Classification of shield boss types

The grip was a plain iron bar – it had no display value, being fixed on the inside of the shield – to which the handle was attached. It was riveted to the reverse of the shield and the longer examples had flared ends for which the rivets could be seen on the outer face. Even the short grips were only rarely fastened directly to the flange of the boss as this involved complicated (and unnecessary) alignments of the rivets used. The handle could be simple (leather and /or textile round the iron bar) or complex, involving a shaped, wooden stringer again covered with textile and/or leather, attached in a slightly off-centre position within the hole (to allow for the knuckles and back of the hand) in one of a variety of ways, commonly by a riveted lap joint, a riveted flush insert into the circular opening or, rarely, by being made in one piece with one of the board planks and secured by the flanges on the grip. The binding material made the handle more comfortable to grip and prevented slipping. Where the handle was in one piece with the board, the central hole was cut as two opposing D-shapes, back to back, with the handle formed by the connecting material between them. The smaller the amount of material removed from the board the less weakened it would be by this, and with a D-shaped hole the hand could be more firmly wedged inside the boss, to give better control. This would have been an important factor when the boss was being used aggressively, effectively as a weapon in its own right – the long spiked apex could be devastating if used against an unprepared opponent.[19] Equally, when attached to a small board the shield was then better-suited for use in parrying blows, for which purpose lightness and ease of manoeuvrability were critical.

The board is not directly evidenced in England, although there are examples from the early Danish bog deposits. The evidence for English boards suggests they were generally smallish and circular, and could be divided into three 'ranges': the smallest 13¼-16½in (34-42cm); the middle range 17¾-26in (45-66cm); and the largest 27½-36¼in (70-92cm), while the commonest types seem to have been 20in (50cm) and 24in (60cm); the later examples shown on the Bayeux tapestry are apparently about 36in (90cm) in diameter. There is every likelihood that the smaller shields were

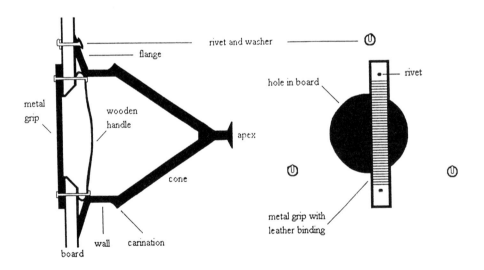

Figure 26 Schematic diagram of a shield boss

---

[19] The Germanic (Batavian) mercenaries who fought in the Roman campaign of conquest are reported to have smashed their shield bosses into the faces of the British warriors opposing them.

intended for use by the relatively younger and weaker men,[20] while only the biggest and strongest men could heft the large boards to shoulder height in combat. To some extent, then, shield size was a reflection of the user's prowess and status, and so the large shield from Mound 1 at Sutton Hoo may not reflect just a large-framed man but a high-status man for whom the ostentation of a broad board was appropriate.

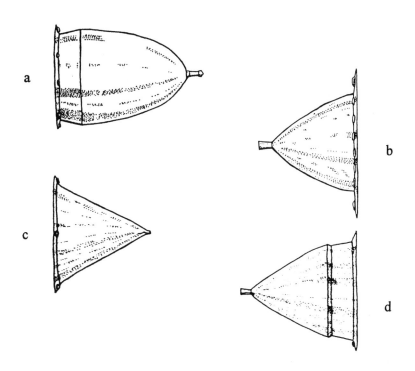

Figure 27 Shield boss types (after Dunning in Evison (1963))
a: Group 7 'sugar-loaf' boss from Sittingbourne, Kent Height (flange to apex) 7½in (19cm);
b: Group 8 boss from Thetford, Norfolk. Height 4¾in (12cm);
c: Group 1 boss from Portsdown, Hants. Height 4¾in (12cm);
d: Group 3 boss from Bury St Edmunds, Suffolk. Height 6in (15cm)

---

[20] It is, of course, perfectly possible that at any given time the men chosen for the shieldwall had the larger available types, while the second rank was equipped with the more modest boards; there is no evidence known to me for men having more than one shield *in battle* (though the rules for viking duellists allowed each man three) yet it is not inherently improbable that wealthy men might have a spare carried by an attendant, given that the wooden board was apparently easily damaged in the fray; in this connection, see the illustration (Fig.36) of an Anglo-Saxon king on p.181, who is accompanied by a youth with no weapon but a shield.

Terry Brown suggests that warriors standing in a solid defensive wall would brace the shield against the left shoulder and knee to withstand the shock of a charge – such a practice would require a large board.

The scarce examples of edge-bindings all attest to more-or-less circular boards. Manuscript and other illustrations consistently show a convex, 'dished' shape for shields but this seems to contradict some of the archaeological evidence. However, some of the longer grips are bent back and, if this is not due to distortion in the grave, may be to accommodate a convex profile.[21] The boards used in the shield are generally between 5mm and 9mm thick, based on the length of exposed shank of the securing rivets, which does not account for any possible tapering towards the edge, nor leather covering for the outer surface. The later the shield is, the thicker will its boards be and the larger the diameter, as a general principle. Although the poetic references to lind 'lime wood' for 'shield' have fixed lime as the wood from which shields were made in popular imagination, Härke shows that alder and willow (or poplar) were the most popular woods in his sample (with over a third each of all examples), followed by maple (10%) and birch (nearly 7%), while lime, ash and oak account for only 10% between all three. Poplar, alder, willow and lime wood are all light, fibrous and tough, while birch and maple are perhaps less resistant to splitting; ash and oak are both heavy woods, the latter being very prone to splitting under impact, and so a poor choice of material for a shield.

Existing remains of English shields point to a construction of boards laid side-by-side, not overlying each other like plywood – although this also has been a popular assumption for many years, which is known from Roman period sites in Britain and elsewhere, and seems to have been used for shield construction during the Middle Ages. At least three planks went into the making of a shield, and Scandinavian evidence suggests as many as nine might be used; they were probably fixed together with glue and ledges, the planks rebated along their edges to form a flush surface, strengthened towards the middle by the long grip riveted across three or more. The curved section of the shield could be produced by steaming and bending the timber over a former. The outer, and possibly also the inner surface was covered by leather which had been applied wet and allowed to shrink onto the board, holding the whole disc tightly together. If the leather were treated with dubbing after it dried, it would not only protect the wood from blows in combat, but also weather-proof it. One of the Laws of King Athelstan specifically outlaws the use of sheepskin on shields; the scarce and fragmentary remains of shield coverings recovered from graves are apparently all cowhide, sometimes tanned. Metal fittings on the shield contributed to the display value and added protection to the user, but against these benefits is the additional weight; some may have been 'patches' to repair a torn cover or strengthen a split board.

Some shields feature iron or bronze studs set symmetrically around the boss, which are probably for decoration as much as anything else; the shield from Sutton Hoo featured elaborately decorated examples which may have held in place some leather figural decoration, while a Continental Alamannic shield had a series of leather strips

---

[21] The *Battle of Maldon* refers to a *cellod bord* which has been translated 'hollowed shield', i.e. convex, although the evidence for this interpretation is not compelling.

radiating in a gentle spiral from boss to rim, rather like a sun-wheel. There is a *prima facia* case for decorated shield boards, given the Germanic predisposition to decoration and display and Tacitus's statement in *Germania* that shields were coloured, although there is virtually no archaeological evidence for the practice. The Sutton Hoo shield with its edge-binding and many metal fittings may be considered typical of the highest level of martial display; less ostentatious but still definitely 'high-ranking' are the gilt and silvered rivets and fittings of a handful of other examples. Manuscript illustrations generally show radiating lines, enclosing dots which may or may not be studs, rivets or appliqué plates. Whether the various units of the *fyrd*, which in early times will have been family- or leader-based, devised a common 'heraldic' motif or not is unknown. Naturally the material culture of various regions dictated preferences in shield size and shield boss form, as in other types of military equipment, jewellery, etc. and it is to be expected that the typology recovered from pagan burial goods is at best incomplete and biased towards the evidence from the best recorded finds.

Härke suggests that the development from the earlier smaller, thinner shields to ones with convex boards and cones in the sixth century marks the tactical change from emphasis on hand-to-hand individual combat to fighting in formations with shields which were able to withstand head-on blows; his analysis of damage and repairs to surviving bosses also supports the proposal that earlier shields were used 'actively' – for parrying and thrusting – while later ones served 'passively' as mere cover. Possibly also the increased height of the 'sugar-loaf' bosses points to its aggressive use in the mêlée, at the same time as the *seax* ousted the axe as the weapon for close-in fighting.

The Body Armour

The damp earth, wondrously frozen,
first bore me from its womb.
I know myself not to have been made with wool's fleeces,
with hairs through high skill, by awareness of myself.
Wefts are not wound on me, nor have I warp,
nor through pressure of bunches does thread resound in me,
nor does a shuttle pass singing through me
nor a weaving-slay strike me from anywhere.
Worms do not weave me in the course of time,
those which make the yellow weaving.
Yet nonetheless widely across the world I am
called a splendid garment for heroes.
Say, with true speech, wise in skilful thought,
wise in words, what this apparel may be.

(Exeter Book *Riddle* 35)

Mec se wǣta wong wundrum frēorig
of his innaþe ǣrist cende
Ne wāt ic mec beworhtne wulle flȳsum,
hǣrum þurh hēahcrǣft, hygeþoncum mīn.
Wundene mē ne bēoð wefle, ne ic wearp hafu,
ne þurh þrēata geþrǣcu þrǣd mē ne hlimmeð,
ne æt mē hrūtende hrīsil scrīþeð,
ne mec ōhwonan sceal āmas cnyssan,
wyrmas mec ne āwǣfan wyrda crǣftum
þā þe geolo godwebb geatwum frǣtwað.
Wile mec mon hwæþre sēþēah wīde ofer eorþan
hātan for hæleþum hyhtlīc gewǣde.
Saga sōðcwidum searoþoncum glēaw,
wordum wīsfæst, hwæt þis gewǣde sȳ.

The Germanic body armour we hear most of took the form of a 'mailcoat' (OE *byrne*, *hlenca*) which was a very costly item. In *The Battle of Maldon*, there are no references to English armour at all, which may indicate that at that date (991 AD) mail was not common among English troops, and which in turn explains the English insistence on keeping the shieldwall intact for protection, according to Nicholas Brooks. He also sees this as a partial reason for Byrhtnōþ's failure at Maldon, where the East Saxon forces would have stood a better chance of victory if they had been equipped to the same standard as their opponents. However, the poem is in many ways a very conservative, traditional piece and it may therefore be the case that the poet deliberately suppressed any mention of body armour which would have detracted from his theme. The coat of ring-mail was certainly known and used in the early centuries of the present era, as there are examples from the Danish bog deposits, as well as occasional references in Anglo-Saxon literature. The evidence of wills and bequests for the mailcoat as a standard piece of war-gear in England is all from the later end of the period.

However in 1008 the *Chronicle* records:

Here the king ordered that across all the English nation ships must be made constantly, that is then [one] from every three hundred hides, and from ten hides one *scegð* [a swifter, lighter vessel] and from every eight hides a helmet and mailcoat.

Hēr bēad se cyng þ man sceolde ofer eall Angel cynn scipu feastlīce wircean þ is þonne of þrym hund hīdum ⁊ of .x. hīdom ǣnne scegð ⁊ of .viii. hīdum helm ⁊ byrnan

This does not mean, of course, that no English warrior before 1008 ever wore helmet and mailcoat, but it does seem that Æþelred was trying to ensure that men presented themselves for military service properly equipped – there was little point in his calling out the *fyrd* if they were to be cut down without striking a blow.

The poet who composed *Beowulf* was aware of the beauty of polished mail, as when the hero first greets King Hrōþgār of the Danes:

> Bēowulf spoke, his mailcoat shone on him
> the net of armour linked by the smith's ancient craft

(lines 405–6)

> *Bēowulf maðelode, on him byrne scān*
> *searonet seowed smiþes orþancum*

Finds of mail from Anglo-Saxon sites are a rarity, although the corroded mass attached to the helmet from Coppergate, York, was patiently restored to its former shape. Probably the only example of a complete mailcoat is that from Sutton Hoo, which even resisted examination by radiography to determine details of its nature and manufacture, again due to its corroded state. The garment was seemingly a thigh-length coat of ring-mail, the individual links ¼in (8mm) in diameter and in rows alternately riveted and butt-jointed (hammered together) to close them. The finished byrnie would have been substantial and heavy, due to the large quantity of rings used, but correspondingly supple and proof against most blows.

Smaller sections of mail occasionally occur in high-status graves, and the famous cemetery at Vendel, Sweden, which has many close parallels to early eastern English material, yielded helmets which had featured a mail 'curtain' hanging from the rim and short face-plate. A mailcoat would be most effective if worn over a leather jerkin, though evidence for such an undergarment is absent until the Middle Ages. Nevertheless, there are representations of men in armour on the decorative plaques of the Sutton Hoo helmet, although it is difficult to interpret what is shown. The 'dancing warriors' (Fig.12, p.73) appear to be wearing knee-length coats with deep cuffs and some form of decorative band along the upper edges which form the collar. This feature has been linked to a find from a minstrel's grave at Cologne, where remains of a gold brocade collar survived as a 'loop' about his neck extending to about waist level. The possibility remains, however, that the coats depicted are ritual robes rather than war-gear – their helmets bear bird-headed horns which seem to have cultic significance whether they are representations of actual headgear or just a method of portraying possession by the raven-god, Wōden. Furthermore, another motif from Sutton Hoo – the rider with raised spear – seems to be wearing a similar garment (judging from the small part of his body not covered by his shield) so this may have been some form of double-breasted harness, possibly covered with small metal plates. The deep, ornamented cuffs of the coats worn by the dancers, the rider and his attackers may represent some form of vambrace, possibly in the form of metal strips attached to the lower arm. Segmented greaves of just this construction were found in one of the Vendel graves, and it hardly seems credible that a folk which could produce the Sutton Hoo helmet could not come up with some form of leg and forearm protection. The figure being ridden down on the 'rider' plate is clearly wearing a mailcoat, though again with edges, collar and cuffs picked out in the same longitudinal strip decoration.

The Franks Casket (see front cover) shows warriors attacking a house, variously armed and all with some form of banded 'kilt' which may represent an armoured tunic, though mail is there apparently represented by rows of circles so the 'armour' must be in the form of strips, for example of toughened leather.

The Helmet

> Plainly visible there on the warriors was
> a braided mailshirt and choicest sword,
> a splendid war-coat, many a helmet,
> a marvellous boar motif.
>
> > (*Elene*, lines 256–9)
>
> *Đǣr wæs on eorle ēðgesyne*
> *brogden byrne 7 bill gecost*
> *geatolic gūðscrūd, grimhelm manig,*
> *ǣnlic eoforcumbul.*

The evidence for helmets among the Germanic nations is not profuse until well into the Later Roman Iron Age, when captured Roman equipment and native copies became associated with warriorhood and, above all, with military leadership. There are many examples of such headgear from Continental Europe from the 500s onwards, though still very few from the British Isles.

The Old English word for 'helmet', *helm*, derives from an original root meaning 'hide' which also gives rise to the words 'holster' (OE *heolster* 'darkness, concealment') and 'Hell' (OE *hel* 'place where one is hidden, grave'), amongst others. The central idea of the group is of 'covering' but significantly not specifically of 'protection'. A 'helm' might therefore be any kind of masking or clothing which hides the wearer.[22] In later times, a distinction is drawn between a 'helm', which is generally an all-in-one article, and a 'helmet' which is divided into a skull and movable vizor, bevor, etc..

There have been only three significant finds of helmets from England, as well as a few 'near misses' – objects which were at first identified as such and later found not to be, such as those from Leckhampton, Gloucestershire (a Romano-British diadem), Souldern, Oxfordshire (an Anglo-Saxon bucket) and Hamworthy, Dorset (a Herzegovnian belt). The genuine finds are known as the Sutton Hoo, Benty Grange and Coppergate helmets.

---

[22] The god Wōden was characterised by his masked and mysterious appearance, which gave rise to his English by-name 'Grim', an epithet applied to many earthworks, e.g. Grim's Ditch, Grimsdyke, etc.

Nevertheless, although there is some physical evidence for the helmet among the early Anglo-Saxon warrior-nobility, there is little doubt that it was not a common piece of military equipment until much later – an edict of 1008 and the later Laws of Cnut are among the first to stipulate that those who present themselves for active service should be equipped with a helmet, amongst other things. Contemporary manuscript illustrations of Anglo-Saxon warriors commonly show one of two forms of headgear: a straight-sided, triangular item with lines suggesting bands at the edges, or a floppy, forward-pointing cap. Either or both of these types of helmet could have been made from boiled and formed leather, of course, which would hardly ever survive archaeologically. These may have been the standard head protection of the English warrior before the later Viking wars (c.990 onwards) dictated an improvement to the standard war-gear of the defenders.

The Battle of Maldon poem, recording events of 991, conspicuously fails to mention helmets in connection with the English forces mustered against the vikings, although the fact that the defenders could not tell who it was that fled on the one remaining horse (it was a thane called Godric, although the troops evidently believed that it was their leader, Byrhtnōþ) may perhaps be related to the rider's face being obscured by some form of headgear.

The Sutton Hoo Helmet

This was one of the most significant of the finds from the remarkable ship burial beneath Mound 1, and it is worth stressing that if the grave had been disturbed and the pieces removed from their setting it is unlikely that the article could have been reconstructed from the mass of rusted iron and bronze fragments which are all that remain today of this great Anglo-Saxon showpiece. Only the nose-piece, the moustache and the eyebrows were recognizable when the helmet was first discovered, and the hard-packed, sandy soil of the mound helped to preserve its shape. Even so, less than half the original surface was actually recovered, so the modern reconstructions still involve a good deal of inference.

The decoration of the helmet is of a common, post-Roman, North Sea Germanic style which led early examiners to conclude that it was of probably Swedish workmanship (its closest known parallels were the helmets found at the cemetery of Vendel, Sweden); only differences in the construction techniques point to its native, English origin. The skull is made from a single sheet of iron, to the rim of which are attached the deep, movable side-pieces and neck-plate, and a fixed face-plate (Scandinavian examples are always made up from iron strips and have hanging iron strips or mail at the rim, not the deep side-pieces of this and the Coppergate examples). The surface of the skull, neck-plate and side-pieces were covered in decorated bronze foils, each tinned to give a lustrous, silvery sheen, in discrete zones: the 'rider' motif on the skull, 'dancing warriors' on the side-pieces, and 'interlaced serpents' on the neck-plate, while 'intertwined snakes' appear in bands on all these surfaces. The tinned plates are held in place by corrugated bronze strips, and the edges of the helmet's various components are finished off with bronze channelled strips.

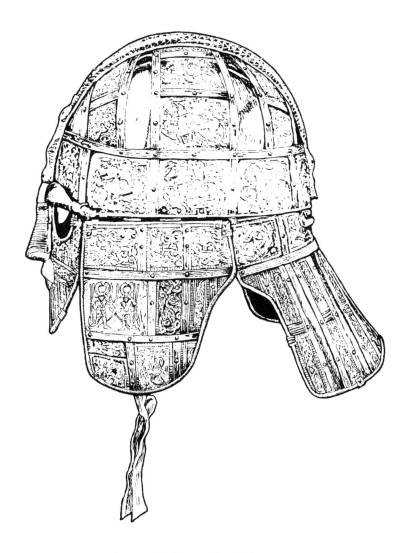

Figure 28 Sutton Hoo Helmet

Across the top of the skull, fore and aft, runs a decorative ridge, finished at each end with a stylized dragon's head, with toothy, gaping mouths and garnet eyes. Confronting the forward-facing head is a stylized flying dragon, also with a similar head to its opponent, but with outstretched wings (which are the 'eyebrows' of the face-plate), a thicker body (the 'nose') and tail (the 'moustache'). The eyebrows themselves finish in boar's heads at the outer ends and have garnets set into their lower edges, while the nose and moustache/mouth are of gilded cast bronze like the eyebrows and dragons' heads. The effect is of a recognizable but 'puzzling' human face made up from random, zoomorphic decorative elements. The rest of the face-plate is covered in long narrow bands of 'interlaced serpents' decoration like that on the neck-plate. There was no discernible buckle among the fragments, but the curved front edges of the side-pieces were clearly intended to abut with the corresponding parts of the face-plate, so the whole would have been drawn tight around the wearer's head, secured perhaps with laces or a thong. Although no interior survived, there were corrosion products on the inner surfaces which could have come from a leather lining which, in turn, would probably have been padded for comfort and additional protection.

The Sutton Hoo hoard dates from the first half of the seventh century, and there have been numerous attempts to link together the two great surviving triumphs of Anglo-Saxon art: the Sutton Hoo treasure and *Beowulf.* The poem, as it survives today, was written down about 1000 AD, but there are clear indications that the present work is a West Saxon copy of at least one other, earlier, Anglian manuscript. This might – and only *might* – have been composed in East Anglia in the 600s by someone within living memory of the great burials by the Deben. If so, the helmet from Sutton Hoo would be of more-or-less the kind the poet had in mind when he described such items. In the poem, the helmet is called *heregrīma* 'raiding-mask', *grimhelm* 'masked-helm' and *gūþhelm* 'war-helm', etc. while its components include *hlēorberge* 'cheek-protector' and *wala* 'wale, wreath'. Seemingly, then, the *grima* references are to the face-plate which conceals the identity of the wearer, while the *hlēorberge* is the side-pieces pulled tight against the cheeks and sides of the head, while the *wala* must be the ¾in (2cm) thick iron band which runs across the top of the helmet. The *wala* is also said to be *wīrum bewunden* 'wound about with wires', which is a fairly good description of the chevron-patterned, silver wire inlay which occurred on the helmet's ridge and eyebrows. If this ridge actually is the *wala* of the poem, then the skull of the helmet must be what is there called the 'roof' – *ymb þæs helmes hrōf hēafodbeorge, wīrum bewunden, wala ūtan hēold...* "around the helmet's 'roof' the head-protector, wound about with wires, the *wala* guarded from without..." (lines 1030–1).

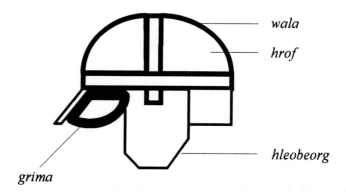

Figure 29 Schematic representation of an early English helmet

The Benty Grange Helmet

This was the first English helmet from the Anglo-Saxon period to be found of which record exists – it was taken from a burial mound at a farm called Benty Grange, near Buxton in Derbyshire, in 1848, along with other metal artefacts such as drinking-cup mounts and hanging-bowl escutcheons. Although the excavator was careful to record the details of his finds, nineteenth century archaeology was not the science it is today, and there are many unanswered questions concerning this and the other articles found in the grave. The helmet itself was described as a "skeleton formed of iron bands radiating from the crown of the head and riveted to a circle of the same metal, which encompassed the brow ... covered with plates of horn disposed diagonally so as to produce a herring-bone pattern" which is surprisingly accurate considering the wild guesses that other contemporary diggers were making about their finds. The report goes on: "on the bottom of the front rib, which projects so as to form a nasal, is a small silver cross ... and on the crown of the helmet is an elliptical bronze plate supporting the figure of an animal carved in iron with bronze eyes, now much corroded, but perfectly distinct as the representation of a hog". This 'hog' or boar figure was not 'carved in iron' exactly, but rather a hollow, cast iron emblem. There were also a number of small silver-ornamented fragments associated with the find, as well as some buckles, though these are perhaps more likely to have served to fasten the body armour than the helmet, judging by Scandinavian parallels. Sadly, though this was clearly the grave of a warrior and a nobleman, there were no finds of weapons in the grave, which strongly suggests that it had been robbed previously – especially bearing in mind that all the finds came from the head and feet areas, the middle portion having thus been rifled and picked clean.

The helmet was cleaned and scientifically examined in 1949 by Rupert Bruce-Mitford, who dated it to the 7th century on account of the filigree and garnet-and-gold decoration on the boar figurine. The construction of the helmet is of iron strips of 1 to 2mm in thickness. The brow band is 1in (2·5cm) wide and holds together all the other strips, which are: two 1in thick bands crossing at right-angles, the one running fore-and-aft being slightly longer (15¾in, 40cm) to project about 2in (5cm) below the brow band as a nasal, decorated with a small inlaid silver cross, and at the back was curved into the profile of the neck. The transverse strip also projected slightly below the brow band and may have had side-pieces dependent from it originally. In the open spaces between the main framework strips were further, tapering iron strips. The metal frame was invisible in use, having been covered with curved, horn plates of which the grain was offset at right-angles on adjacent plates to give a chevron effect (the use of horn – a tough but light material – in this manner is almost unparalleled in this period); the metal itself was covered with more horn strips, which were held in place by decorative silver rivets and the small, silver, wheel-headed cross surrounded by tiny silver studs was fixed onto this surface. The spaces between the neck projection and side projections were apparently also filled by curved plates of horn, although there was no evidence for any face-plate or eye protection having been fitted.

The boar figurine which surmounted the helmet is in contrast to the wheel-headed cross on the nasal and the other cross symbols found on other articles in the grave, as appliqué ornament on the drinking cup, for example. Similar items are represented in Vendel- period art, where they are proportionally much larger and more impressive – perhaps artistic licence is to blame for this, making the important things larger than life. The figure was constructed of hollow, D-sectioned bronze castings fixed back-to-back with silver rivets, with a 2mm gap between the halves to accommodate what was probably a strip of stiff fur forming the boar's bristles. The surface of the body was covered in a ferrous material and dotted with tiny silver studs, the projecting ends of which were gilded,[23] while its hips and shoulders were made from tiny gilded silver plates (re-cycled Roman material). There was a socket for a tail although this was not found (apart from a tiny bronze fragment), while to the head a great deal of jeweller's work had been devoted – the eyes were garnets set in gold sockets with filigree wire edging, the muzzle and tusks were made from gilt bronze sheet while the (missing) ears may have been gilt bronze castings. The whole figure was fastened with rivets to a small bronze plate which stood slightly forward of the crown, for maximum visibility.

Quite what the message to the viewer was supposed to be is hard to say, since symbols from both Germanic heathendom and Christianity were prominently displayed. The boar was a powerful emblem of the wealth-and-fertility gods (the Norse *Vanir*) whose protection clearly extended onto the battlefield, and which was supposed to guard the life of the warrior who bore it,[24] yet the wheel-headed cross was presumably an overtly Christian symbol at this date, having replaced the fish as the standard device for the church. It may be that the warrior in the howe at Benty Grange was a political 'convert' to the new religion who nevertheless put his faith as much in the old ways as any of the new learning. Clearly his family and friends held to the traditional burial ritual for pagan Germanic warriors and interred him with his war-gear and intimate possessions.

The Coppergate Helmet

This is the most recently discovered helmet from the Anglo-Saxon period, which was unearthed during the dig at York in the 1980s, carefully buried in a wooden-lined shaft It is in several parts: the composite skull, two deep, curving side-pieces, a mail curtain extending from the side-pieces around the back of the helmet like a mediaeval *aventail*, brass edge-bindings and a copper-alloy ridge and nasal fitting. The skull is made up from iron bands running fore-and-aft and side-to-side as for the Benty Grange example, attached to a brow band, the spaces between being filled by iron sheets, without any surviving evidence for padding or a lining (which could, in any

---

[23] If there is some symbolic meaning to the boar then it should be borne in mind that the Norse god *Freyr* (a third function, peace-and-plenty divinity) had as his cult animal the boar *Gullinbursti* 'Golden Bristles'.

[24] For more on boar symbolism, see p.50.

case, have taken the form of a separate item much like the mediaeval 'arming cap'). The brow band has two shallow 'arches', decorated with brass dragon-ended eyebrows, let into it which form the rim of the eyes while to the area between these is added the nasal, a cast bronze piece with fine, interlaced animals along it. Gripping the top of the nasal in its mouth is a cast dragon head which forms the attachment for the crest, a copper-alloy strip, bordered by thin mouldings, bearing the inscription in large and decorative insular capitals:

IN. NOMINE. DNI. NOSTRI IHV. SCS. SPS. D. ET. OMNIBUS DECEMUS. AMEN. OSHERE. XPI.

"in the name of our Lord Jesus, the Holy Spirit, God and all, we pray. Amen. Oshere. Christ."

while the same inscription (partly damaged) seemingly ran across the transverse decorative crest which ran from just above the brow band across the top of the helmet. On the basis of the script and the decorative style, a date in the late 700s has been assigned to the helmet. *Ōshere* is a masculine personal name, and the initial element *ōs-* 'heathen god' is known to have been popular among the members of the dynasties of both Bernicia and Deira, judging from later king-lists and the testimony of Bede, although this actual combination of elements does not seem to have occurred in the name of any recorded king.

The lower rim of the helmet has a broad brass coping strip to which the side-pieces were attached with large hinges. The side-pieces themselves hung down and forward, and were secured by thongs attached to a small, central rivet on each. To the back edge of the side-pieces was attached a ring-mail curtain, the top rings of which passed through the coping strip of the rim.

The Seax

...At his side lies his deadly foe,
sick with *seax* wounds...

(*Beowulf*, lines 2903–4)

...*Him on efn ligeð ealdorgewinna*
siexbennum sēoc...

The *seax* can be considered as either a large dagger or a short, single-edged sword, rather like the later cutlass or sabre. Its origins are difficult to determine, but probably represent a natural development to weapon status from household and hunting implements. Single-edged swords are found in Scandinavia in the Germanic Iron Age, and may have contributed to the rise in use of the weapon during the Migration Period. Early forms of *seax* are fairly common in 5th century Frankish graves, and only later

146

do they come into favour on this side of the Channel; this is surprising in as much as the weapon gave its name to the people known as *Seaxe* 'Saxons' who were important in the Germanic settlement of Britain, judging by the Saxon polities which arose in the 6th and 7th centuries – the *Eastseaxe*, *Westseaxe* and *Sūðseaxe* (East, West and South Saxons now remembered as Essex, Wessex and Sussex).

An alternative term found in some books is 'scramasax', which is used to denote the seax in its guise of 'weapon' and to distinguish it from the smaller and humbler domestic or hunting knife. On the one hand, there is no clear evidence that the Anglo-Saxons would have recognized any such distinction, since both spear and bow were hunting tools as well as weapons, apparently without distinction of name; and on the other hand, the term 'scramasax' is itself only used by Gregory of Tours in the *History of the Franks*, and there not precisely – one such is said to have been used to murder somebody, but that does not of itself mean that it had to be an item of battlefield equipment.

The typological classification of the weapon generally in use follows the system devised by Bohner for the Frankish finds: three main categories are described as:–

type	description	Continental dating
Class A	the narrow / small seax	5th–6th century
Class B	the broad seax	7th century
Class C	the long seax	8th century

Table 16 Classification system for the seax

The English weapons generally correspond with the Frankish in date (as far as can be determined) but have specific characteristics which suggest that they have been made in Britain, not brought in from Francia. Among these insular traits are lighter, flimsier blades and smaller upper guards to the hilt. Perhaps more significantly, the English seax sometimes has a much longer grip and the upperguard is curved away from the blade, suggesting that these weapons have been adapted for two-handed use – if so, they are almost unique in early Germanic battlefield weaponry, since not even the spear was intended to be used without the protection of a shield as well. However, the later long-hafted axe certainly required two-handed use, and it may be that the long-hilted seax was a fearsome weapon in the hands of a practised user.

English seax blades, which are commonly of pattern-welded construction, appear to have developed a distinctive shape, whereby the profile of the back is angled from the tang outwards and then sharply in towards the point (the 'broken-back' blade form), a feature which is also found on domestic knives both here and on the Continent; in contrast, the earliest examples of the weapon, as also the later Frankish ones, feature a shallow rounding towards the point. The long blade made in 'broken-back' form seems to be unique to England. Later Norse seaxes appear to have developed due to contact with England during the Danish wars. Though pattern-welding became unfashionable for swords in the 8th century, perhaps due to the expense involved, it was still applied to seaxes and some of the finest, most ornately decorated weapons date from the period after sword production went over to plain steel.[25]

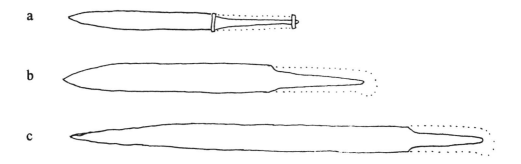

Figure 30 Seax types (after Gale)
a: Class A, Narrow Seax; b: Class B, Broad Seax; c: Class C, Long Seax

The wooden, horn or bone hilt of the seax was fixed to the short tang, perhaps by compression binding with organic material such as cloth or leather, which has since perished, to prevent splitting along the grain of the material. Examples with pommels are not often found, so the seax's hilt or handle must have been of a different order from that of the sword in those cases – no rivet holes or notches are in evidence to suggest any of the other normal hafting techniques for tools.

The shorter types of seax are far more common than the long seax (Class C) which may indicate that this type alone should be considered as a weapon rather than a general-purpose tool. The blade length of between 21¼ and 30in (54 and 76cm) for Class C relates quite closely to the equivalent sword blade length range, while for Classes A and B the range is from 3¼ to 14in (8 to 36cm), but many such have a length of around 9½in (24cm). There is evidently a distinction in function between the two blade forms, especially as there are virtually no finds in the intermediate (14½ to 20¾in, 37cm to 53cm) range. It is hard to imagine a knife with a 3¼in (8cm) blade being used in warfare (except as a last resort!). It therefore seems likely, on *a priori* grounds at least, that warriors had knives of various kinds, and that the most splendid of these were decorated and valued every bit as much as swords or helmets or mailcoats.

---

[25] See above, p.108, for more on sword-making.

Seaxes of all types were often decorated, usually with grooves or inlaid metal of contrasting colour (notably silver), generally in the form of plaited wire strips laid with opposing edges next to each other to give a herringbone effect. Inlay could also spell out the name of the owner or maker, such as the tiny example from the Thames at London bearing the name *Ōsmund*, while that from Battersea features the name *Bēagnōþ*, decorative interlaced lozenges and an entire *fuþorc* or runic alphabet.

It seems that the weapon was kept in a sheath, often of leather with a tooled design – examples survive from London and York. The sheath itself was a folded flap of leather, riveted along its lower edge, sometimes with small buckles and reinforcements at the mouth and point to prevent wear. There are also a few early examples of seaxes with wooden scabbards, from England and the Continent. Evidence from graves and figural representations shows that the weapon was worn across the stomach, blade uppermost and with the hilt at the right-hand end (although the long seax would have probably been somewhat unwieldy in this position). This would have made withdrawal quicker and easier, and by preventing the seax from resting on its cutting edge, the sheath and the edge would both have been protected from undue wear. The small buckles may have fastened straps which stopped the weapon from falling out. There are no certain manuscript illustration of seaxes, partly because English artists generally followed Continental models in their drawings: we cannot assume from this that seaxes went out of use, or were worn in such a way as to be out of sight to a casual observer (e.g. like the *scéan dubh*).[26]

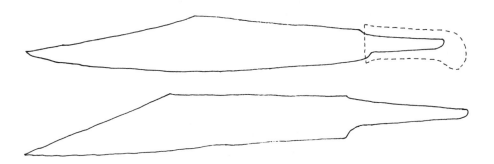

Figure 31 Broken-backed seaxes (after Gale)

References to seaxes are not as common as those to swords, but there are enough to show that the word was in common use. As an example, from *Beowulf* there is the fight scene where Grendel's mother has pinned the warrior to the floor of her underwater dwelling:

---

[26] See Fig.11 p.57 for an 8th century example of a seax worn across the midriff.

"[She] bestrode the hall-guest then and drew her seax,
broad and bright-edged, [she] wanted to avenge her son,
her only offspring. About his shoulders hung
a braided breast-net which protected his life
against point and against blade, denied entry."

(lines 1545–9)

Ofsæt þā þone selegyst ond hyre seax getēah
brād [ך] brūnecg, wolde hire bearn wrecan
āngan eaferan. Him on eaxle læg
brēostnet broden þæt gebearh fēore,
wið ord ond wið ecge ingang forstōd.

The 'braided breast-net' is a mailcoat, described with typical Anglo-Saxon poetic imagination. Other names for the weapon include 'hand-seax' (*handseax*) and 'thigh-seax' (*ðēohseax*), the first suggesting the small knife and the latter the longer weapon which hung at the thigh because it was too large to be slung across the stomach in the normal manner.[27]

The Bow

AGOF[28] is my named turned round
I am a splendid creature created through struggle,
when I bend and from my bosom goes
a deadly missile I am prepared
so that I sweep that life-bane far from me,
When the master who made this punishment for me
lets go my limbs, I shall be longer than before,
until I spew forth – mixed with destruction –
the dire poison which I swallowed before.
From none among men does that leave
easily, of which I spoke before,
if what flies from my belly touches him
so that he pays for the deadly drink with his power,

---

[27] More linguistically transparent than the 'sword' names given above (p.102) are the words related to the Old English word *seax*, *sax* 'knife, dagger, short-sword' (Old Saxon and Old High German *sahs*, Old Icelandic and Old Frisian *sax*) all based on a Proto-Germanic root **saχ-* 'cut' and further connected to Latin words such as *secula* 'cutting tool'; the root **saχ-* also gives rise to the Old English words *secg* 'blade, sword' and *sagu* 'saw'. Further related terms include Latin *saxa* 'rock, stone' reminding us that the earliest cutting implements were the broken splinters of flint used by Stone Age peoples.

[28] 'Agof' is said to be the reversed spelling of the creature's name, but somewhere in transmission the original 'agob' has been silently altered; 'agob' turns into 'boga', the OE word for 'bow'.

with his own life, for full atonement.
Unbound, I will obey no-one
unless tied with cunning. Say what I am called.

(Exeter Book *Riddle* 23 'bow')

AGOF is mīn noma eft onhwyrfed,
ic eom wrǣtlīc wiht on gewin sceapen.
Þonne ic onbūge Ꝫ mē of bōsme fareð
ǣtren onga, ic bēom eallgearo
þæt ic mē þ forhbealo fēor āswāpe,
siþþan mē se waldend se mē þæt wīte gescōp
leoþo forlǣteð ic bēo lengre þonne ǣr
oþþæt ic spǣte spilde geblonden
ealfelo attor þæt ic ǣr gēap.
Ne tōgongeð þæs gumena gehwylcum
ǣnigum ēaþe þæt ic þǣr ymb sprice
gif hine hrīneð þ mē of hrife flēogeð
þæt þone māndrinc mægne gecēapaþ
full wer fæste fēore sīne.
Nelle ic unbunden ǣnigum hȳran
nymðe searosǣled. Saga hwæt ic hātte.

The word 'bow' (OE *boga*) is related to its homonym 'bow' meaning 'bend, flex' (OE *bugan*) and simply means 'that which bends' – a concise description of the weapon. The evidence for bowmanship among the early Germanic peoples is sketchy and largely based on the finds of metal arrowheads – arrows tipped with organic material such as bone or antler, or fire-hardened ones, are poorly attested since they tend virtually to vanish in normal grave conditions. Nevertheless, from the available evidence, it seems that the use of the bow was more popular in continental *Germania* than in Scandinavia proper. The Danish bog-find from Ejsbol provided 675 arrowheads, but not a single bow was found, although at Nydam, along with several hundred arrows, as many as thirty six bows were recovered. Quivers, too, are often found, with an average capacity of about twenty or more arrows. This suggests that the 675 arrowheads from Esbjøl would represent the ammunition of thirty or so men, though for obvious reasons, arrows are more likely than other weapons to be scattered on a battlefield, and less likely to be recoverable. The early continental Germanic evidence of grave finds suggests that bowmen may have been armed with axes also, in which case they could have joined in the fray once their arrows were spent. In Thuringian and Lombardic law, the bow was the weapon of the lowest classes due for military service, and by implication the only weapon they could be expected to afford. In contrast, the Alamannic cavalry were actively encouraged in the use of the bow, presumably due to contact with horse-archers such as the Huns and Avars.

The 8th century Swabian cemetery at Oberflacht produced a series of arrow-shafts, each 24in (60cm) long, and tapering bows of yew, of between 6 and 7ft (1·83 and

2·10m) long, true 'longbows' in any sense. There are also some later finds of arrows from Scandinavia, showing both triangular and quadrangular sections. A remarkably heavy melting of snow in Oppedal, Norway, in the mid-1930s allowed the locals to gather arrowheads which had been used in reindeer hunting in viking times and had lodged in the snow and ice of the mountainside; these and other Scandinavian arrows were mostly fixed by pointed tangs rather than sockets. Pictish pictorial evidence suggests that in the 7th century a rudimentary form of crossbow was in use in Scotland, although there is no more direct archaeological evidence than a possible crossbow nut found in a crannog with two heavy iron quarrels. (The English sources are silent on the use of this weapon, which was previously thought to have been introduced by the Normans.)

The obvious archaeological evidence for the early English use of bows and arrows would be the discovery of metal arrowheads in Anglo-Saxon graves. There are a number of problems associated with this, however, not the least of which is that many small, pointed objects may be classified variously as arrowheads or spearheads depending on which category the writer feels they more probably belong to: there is no rigid typological distinction between the smaller types of spearhead and the normal arrowhead.[29] Swanton's classification system for spearheads[30] takes this into account and the commonest arrowhead form in use throughout the Anglo-Saxon period – the leaf-shaped blade with cleft socket – is identical to his spearheads of Type C1, but, as Manley has shown, the smaller 'spearheads' may be between 4-8in (10-20cm) long, while arrowheads regularly fall around the 4in (10cm) length (and some Scandinavian types can be up to 6in, 15cm). Other considerations are that arrows may have had perishable, organic tips, or have been simply hardened in fire (in which case they will not normally survive in the earth), and that small iron objects would usually rust and would probably be overlooked except in the most rigorous and meticulous excavation.

It is unlikely that special military arrows were manufactured, since the bow was not the first choice of military weapon among the English. Hunting arrows, whether tipped or not, which could bring down game would suffice for use against lightly-armoured troops. The function of the arrow is to strike with as deep a wound as possible, against animals and/or men, and to this end the prudent bowman maintained a choice of arrow types[31] – where arrowheads survive in graves, they are often a mixture of 'barbed' and 'bolt' forms.

---

[29] This problem was brought into focus in the case of the famous 'Ice Man' glacier body discovery, where the small knife at his belt had a flint tip which would certainly have been described as an arrowhead if the whole implement had not survived intact.

[30] See above, p.119, for a tabulation of the commonest spearhead types.

[31] While apocryphal stories of poisoned arrows are known, there is no hard evidence for this practice. There are two occurrences of the phrase *ættrene ord* in *The Battle of Maldon* which can be literally translated 'poisonous point' but these both refer to spears, and are in any case literary metaphors better rendered as 'deadly point'. Notwithstanding this, the incidence of blood-poisoning resulting from wounds must have been quite high (early mediaeval weapons were not normally cleaned to modern surgical standards!) and this may have given rise to the idea of the venomous blade.

English bows of the Anglo-Saxon period were of the 'longbow' type, even though they were seemingly only drawn to the chest, not the ear as for the classic mediaeval English and Welsh longbow. One find from Chessel Down was 5ft (152cm) long – shorter than the Oberflacht maximum of 7ft (210cm), but a powerful weapon none the less. The bows on the Bayeux tapestry seem to be about 49ins (125cm) long, but detailed inferences based solely on that work's evidence should not be made. The range of the bow depends more on the strength and skill of the bowman than the tensile strength of the weapon itself. Assuming that men accustomed to hunting would be reasonably proficient in its use, a range of between 285 and 600yds (260 and 550m) has been proposed, although F. M. Stenton was inclined to put it at no more than 100yds (90m).

The *Beowulf* poet knew of the bow and arrow as a weapon of the chase, and described a hunting accident whereby a youngster caused the death of his elder brother:

> For the eldest unfittingly was
> the bed of death laid out by his kinsman's deeds
> once from his horn-bow Hæðcyn
> killed him with an arrow, his noble loved one,
> he missed his mark and shot down his kinsman,
> his own brother, with a bloody shaft.

(lines 2435–40)

> *Wæs þām yldestan ungedēfelīce*
> *mæges dædum morþorbed strēd*
> *syððan hyne Hæðcyn of hornbogan*
> *his frēawine flāne geswencte,*
> *miste mercelses ond his mæg ofscēt,*
> *brōþor ōðerne, blōdigan gāre.*

The *hornboga* 'horn-bow' may be a composite bow of wood and horn, if it is not just a poetic way of expressing the weapon's curvature. Later in the poem, the warrior Wīglāf describes his dead lord as the folk prepare his funeral pyre, in terms of the battles he has survived, in a quite detailed account of the effects of archery in war:

> "...Now the embers shall devour
> – the bright flame grow – the warriors' strong man,
> who often endured the iron-shower
> when the storm of darts powered by strings
> sped across the shieldwall, the shaft held to its task,
> keen in its feathered flights it followed the barb."

(lines 3114–9)

> *"...Nū sceal glēd fretan*
> *– weaxan wonna lēg – wigena strengel*
> *þone ðe oft gebād īsernscūre,*
> *þonne strǣla storm strengum gebǣded*
> *scōc ofer scildweall, sceft nytte hēold,*
> *feðer gearwum fūs flāne fullēode."*

There is, though, little direct descriptive evidence to suggest that the English used the bow in war on any but the smallest scale, other than the few references in *The Battle of Maldon* to the two sides harming each other only "through arrow's flight" (*þurh flānes flyht*, line 71) and in the initial stages "bows were busy" (*bogan wǣron bysige*, line 110), while towards the end Æscferþ's contribution was that "he sent many arrows speeding forth – sometimes he struck a shield, sometimes wounded a warrior" (*ac hē fȳsde forð flān geneahhe, hwīlon hē on bord scēat, hwīlon beorn tǣsde*, lines 269–70). Furthermore, as Nicholas Brooks has suggested, if Wulfmǣr could pick up and throw back a spear (line 156) there is no reason to think that bowmen would be unable to shoot back the other side's arrows.

In post-Conquest times we have the surprising statement of Henry of Huntingdon that the English did not know the use of archery in war, yet there is some evidence to show that the bow was a popular hunting weapon which was simply not considered sufficiently 'noble' as an instrument of warfare. On the 7th century Franks Casket lid, the warrior named in runes as *Ægili* (i.e. Ægel or Egil) is depicted shooting at an attacking force from the window of his house, one man having been felled by an arrow in the chest while the foremost of the advancing assailants has two stuck in his shield with a third about to strike his helmet. Egil, in common with other Anglo-Saxon illustrated bowmen, does not have a quiver, but seems to have one further arrow propped against the windowsill ready for use, while a woman seated behind him is apparently making more; yet these circumstances are clearly not those of normal warfare: the bow-wielding warrior is being attacked in his house and having to improvise with the weapons he has to hand. Elsewhere, and at the other end of the period, the Bayeux tapestry clearly shows an archer among the English troops, though he is in something of a minority, surrounded by the armoured sword-, axe- and spear-wielding warriors of the English shieldwall, and significantly he seems to be only chest-high to the regular infantrymen around him. Many of the English soldiers there have shields with numerous arrows sticking out of them, and the Norman archers are shown operating in conjunction with their cavalry, giving covering missile attacks while the horsemen advance. (One even appears on horseback chasing the routed English.)

If bowmen were not front-line troops in the Anglo-Saxon military hierarchy, it may be that their role was rather with the other non-combatants in protecting the waggons and packhorses than in offensive action. Again, if the bowmen were of lowly status – and they need not always have been, as the archer in *The Battle of Maldon* was clearly of enough importance to be a hostage – it could be argued that they were left behind by the main army and were only expected to play the part of snipers and skirmishers, harassing the enemy without engaging him in a straight fight. Brooks remarks that the archery at Maldon was such as to wound the foe without apparently being deadly in its effect.

It would be instructive to know the source of a later addition to manuscript 'C' of the *Chronicle*, describing events at Stamford Bridge where Harold's English army took on the forces of his brother, Tostig, and the Norwegian adventurer Hárald Harðráða. Describing the Norse king's defeat and the rout of his army, the manuscript says:

... and the Northmen fled from the English. Then one of the Norwegians was there who withstood the English army, so that it could not cross over the bridge nor gain victory. Then one Englishman shot with an arrow but it achieved nothing, and then under the bridge came another one and pierced him beneath the byrnie. Then Harold king of the English came over the bridge and his army onwards with him and made a great slaughter there of Norwegians and of Flemings, and the king's son Edmund allowed Harald to proceed home to Norway with all the ships.

(*ASC 'C'* s.a. 1066)

ꝺ þa Normen flugon þa Englisca. Ða wes þer an of Nor wegan þe widstod þet Englisce folc, þet hi ne micte þa brigge oferstigan ne sige gerechen. Ða seite an Englisce mid anre flane ac hit nactes ne widstod ænd þa com an oþer under þere brigge end hine þurustang en under þere brunie. Þa com Harold Engla chinge ofer þere brigge ꝺ hys furde forð mid hine ꝺ þere michel wel geslogon ge Norweis ge Flæming ꝺ þes cyninges sunu Hetmundus let Harold faran ham to Norweie mid alle þá scipe.

Unfortunately, the handwriting and language in which this addition is made dates from the 1200s and consequently the description of events may be a later embroidering of some minor incident. Nevertheless, the implication is clearly that the English archer shooting from a distance could do nothing to dislodge the Norwegian on the bridge, and that only the quick-thinking of another man saved the day. It is not clear whether this man who felled the viking did so by stabbing him or possibly shooting him at close range and from a place of concealment beneath the bridge, as *þurustang* 'through-pierced' can bear either sense.

The bow, then, was never the first choice of weapon of the English 'professional' warrior and seems probably to have been largely reserved for hunting. The lower orders, however, may perforce have had to use it when summoned to war, due to its relative cheapness and the fact that such men already had a bow for hunting. Bows are not the weapons of heroes in Germanic tradition, who generally prefer to slog it out with spear and sword; they are not prestigious, decorated *māþmas* handed on with pride from father to son – they are just cheap, crude staves with a length of string attached.

As a postscript to this section on missile weapons, Old English glosses the sling (Latin *ballista*) as *stæfliðere* 'staff-pouch', while *liðere*, *liðera* occur as words for 'sling'.[32] Again, there is no evidence that these were regularly used in warfare, normally being hunting weapons. Also, the Exeter Book has a riddle which I quote below:

> I am the protector of my herd,
> retained by fastening wires, filled within
> with noble treasures. Often in the daylight
> I spew spear-terror; greater is success
> because of my filling; the lord beholds
> how war-spikes fly from my belly.
> Sometimes I begin to swallow dark things,
> polished battle-weapons, bitter points,
> fearful deadly spears. My contents are gainful,
> a fair womb-burden dear to proud men.
> Men remember what passes through my mouth.

(Exeter Book Riddle 17)

> *Ic eom mundbora mīnre heorde,*
> *eodorwīrum fæst, innan gefylled*
> *dryhtgestrēona. Dægtīdum oft*
> *spǣte sperebrōgan, spēd biþ þȳ māre*
> *fylle mīnre; frēa þæt bīhealdeð*
> *hū mē of hrife flēogað hyldepīlas.*
> *Hwīlum ic sweartum swelgan onginne*
> *brūnum beadowǣpnum, bitrum ordum,*
> *eglum attorsperum. Is mīn innað til,*
> *wombhord wlitig, wloncum dēore.*
> *Men gemunan þæt mē þurh mūþ fareð.*

This has been construed as either 'ballista' or 'catapult' and although neither kind of weapon is known to have been in use in England at that time, the fact that a riddle could be composed for an English-speaking audience presupposes that the intended audience would be familiar with the concept of such a war-machine at the very least.

---

[32] These words are based on the noun *leðer* 'leather' and mean '[thing made from] leather'. Men with slings are shown on the lower margin of the Bayeux tapestry, where they are apparently hunting birds.

Miscellania

Aside from weapons as such, there are a number of other items of a vaguely military character which ought not to be passed over. Among these are some of the artefacts from Sutton Hoo Mound I, which have about them an air of dignity and implicit threat which put them firmly in the category of war-gear even if they have no obvious place among the more usual tools of war.

The War-hammer

Evidence for the use of hammers as weapons in northern Europe is not plentiful, but there is a general assumption that the Scandinavians used such weapons and that the parallel North Sea cultures of early England may have done likewise. The theory rather rests on the Norse stories of the god Þórr (Thor) whom the English knew as Þunor (i.e. 'thunder') and who was certainly worshipped by the early Anglo-Saxon migrants. The weapon used by Þórr was the massive hammer Mjolnir 'miller, crusher' which could fly from the god's hand, destroy a foe and return to him. This weapon is probably to be seen as a figurative interpretation of lightning which was observed to strike suddenly, and might kill a man or fell a tree, but on examination there would be no sign of the weapon which had caused the damage.

However, there is nothing intrinsically unlikely in the use of the domestic or farmyard hammer as a weapon, particularly by folk who have to make the most of the tools available to them.[33] As a missile weapon, the hammer can be thrown with greater effect if it is attached to a length of chain or rope and swung round the body to build up momentum before release, exactly like the 'hammer' used in the Highland games. The many small hammer amulets found in heathen English and viking graves are often equipped with a suspension loop such as would be appropriate to a missile weapon, and pictorial representations on runic stones also have this feature. The early English amuletic examples show very long, thin handles while the Scandinavian ones are characterized by short, stumpy hafts. The Icelandic story of the making of the god's hammer by the dwarves specifically says that the handle came out rather shorter than normal.

There is further evidence, however, from the Bayeux tapestry where, in the battle scene showing the English shieldwall, what appears to be a mace is shown heading right-to-left, i.e. as if having been thrown by the English towards the advancing Norman cavalry. (Fig.1, p.21) The head of this weapon is admittedly tri-lobed and not a very close match to the shape of the hammer associated with Þórr, but it is not unlikely that the form would have developed in time. The final panel of the tapestry shows the defeated English fleeing the field, some bearing the same tri-lobed weapons;

---

[33] There are traditions of the use of the hammer as a weapon by the Goths. St. Saba, a Gothic martyr, died when a warrior snatched up a 'pestle' and hurled it so that it struck the holy man's chest, according to Sozomen's account. Ammianus describes Goths fighting with fire-hardened clubs, which may reflect the same proficiency with the hammer as a weapon of war.

these men have no armour and are travelling on foot, hence they may represent the remnant of the rank-and-file of the *fyrd*.

A mace is itself nothing more than a streamlined, slightly upmarket club, which was known to the Anglo-Saxons as a *sāgol* and widely used in hunting. Possibly, if the lower orders were forbidden to carry arms, the *sāgol* was their principal means of self-defence,[34] rather like a *shelalagh*.

Pole-arms

A *sāgol*, apart from being a club, could also be a rather longer weapon, such as a quarterstaff or pole. The mediaeval English tradition of staff-fighting may even go back to Anglo-Saxon times; although there is very little evidence for any such techniques in use among the lower orders (who were denied legal access to the normal weaponry of the day) there is equally no reason to suggest that the technique had been introduced in post-Conquest times.

Old English used the word *stæfsweord* 'staff-sword' to describe a particular kind of weapon which sounds as if it should have been a pole-axe or some similar, long-shafted weapon with a long pointed blade, but apparently different in kind from the normal form of spear.[35] There are Icelandic saga references to a weapon called a '*høggspjot*' (hewing-spit) which may be a similar cut-and-thrust device.

The Whetstone

The whetstone from Sutton Hoo Mound I (Fig.3, p.31) is virtually unique. It has been interpreted as a 'sceptre' and in as much as this word implies a symbol of kingly power the whetstone may be so described. It is not a 'sceptre' in the classical sense of a rod with a decorated finial, however; it consists of a long, heavy stone carved into a square-sectioned bar, at the upper and lower ends of which are carved finely-detailed bearded or clean-shaven human faces. The bar finishes in a round 'door-knob' at each end, painted red and enclosed at the base in a bronze cage with a small, cupped foot. The top fitting ends with a large bronze circlet surmounted by a bronze stag figurine.

There are no clear parallels for this object anywhere in Europe, although decorated whetstones of a very different kind do occur in Wales, Scotland and Ireland. The small stag figurine is one of the few three-dimensional sculptures from Anglo-Saxon times. The stone had never been used for sharpening, which tends to suggest that it had primarily symbolic significance. If so, the role of the warlord as giver and ruler of weapons is called to mind, and nothing could symbolize the lord's power over his men better than his bearing a ritual whetstone. That said, the piece remains an enigma.

---

[34] That a club was not considered a 'weapon' in the narrow sense is supported by the fact that William of Normandy's half-brother, Bishop Odo of Bayeux, was forbidden to carry arms because of his holy office yet went to war in full armour, equipped with a helmet and a wooden club (*baculu[m] tenens,* according to the tapestry).

[35] But spearheads of the more elongated type, such as E3, could plausibly be described by such a title (Fig.22, p.122) as could the sword-shaped type G (Fig.23, p.123).

Figure 32 Two armoured English warriors based on a detail in the Bayeux tapestry. The one on the left has a full-length mailcoat and 'teardrop' shield, while his companion, a 'cumbolwiga' or standard-bearer, has a convex circular one with a spiked boss.

The Standard

Close by the whetstone in the mound, the excavators found a long iron pole which has defied classification. It is a square-sectioned rod 5½ft (1·7m) long with an iron 'cage' attached at the top. The upper part of the cage is an iron grille, each corner of which is fashioned into a stylized horned animal's head. The foot of the rod is split into a v-shaped 'soil-spear' which would presumably have been thrust into the ground to make the whole object stand upright by itself, although it is very small and could hardly have worked well for this purpose.

The purpose of the stand is still unknown. It has been suggested that oil-soaked rags might be wrapped round the grill and ignited to make a 'flambeau', or that it could be a rather ornate type of royal standard such as was used by the Northumbrian King Edwin, according to Bede. Its location in the grave with the whetstone suggests that the two mysterious objects share some common significance or purpose.

However, it should not be forgotten that military standards or pennants were used throughout the Anglo-Saxon period, and that there is no reason to suppose that the Sutton Hoo warrior-king would have gone into the next world without his own. The standards shown on English coins (Fig.33, p.163) and the Bayeux tapestry are small, rectangular and with a dagged trailing edge; Roman coins show barbarian standards of almost identical design from perhaps 800 years earlier. The simple, geometric designs depicted (mainly crosses and circles) could easily have been made either by appliqué shapes or by embroidery. The tapestry's depiction of what appears to be Harold's personal standard is in the form of a reddish dragon (Fig.32, p.159) which is probably of a type based on the windsock principle – a moulded head with gaping mouth is attached to a fabric bag which inflates as the breeze (or passing air, if carried by a rider) fills it, giving the dragon the appearance of flying overhead.[36]

The Horn

Although not strictly an item of military equipment in the narrow sense, the horn seems to have played some part in warfare. It was, with the flag, the principal means of signalling available to early armies, and was no doubt used for fanfares, for alarms and possibly even for musical purposes. There are illustrations from the Anglo-Saxon period showing the playing of harps and various kinds of wind instrument, though all appear to be in domestic contexts.

Travellers were required by law to wind their horns as they passed along, and any group found off the king's highway travelling without doing so was to be considered with suspicion as potential raiders or bands of thieves. Armies presumably marched to the sound of horns, since the woeful remnant of a warband besieged in Raven's Wood have their first inkling of rescue when they hear the sound of horns:

> …Rescue happened after,
> to the sorrowful men at dawn,
> once Hygelāc's horn and trumpet's
> song they heard, when the good man came
> with the folk's duguð travelling behind.
>
> (*Beowulf*, lines 2941–5)

> … *Frōfor eft gelamp*
> *sārigmōdum somod ǣrdæge,*
> *syððan hīe Hygelāces horn ond bȳman*
> *gealdor ongēaton, þā se gōda cōm*
> *lēoda duguðe on lāst faran.*

Archaeological evidence for horns (and other instruments) is poor, but this is explained by the perishable nature of the material. One possible example was unearthed in a (probably royal) burial at Broomfield, Essex, described as a drinking horn in the literature but lacking the ornate metal fittings such vessels usually have.

---

[36] Compare the description of the fluttering raven banner on p.76 for a Scandinavian parallel.

III. Warfare

… Then battle was nigh,
glory in combat, the time had come
when doomed men had to fall there.

(*The Battle of Maldon*, lines 103–5)

… Þā wæs feohte nēh,
tīr æt getohte, wæs sēo tīd cumen
þæt þǣr fæge men feallan sceoldon.

III. Warfare

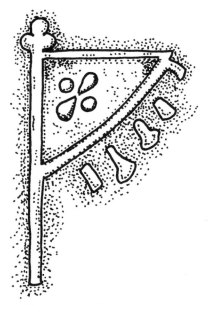

*Figure 33 War-banner from an Anglo-Saxon coin
with simple cross design and tasselled lower edge*

Society begins with an act of violence – for example, in the northern tradition, as in many other early cultures, it is only after *Óðinn*, *Vili* and *Vé* have destroyed *Ymir*, the primal being, that they can create the world from his flesh. This primal act of destruction is itself pregnant with an act of creation, or at least of empowerment to creation. The earliest human societies came about through their members' need to work together if they were to succeed in their new role as carnivorous predators, and the earliest social acts were those of catching and despatching prey, dividing and eating it.

Many early cultures sought to recapture this moment of mythic or 'sacred' time by replicating the destruction of the being: we call this 'human sacrifice'.

Where the economy of a society is not particularly labour-intensive, and especially where a combination of hunting and agriculture still only provides subsistence levels of food production, there are important questions involved in the place and importance of the individual; it can then be crucial for each to demonstrate his worth as a net contributor to the society. This leads to an interesting dilemma: how does one deal with criminals and captives? Prisoners-of-war have no reason to expect mercy from their conquerors; thieves, murderers, adulterers and the like have little prospect of gentle treatment from those they have wronged. But what to do with such people? They must either be turned out (where they continue to pose a threat) or held (where they have to be fed). Making them into slaves is one solution, where there is capacity for productive work, but among small-scale herdsmen and farmers such as the early folk of northern and western Europe, slaves are as much a liability as an asset – extra mouths to feed. It therefore follows that the captives and criminals have to be removed from the economy; the two obvious ways of achieving this are putting them to death (effective but wasteful) and selling them on elsewhere (profitable but not always an option). Simple hanging or beheading are reasonably efficient means of getting rid of the unwanted, but where it is possible to turn such practices into a religious rite which will benefit the community, the inherent wastefulness of the act can be avoided. According to this reasoning, therefore, every life taken in ritual sacrifice enriches the society which takes it, while a life spared is just another mouth to feed.

It is with this in mind that we read of the Germanic practice of religious sacrifice, whereby those captured in war were ritually destroyed – not just killed, but their entire presence wiped off the map of human existence. We have the testimony of Orosius, writing of the *Cimbri*, the Germanic tribe which gave its name to 'Himmerland' in Denmark, that in accordance with a vow they had taken, this folk's warriors set about the wholesale destruction of a defeated foe: ripping up their clothing; hurling their treasures into a river; hacking their riding tack, armour and weapons to pieces; drowning the horses and hanging the men from trees. The Cimbri are usually presumed to have offered their enemy to *Wōðenaz*, the Germanic god who presided over war and death, and to have been content with victory over their adversaries; the defeated warriors and their equipment belonged to the god and had to be ritually destroyed to send them to him. It is presumed that very similar circumstances surrounded the disappearance of the Roman legion commanded by Varus which entered the northern forest where Arminius's men were waiting for them; the Roman troops were never seen again.

Hanging from trees seems to have been the approved, traditional method of sending captives into the next world. It is mentioned in connection with the *Semnones*, who worshipped once a year in a sacred grove the god called by Tacitus *Deus Regnator Omnium* 'God Ruler of All',[1] beginning their devotions with a human sacrifice. Even *Beowulf* has echoes of the practice, as when a band of warriors who had been driven from the battlefield took refuge in *Hrefnes holt* 'Raven's Wood' and were taunted by their enemy:

> Then the great army encircled those who had escaped the sword,
> wearied by wounds; [he] frequently promised woe
> to the wretched troop throughout the night,

---

[1] Interestingly, 'ruler of all' is a phrase used of Christ in some Old English texts, e.g. *eallwealdend* in Ælfric's *Lives of Saints*.

he said that in the morning with sword's edges
[he] meant to destroy [them], some on gallows-trees
as play for birds...

(lines 2936–2941)

Besæt ðā sinherge sweorda lāfe
wundum wērge; wēan oft gehēt
earmre teohhe ondlonge niht,
cwæð hē on mergenne mēces ecgum
gētan wolde, sume on galgtrēowum
[fuglum] tō gamene ... ...

Death in battle is one thing, and ritual murder in cold blood after a battle something entirely different, we might think; but with the absolute duty of vengeance for fallen kinsmen heavy on their minds, it is hardly surprising that the victors often destroyed those they had overcome in anger, whether Wōðenaz had been invoked or not.

Death as a legal punishment also played a major part in Germanic life. Tacitus notes that there were two principal methods of execution: traitors and deserters were hanged on trees as an example to others, while the cowardly, lax and effeminate were pressed down into bogs so that their crimes might be hidden.[2] While the latter method does not seem to have remained in use among the English in Britain,[3] hanging was certainly a legal means of execution in Anglo-Saxon times, and many captured vikings ended their days on English gallows. Although this practice was sanctioned by the king's legal code and the church, it is clear that as a death-rite hanging is of greater antiquity than its Christian practitioners could have known. It is interesting to refer to the story in which that great northern warrior and troublemaker, Starkaðr, had been advised that a sacrifice to Óðinn (the Scandinavian counterpart of Wōðenaz) was required, and the victim should be King Vikar, with whom he was travelling. Starkaðr persuaded the king that they should fool the gods by staging a mock-sacrifice: the king should stand on a block, with a calf's intestine round his neck attached to a fir tree's branch while Starkaðr prodded him with a wand.

Then Starkaðr thrust at the king with the wand and said "Now I give thee to Óðinn!". Then Starkaðr let go of the fir bough. The wand became a spear and pierced through the king. The block fell from beneath his feet and the calf's intestines became strong as wood and the bough rose up and lifted the king up among the branches, and there he died. (*Gautrekssaga*)

Þá stakk Starkaðr sprotanum á konungi ok mælti "Nú gef ek þik Óðni!". Þá lét
Starkaðr lausan furukvistinn. Reyrsprotinn varð at geir ok stóð í gegnum

---

[2] Danish peat bogs have yielded numerous bodies of men and women executed in this way.

[3] There is some slight evidence for certain individuals having been buried alive in the pagan period in, for example, Sussex. This may mean they were merely stunned at the time of their internment, but it is far more likely that they were suspected of witchcraft and were pinned down into the grave to avoid the possibility of their walking after death.

koninginn. Stofninn fell undan fótum honum en kálfspparmarnir urðu at viðu
sterkri en kvistrinn reis upp ok hóf upp konunginn við limar, ok dó hann þár.

The war-god was not easily cheated of his victims, even though this was a double-death of simultaneous stabbing and hanging, such as are known from other evidence to have been associated with the Óðinn cult. Yet there is no suggestion that King Vikar was a criminal whose death was a legal requirement; it seems to have been a case of Óðinn favouring certain kings with victories for a while, then withdrawing his favour and exacting a terrible price for his support.

However, there were other ways for victims to meet their end, as archbishop Ælfhēah (now known as St. Alphege) found out when he gave himself up as a hostage to a viking army and forbade anyone to raise a ransom for him:

> ...then the raiding army became very agitated against the bishop because he would not summon up any money for himself, but [rather] he forbade that anyone should hand over anything in exchange for him; they were also very drunk, for wine had been brought there from the south; then they took the bishop and led him to their meeting on the Saturday night, the eve of Sunday after Easter, and shamefully killed him there, stoned him to death with bones and the heads of oxen, and then one of them struck him with the flat of an axe on the head so that with that blow he sank down and his holy blood fell onto the earth...

> *(ASC 'C' s.a.1012)*

> *... wearð þā se here swȳðe āstyred angēan þone bisceop for þām ðe hē nolde him*
> *nān feoh behātan ac hē forbēad þæt man nān þing wið him syllan ne mōste; wæron*
> *hī ēac swȳþe druncene, for ðām þær wæs brōht wīn sūðan; genāmon þā ðone*
> *bisceop, læddon hine tō hiora hūstinge on ðone Sunnanæfen Octabas Pasce þā*
> *wæs xiii kl.mai and hine þær ðā bysmorlīce ācwylmdon, oftorfedon mid bānum*
> *and mid hrȳþera hēafdum, and slōh hine ðā ān hiora mid ānre æxe ȳre on ðæt*
> *hēafod þæt mid þām dynte hē nyþer āsāh and his hālig blōd on þā eorðan fēol...*

Ælfhēah was not killed simply for sport – his status as a priest meant that he was accorded a sacrificial ritual death, similar to that which an earlier heathen army had meted out to the fiercely unrepentant Christian King Edmund of the East Angles.[4] It is worth noting that the method of putting the enemy priest-king to death – throwing missiles at him – mimics the sacrificial death of the northern god *Baldr*.

Finally, it is worth stressing that the modern notion of linear time was still something of a scientific abstraction among even the Christian Anglo-Saxons, whose attitudes to life and death seem to have been governed by the world-view of their heathen forebears. They believed that at a given time some men were 'fey' (*fǣge*), doomed to die – a reaction to the uncertainties of warfare and accidents not unlike that of many modern soldiers who have faith in the idea that "if it's got your name on it, there's nothing you can do". The converse of this is also held to be true, of course, that

---

[4] See below p.212 for Edmund's fate at the hands of the vikings.

"you're all right until your number comes up". Tied in with this idea is the concept of *wyrd* 'the course of events' which is the underlying structure of time; it is this pattern which the Anglo-Saxons tried to read in the world about them. *Wyrd* was not exactly 'implacable fate' but rather 'the way of the world, the way things happen'. As the *Beowulf* poet observed:

> ... *Wyrd* often saves
> an undoomed hero as long as his courage is good.

(lines 572–3)

> ... *Wyrd oft nereð*
> *unfægne eorl þonne his ellen dēah*

The implication is that while a man's courage holds out, he has a hope of winning through since *wyrd* 'the way things happen' will often work to help such a man, as long as he is not doomed; conversely, if a man *is* doomed then not even his courage can help him stand against 'the course of events'. While hardly a very comforting viewpoint for a man who thinks he may be doomed, this outlook[5] no doubt helped many a warrior keep his spirits up in difficult circumstances.

The Nature of War in Anglo-Saxon England

Warfare in the modern sense – entire nations giving over their collective efforts and industrial output to the prosecution of a particular campaign against a specific enemy – is a relatively modern phenomenon. Warfare in the ancient sense was a state of hostile relations between polities which was rather more confined to the ambition and prestige of individuals. As such it was not a quantum (war~peace) situation, but one stage on a scale of hostilities. It should be remembered that until relatively recent times in most European communities strangers from outside the farm/village/town were regarded with deep suspicion, and for most people love, peace and friendship were confined to the (extended) family and a handful of trusted individuals: everyone else was a potential foe. In these circumstances, aggression could never be far from the surface, since any indication that there was reluctance to defend oneself could be interpreted as an invitation for others to attack.

At the height of the wars against the vikings, which he stood a very good chance of losing, King Alfred of Wessex greeted a Norwegian traveller called *Ohtere* (i.e. Ottar) at his court and extended his hospitality to the seafarer, listening eagerly to his tales of exploration in northern waters and apparently treating him with courtesy and honour. One could hardly look for a better indication of the spirit of those times: the viking

---

[5] As a model of time and history for a reflective and cautious people such as the early English were, this makes sense of the obviously arbitrary nature of death in war (and peace) and the development of historical processes. The Christian explanation of these matters – God's providence making itself felt through the imperfect and arbitrary nature of the world – was evidently felt to be lacking conviction.

campaigns against Wessex were being carried out by leaders of great skill and guile, yet both Alfred and they knew that their authority and success rested in the end on their personal reputations and 'luck' – the deaths of one or two prominent chiefs could spell the end of the vikings' campaigning, as the armies split up into their constituent units, the ties of loyalty and promises of support suddenly broken with the removal of the central characters. Alfred had no real need to fear that Ohtere was a spy working for the Danes, since the Norwegian had no reason to follow raiders and plunderers: he was a merchant and a developer of new markets, an explorer and a farmer, with nothing to gain from hostility towards the West Saxon court.

Kings in Anglo-Saxon times generally went to great lengths to control trade – many established trading centres (OE wīc) in the seventh century in order to ensure that commercial business was conducted where it could be properly recorded, and taxed. The economic aspect of kingship could be vital, and no reasonably intelligent king can have failed to see the potential profit in well-organized campaigns against wealthy neighbours. If no other benefit accrued to the aggressor, there would at least be a supply of slaves, cattle and other moveable property for sale in the wīc, captured from the opposition in the early phases of the incursion. Kings needed wealth – especially in the form of 'prestige goods' such as jewellery, armour, weapons and tableware – with which to reward their supporters at such public occasions as custom dictated (e.g. the symbel). When normal mercantile trade was thin and the tax-base was correspondingly poor, aggressive warfare was simply another way of acquiring these things. Needless to say, the more successful a king became through controlling a lucrative trade, the more tempting a target he made for his less fortunate neighbours.[6]

War was always most probable where there was a boundary, with competition between those on either side. This was certainly true in the days of the Heptarchy, where the smaller players were gradually reduced to mere satellites of the major powers. It was no less true under Athelstan, whose prominence made his newly-reconquered English state a target for the Welsh, Scots and Norsemen beyond its frontiers. Even within the later 'united' England, there was always the possibility of dissension from the once-independent regions such as the West Welsh (Cornwall) and the ex-Kingdom of York. From these examples, it is evident that war was more often about lordship, indeed overlordship, than about internal feuding or external takeover. For years after the extinction of their own dynasty, the Mercians in the West Midlands were decidedly unenthusiastic about submitting to the West Saxon royal line, their hereditary foes over many generations.

---

[6] The system was developed to keep prestige goods in circulation. Warriors took booty from the foe, and handed it to the lord who kept it in the collective tribal store (OE hord); it was later redistributed among the warriors and at some point could be lost to a foe. The supply of such goods was constantly replenished by the work of smiths who produced new artefacts, to counteract the effects of natural attrition (accidental loss, irreperable damage, etc.) and active human removal (deposition as grave goods, deposition as votive offering to gods, etc.). Nevertheless, the competition for the means of acquiring prestige goods was always present among early chiefs whose own reputation and power depended on these resources.

Figure 34 An open order shieldwall from a detail in the Bayeux tapestry.

Bruce Lincoln has defined early warfare as 'organized and coherent violence conducted between established and internally cohesive rival groups ... it is neither individual, spontaneous, random, nor irrational'[7] which is a good enough working description for our purposes. War can come about for a variety of reasons, but usually these can be reduced to the competition for resources; even religious wars such as the Crusades, while having as their outward aim the conversion or extinction of unbelievers, always have a political dimension which serves the material purposes of the aggressor group. Religious wars have one distinct advantage over overtly political ones: they provide motivation for warriors who often actually stand to gain very little materially in return for the dangers they face. In the case of the Norse worship of Óðinn, warfare became an end in itself, virtually a religious act – the greater the number of enemies slain, the more devout the warrior was held to be – and at the same time death in battle ensured a seat in the war-god's hall. Religion, then, could be used to further political and economic ends.

Another reason for warfare is, paradoxically, its unifying effect – the creation of a mythic, demonic, alien enemy which must be overcome if the common good (*our*

---

[7] *In Death, War and Sacrifice: Studies in Ideology and Practice.*

common good) is to be safeguarded.[8] Uniting against the foe, the bonds of friendship and allegiance within the group are strengthened, emerging and potentially dangerous tensions are put aside for the moment. Skilful leaders can dispel potential discord by channelling the group's aggression outwards against an external target, rather than letting it be focused on some internal dispute. Equally, the opportunities for a leader's personal advancement are greater in a time of war than otherwise, as separate peoples under a common threat draw together into military alliances.

Most men will fight if they are angry enough, but anger alone is not sufficient – it does not normally last long enough to fight a campaign before fear of the situation takes over, and it is not easily channelled, is too headlong and reckless. If the warrior is to expose himself to danger regularly and over a sustained period, he must be persuaded that his actions are justified or necessary, that they serve some higher purpose and that it is right to face risks for the greater good. In order to bring warriors to the point where they are willing to tackle, fight and kill other men, it is necessary to establish two conditions: the warrior must know himself to be a member of a group to whom he owes great loyalty[9] by virtue of kinship, or common traditions, or common language, or whatever; and he must believe his enemy to be wholly outside this group, an 'alien' who poses a threat to the existence, prosperity or freedom of the group, and against whom it is therefore legitimate to use violence as a means of thwarting these ambitions. (Naturally, these conditions will usually be met on both sides – each side will view the other as a threat.) The normal injunction against taking human life, which exists in all societies – though with various different exceptions in each – is not merely suspended in time of war, but moreover the act of killing is rather celebrated than condemned.

Different levels of hostile relations exist, corresponding to the numbers of people actively involved and the level of violence. The lowest level and the commonest is the brawl, between individuals or at most a few men, resulting in injuries and only in extreme cases in loss of life – such events as wayside robbery, neighbourly disputes, etc. These matters could generally be settled there and then, but if there was lingering resentment, and particularly if someone had been killed, then the next level would be attained: the feud (OE *fæhð*). This was a state of hostility between kindreds, often consisting of dozens of people, but usually only the nearest male relatives to the aggrieved (or deceased) were expected to act aggressively; the rest of the kindred provided moral support. A feud could potentially go on for generations and claim many lives since it would become a tit-for-tat, life-for-a-life game of one-upmanship;

---

[8] There is a pattern of oppositions here:

us	:	them
behind the shieldwall	:	beyond the shieldwall
defensive behaviour	:	threatening behaviour
solidarity	:	hostility
etc.		etc.

[9] See the mention of *secg* above p.77.

hence many Christian kings[10] passed laws to try to contain the effects by allowing the aggressor's kindred to pay a fixed sum of money (OE *wergild* 'man-price') to the injured party's kindred, which restored the family honour and satisfied the absolute duty of vengeance for a kinsman. It is interesting to speculate that, if a family group unilaterally decided to forgo the practice of *fæhð* it could be wiped out with impunity, as there would be no need to fear reprisals. A man's fierce and numerous relatives were his best insurance against attack where his kindred and its reputation were known, and we have already noted that one of the first things asked of a newcomer was to disclose his father's name and his ancestry.[11]

Beyond feuding was the general state of endemic rivalry between whole regions (or tribes) often the result of ancient grievances – stolen women, unavenged killings, broken promises and alliances – which coloured dealings between tribal leaders and could, if the opportunity arose due to increased military capacity on one or other side, lead to open warfare with full-scale raids and incursions. At what point the Anglo-Saxons made the distinction between this endemic strife and all-out war is unclear, since much of the vocabulary of warfare is poetic and consequently not that normally used to describe or narrate events.

OE verse celebrates many aspects of the military life and suggests that for the greater part of the population death by violence was a perpetual possibility. The risk seems to have been greatest among the higher status groups, but this may be a reflection of the poets' concern with the leaders and warriors rather than with the farmers and craftsmen over whose land the combats were fought. One poem – the *Fortunes of Men* in the Exeter Book – details a number of ways in which man's (not necessarily the aristocrat's) life could be ended, including:

> …hunger shall despoil one, bad weather shall drive one down,
> a spear shall destroy one, battle ruin one…
>
> (lines 15–6)

> *sumne sceal hungor āhīþan, sumne sceal hrēoh fordrīfan,*
> *sumne sceal gār āgētan, sumne gūð ābreōtan*

while in the same collection of poems the *Gifts of Men*, setting out the various skills which a youth might attain, states:

> …one shall be hard in war,
> a battle-skilled warrior where shields clash…
>
> (lines 39–40)

---

[10] The feud is directly the concern of the kindred groups involved; in order to weaken family ties and strengthen their own position, kings resorted to more abstract legal instruments – law-codes, courts and the 'king's justice'.

[11] Feuding was never successfully suppressed in mediaeval times – it was even exported to North America – and probably served as an effective deterrent to wanton violence in a time before apprehension and punishment became the responsibility of a statutory body of policemen.

...sum bið wiges heard,
beadocræftig beorn, þær bord stunað...

Nevertheless, warfare and the upper classes were closely associated in the verse tradition, and it is mostly the kings and nobles whose triumphs are celebrated, as in the *Maxims*:

...In a hero shall battle,
war arise ...

(I, lines 83–4)

....Gūð sceal in eorle,
wīg geweaxan...

Good companions shall encourage a young noble
to warfare and to ring-giving;
courage shall be in a hero, a sword against a helmet
shall be expected in war...

(II, lines 14–17)

Geongne æþeling sceolan gōde gesīðas
byldan tō beaduwe and tō bēahgiefe;
ellen sceal on eorle, ecg sceal wið helme
hilde gebīdan...

and throughout *Beowulf* and the other heroic verse. Generally speaking, the mention of the *ceorl* as a warrior is exceptional,[12] and the warrior grave-goods of the early Anglo-Saxon period coupled with the increasing social stratification of the later period all suggest that 'professional' warriors were a special grade of men in English tradition.

Major campaigns against organized polities were by no means uncommon (they grew to be virtually endemic at some periods under viking attacks) and for the early Christian period (from c.600 to c.850) based on the ASC and other records, Guy Halsall has calculated that the kingdoms of the Heptarchy fought each other or the Welsh on average about every 20 years (i.e. once per generation), while one or other across the country was engaged in battle on average every three years. These figures are to be regarded as the minimum, however, since there were many wars which did not figure in the ASC – virtually the whole of East Anglia and the south east is ignored except when they came up against Mercia or Wessex. Even for these kingdoms, the earlier annals mention battles only when they were remembered due to the death of some king or noble – other fighting is lost to the record. Halsall suggests that with an active service life of 25 years (say, 15 to 40 years of age) the average warrior would, on this reckoning, see action only four or five times (if he survived

---

[12] See above, p.82, for more on the *ceorl* as warrior.

every encounter!) – an improbably low and unconvincing figure given the apparently central role of warfare in Anglo-Saxon social organization and culture. More likely, he proposes, is the notion that the ASC and other major sources, such as Bede, have recorded only the most prominent and large-scale military engagements and that there was a widespread background of low-key, small-scale conflict in which the risk of injury or death was relatively low and which had something of a symbolic or ritual nature – a show of force to intimidate an aggressive neighbour, more than a serious attempt to overwhelm or destroy it. This practice may be linked to the fact that campaigning was normally conducted during the summer months only – small-scale raids might be mounted by a king and his retainers to subdue a potential enemy or retaliate for a previous raid, almost as a kind of sport or diversion from the monotony of courtly life, keeping their warlike skills honed and training the youngsters without serious risk. One advantage of this raiding was the gaining of *gafol* 'tribute' by means of which the aggressor's attack could be bought off.[13]

Halsall further suggests that war parties were expected to use particular routes – many OE charter boundaries mention military roads, called variously *fyrdstræt* 'army-street' or *herepæð* 'raiders-path' which were presumably the routes taken by warriors going about their business, and where watch was kept by the king's officials. In *Beowulf*, upon beaching in Denmark, the Geatish troop is met and challenged by a man called an *ombeht*:

> The watchman spoke where he sat on his steed,
> an unafraid king's man

(lines 286–7)

> *Weard maþelode ðær on wicge sæt,*
> *ombeht unforht...*

This word *ombeht*, which is ultimately of Celtic origin,[14] is widely used to describe a royal official. A similar function was performed by the West Saxon *gerēfa* 'reeve' *Beaduheard*, who met his death after challenging a group of vikings at Dorchester:

> Here King Beorhtric took Offa's daughter Eadburg [to be his wife] and in his time first came 3 ships and then the reeve rode there and meant to take them to the king's estate, for he did not know what they were, and he was slain. Those were the first ships of the Danish men which sought out the land of the English folk.

(ASC 'A' s.a. 787)

---

[13] Handing over *gafol* is something of a two-edged sword, after all. While it can buy valuable time in which to set up an effective defence, it can also serve as an inducement for the aggressor to come back for more – this is exactly what happened with Æðelred and the Danegelds of the late 900s and early 1000s. Equally, if the money for the geld is not readily available and has to be extracted from an unwilling populace, there will be a high incidence of evasion; some may find the payment beyond their means, and be forced to sell their possessions and livelihoods to meet it, or else absent themselves entirely (as refugees or as wolfsheads).

[14] Its origin is usually ascribed to Gaulish *andabactos* 'servant'; it occurs in Norse saga literature as *ambatt*, a word for an Irish captive, and in Gothic as *andbahts*.

787. Hēr nōm Beorhtric cyning Offan dohtor Ēadburge ꝺ on his dagum cuōmon ǣrest .iii. scipu ꝺ þā se gerēfa þǣrtō rād ꝺ hīe wolde drīfan tō þæs cyninges tūne þȳ hē nyste hwæt hīe wǣron ꝺ hiene mon ofslōg. Þæt wǣron þā ǣrestan scipu Deniscra monna þe Angel cynnes lond gesōhton.

In both these cases, it seems that the official was mounting guard over an established approach route which may have been conventionally used for purposes such as raiding and trading. It may have been one of the 'rules of war' (along the lines of the mediaeval chivalric code, or the modern Geneva Convention?), suggests Halsall, that a king's appointed official was not to be killed out of hand; similarly, poets, heralds, women and relatives of the victors who happened to find themselves on the losing side, as for example after the taking of the vikingcamp at Benfleet:

> …and Hæsten's wife and his two sons were brought to the king and he gave [them] back to him because one of them was his godson and the other was [that of] ealdormann Æðelred …   (*ASC 'A'* s.a. 894)

> *… ꝺ Hæstenes wīf ꝺ his suna twēgen mon brōhte tō þǣm cyninge ꝺ hē him eft āgēaf for þǣm þe hiora wæs ōþer his godsunu ōþer Æðeredes ealdormonnes…*

Figure 35 A pair of fighting warriors from the detail of a helmet plate from the cemetery at Vendel, Sweden. The warriors are bare-headed and attacking with sword and shield, their spears having been discarded after piercing mailshirt and shield. Two different styles of armour are depicted: the left resembles that worn by the 'dancing warriors' from Sutton Hoo, while the right is seemingly a coat of plates.

Another possible 'rule' concerned the notion of a 'fair fight', with both sides drawn up formally on open and even ground; this may have been the factor which prompted the

English leader Byrhtnōð to allow the vikings across the causeway at Maldon, without comment from the contemporary chronicle entry or the poet who made the verse record of the encounter, unless we follow Tolkien's rather overworked reading of the single word *ofermōd* as explicit criticism, which has done much to ruin the *ealdormann*'s reputation among modern historians. The battle at Maldon ensued because of Byrhtnōð's refusal to pay *gafol* 'tribute', which may have been a normal strategic move for a kingdom not able to mount a credible defence: in the early wars of the various English kingdoms with each other and the first viking armies there are many instances of leaders buying time by handing over material wealth. Some, like Alfred, used the time they had bought to plan an effective system of defence and counter-attack; others, like Æðelræd Unræd, squandered it on internal rivalries and witch-hunts. Nevertheless, it seems that tribute was acceptable under certain circumstances, but where there were personal grudges to settle it may not have been possible to buy the enemy off.

It was apparently customary in war to take hostages. Some, like the nobleman Imma in Bede's story, were for sale into slavery once transport could be arranged. Others could be held for ransom by wealthy kinsmen. Hostages were generally treated well and were accorded something approaching 'guest' status in some cases, such as that of the Northumbrian Æscferð who was present at the battle at Maldon in 991:

> The hostage began to help him eagerly:
> he was from a stout kindred in Northumbria,
> the son of Ecglāf, his name was Æscferð,
> he did not weaken at all at the war-play
> but rather he sped forth many arrows...
>
> (*The Battle of Maldon*, lines 265–9)

> *Him se gȳsel ongann geornlīce fylstan:*
> *hē wæs on Norðhymbron heardes cynnes,*
> *Ecglāfes bearn, him wæs Æscferð nama,*
> *hē ne wandode nā æt þām wīgplegan*
> *ac hē fysde forð flān geneahhe*

Here, the hostage was allowed to take part in the battle, though only with the low-status weapon of bow and arrows; as to why a Northumbrian should be a hostage to a southern English leader, we may look to the political ties of the north with the Norsemen, through the Kingdom of York and so on, which made Norse rulers more attractive to many northern Englishmen than the West Saxon dynasty. It may have been necessary to keep the leading Northumbrian families in check by taking away a few of their younger men as a token of their good faith.

Swearing of oaths was another way of calling a temporary peace – again, surely such would only have been possible if there were traditional rules of conduct, which allowed an army to disengage and retire once beaten without suffering wholesale slaughter at the hands of the victors. The oaths were normally of 'peace and friendship' (ON *friþ ok griþ*) and amounted to an admission of failure and acknowledgement of military inferiority by the defeated party; some kind of lordship of the victor over the vanquished was implied, as the latter undertook to leave:

876. Here the enemy army stole into Wareham from the West Saxon army, and afterwards the king made peace with the enemy, and they then gave hostages, who were the most honoured [men] in the army, to the king and then swore oaths to him on the hallowed ring, which before they would not do for any people, that they would quickly go from his kingdom... *(ASC 'E' s.a.876)*

Hēr hine bestæl se here intō Wærhām West Seaxna fyrde ʒ siððan wið þone here se cyning frið nām ʒ him þā gīslas sealdon þe on þām here weorþuste wæron tō þām cyninge ʒ on him þā āðas swōron on þām hālgan beage þe hī ær nānre þēode dōn noldon þet hī hrēdlīce of his rīce fōron...

This unprecedented victory for Alfred and the West Saxons was short-lived, though:

... and through that the raiders with horses then stole away by night from the defending army into Exeter... *(ASC 'E' s.a.876)*

...ʒ hī þā under þam hī nihtes bestælon þære fyrde se gehorsade here intō Exanceastre...

Later Norse saga evidence implies that once the battlefield had been marked out with hazelwood twigs, neither army could leave it with honour until the matter had been decided by force of arms – while this has parallels in the rite and tradition of duelling, it is not known to have been regular practice among the early English. There is also a suggestion in the account of St. Guthlac's early military career that it was in some cases normal to return part of the booty taken in war, though this may be no more than the hagiographic eulogizing of the chivalrous nature of the hero-turned-saint.

Serious warfare, by contrast – where kings were toppled, polities overthrown and nations absorbed – seems to have had less to do with such fair play, as the vikings' treacherous oaths suggest. The practice of handing over *gafol* 'tribute' or *geld* 'payment', for example, was not available where the side with the upper hand chose to refuse it. Under those circumstances, it was a case of fight and face total defeat, or surrender. There are enough instances of entire nations being decimated and absorbed by their conquerors (for example, the West Saxon eradication of the *Wihtwære* on Wight) to show that, although there may have been provision for a negotiated peace, there were also times when the foe was implacable, whatever concessions were made. This may have been due to a breakdown in the normal conditions of warfare – one side consistently managing to 'score points' off the other until the cumulative insults induced a level of stress which could only be resolved by a serious campaign, a chance to settle scores. Where economic considerations were uppermost, a large and powerful kingdom may not have been content to spoil the economic base of a rival – it could be rebuilt fairly quickly as long as the men with the necessary expertise remained in place – and chose rather to absorb it by conquest. Kent, Mercia and Wessex fought over the East Saxon commercial centre of London, and it changed hands many times before the Danish wars put all but the latter off the political map. The evidence of the conflict with the Danes also shows that wars could be fought to throw off such external ties, to redress the balance of power and to assert independence and autonomy – often a new ruler began his reign with a campaign to symbolize the break with the past, the fresh start to a period of military self-determination. Each new king had his own allies and enemies, his own scores to settle and debts to repay; conversely, a new king would no doubt be tested out by his opponents, to see whether he could organize effective resistance to attack.

Halsall's analysis of the siting of battles between the years 600 and 850 (but excluding civil strife and viking attacks) shows a remarkable fact: nearly all named and identifiable sites are *either* at an ancient monument (hill-fort, barrow, dyke, earthwork, standing stone or deserted Roman city) *or* at a river crossing. There is little tactical advantage in these sites – the battles were fought before Alfred began the Anglo-Saxon refurbishment of the land defences with the erection of fortified sites at strategic points – and if the events at Maldon are anything to go by in respect of river crossings, the watercourse itself was not the point of contact for the opponents, though it may have kept the two sides apart while they mustered and formed up. Crossing the water was a risky business, as it could hardly be carried out in battle formation, so not only could neither army reach the other at the ford, neither could safely cross the ford either. Most probably, the sites were chosen because of the ease of access to them (particularly fords, on well-used roads over large rivers) and the fact that they were well-known. The roads may even have been those known as *herepæð* or *fyrdstræt*. Without effective scouting and communications, it would have been difficult for armies to engage each other in the field; what could have been easier than to occupy some famous landmark or place and wait for the other side to show up? Indeed, the very act of occupation of a symbolic spot such as a barrow, with all its ritual and totemic overtones, may have constituted a challenge to the local, defending army's honour.

The reasons given for the early campaigns are mostly 'personal' in the sense of grievances over insults, often from long before. Where a tribe felt it had some wrong to right, the memory of it and the stain on their character would be handed on for years, even generations, and could prove impossible to settle. Under conditions where there were many such grievances on both sides in a possibly long and bloody conflict, tribal loyalties would be reinforced at each new outrage (by *their* side) and each new vengeance (by *ours*). Obviously, when aggression can be turned outwards by uniting against a common foe, the internal cohesion of the kingdom or tribe increases – conversely, under peaceful kings such as Edgar and Edward the Confessor, there was an increase in civil unrest and internal disputes – a time of peace was not the unalloyed benefit we would expect.

Strategy and Tactics

...The army shall come together,
a troop of glorious men...

(Exeter Book *Gnomic Verses*, lines 31–2)

...Fyrd sceal ætsomne,
tīrfæsta getrum...

It is difficult to say much about the earlier battles of the English due to the very little evidence that has come down to us – we are lucky if we know who was fighting whom, the names of the men who led the armies and where the battle was fought. Nevertheless, settling disputes by battle rather than tribute or diplomacy seems to have been fairly frequent practice in early England, and seldom does a decade pass in which there are no battles fought. This is contrary to the Continental evidence, which indicates that leaders such as Charlemagne generally avoided battle unless they believed that they had a good chance of winning, preferring other forms of warfare instead, such as ravaging the enemy's land. One reason for this is that prior to the Danish wars, there were few real strongholds in England and so armies tended to meet in the open country rather than attack each other's fortresses. Even trading sites were largely undefended, until Alfred's experiences suggested that fortifying the places where wealth was held would be a good idea; considering the great pains kings went to control trade and generate tax income, this lack of basic protection in such violent times is all the more remarkable. Military earthworks in the pre-viking era consisted largely of bank-and-ditch ramparts which were expected to deny access along roads and to mark off boundaries between folk, such as Offa's Dyke and the numerous other such enterprises. Nevertheless, there is little evidence for full-scale siege warfare in early England, possibly since this requires immense planning to be successful and the siege camp can rapidly degenerate into a hotbed of disease.

Under Edward the Elder, the construction of strongholds (OE *burh*) took on a new importance and it is fair to say that it was largely by this means that the West Saxons were able to contain the viking menace. The forts acted as secure fixed points in a fluid situation, and were used as bases from which any nearby Danes could be harried until they withdrew. The forts seem to have been constructed sufficiently well that they were capable of resisting even a determined viking attack:

Then after those [events] a large army gathered from the East Angles and the land of the Mercians and travelled to the fort at *Wigingamere* [site unknown] and besieged it from outside and attacked it long into the day and took the cattle which was outside, yet the men who were inside defended the fort and then they [the vikings] abandoned the fort and travelled away. (*ASC 'A'* s.a. 921)

Þā eft æfter þām þā giet gegaderode micel her hine of ēast Englum ⁊ of Mercna lande ⁊ fōran tō þære byrig æt Wigingamere ⁊ ymbsǣton hīe ūtan ⁊ fuhton lange on dæg on ꝩ nāmon þone cēap on būtan ꝩ þā men āweredon þēah þā burg þe þær binnan wæron ꝩ þā forlēton hīe þā burg ꝩ fōron āweg.

'Combined operations', with land forces supported by the fleet, were also undertaken during the reign of Athelstan:

> Here Athelstan travelled into Scotland with both a land army and a ship army and ravaged it greatly.　　　　　　　　　　　　　　　(*ASC 'E'* s.a. 934)

Hēr fōr Æþelstān cyning on Scotland ge mid land here[15] ge mid scip here ꝩ his micel oferhergode.

A similar manoeuvre was repeated by Earl Siward in 1054, and against the Welsh in 1063 by Harold. The combination of land-based destructive power and seaborne reinforcement was apparently learnt from the vikings, who often sent part of their forces around English-occupied lands (to avoid battle) and part round the coast by ship. Although neither force was full-strength and both could, in theory, have been picked off singly by the English, this fail-safe policy seems to have worked well enough since frequently both divisions got back to their eastern coastal base unharmed.

The basic tactical unit, in the early wars between the kingdoms of the Heptarchy and their neighbours, was the *werod* consisting of the lord, his immediate followers (*gesīþas*) and their supporters. Thus, in a notable victory over the Scots of Dal Ríada, the Northumbrian king Æðelfrið lost his brother, Þēodbald, together with his whole troop in what was otherwise an overwhelming English victory: the implication is that Þēodbald joined battle along with his *werod* and they were cut down because they were engaged independently and perhaps became isolated from the rest of the host. The basic strategic unit, in later armies at least, was the *scīr*, who maintained their own leadership, command and communication structure even when acting in concert with other shires in the national *fyrd*. There are many examples in the *Chronicle* of whole shires acting in concert independently of the national leadership. To quote two late cases with unfortunate results:

> 999. Here the *here* came back around the Thames and went up along the Medway then to Rochester and then the Kentish *fyrd* came against [them] there and they locked in combat there, but alas that they too readily gave way and fled because they did not have the reinforcements that they ought to have had...
>
> 　　　　　　　　　　　　　　　　　　　　　　　　　(*ASC 'E'* s.a. 999)

Hēr cōm se here eft ābūton Temese ꝩ wendon þā ūp andlang Medewægan tō Hrofescēastre ꝩ cōm þā sēo Centisce fyrde þær ongēan ꝩ hī þær fæste tō gedere fēngon ac wālā þ hī tō hrāðe bugon ꝩ flugon forþām þe hī næfdon fultum þe hī habban sceoldon...

---

[15] Note that here, since the English forces are moving outside their own country, they become a *here* 'raiding force' not the normal *fyrd*.

1016. The *here* travelled back to Mercia. When the king heard [of this] he gathered all the English nation for the fifth time and went after the *here* and overtook it at Ashingdon[16] [Essex] and they locked in combat there. Then ealdorman Eadric did as he had often done before, began the rout with the *Magonsætan*[17] and thus betrayed his royal lord and all his folk...

(ASC 'F' s.a 1016)

Se here fērde eft intō Myrcen. Ðā gehyrde se cing ðā gegaderode hē fifta siððan eal Engla ðēode ⁊ fērde æfter ðan here ⁊ offērde hine at Assandūne ⁊ ðār tōgædere fæstlīce fēngon. Ðā dyde ēadrīc ealdorman swā hē oft ǣr dyde, āstealde þone flēam ārest mid Magesǣtan ⁊ swā āswāc his cynehlāford ⁊ ealle þēode ...

On the Field of Battle

It was a hard meeting there, firm stood
the warriors in the strife, fighters fell
wearied by wounds, the slain dropped to the ground.

(The Battle of Maldon, lines 301–4)

Þǣr wæs stīð gemōt, stōdon fæste
wigan on gewinne, wīgend cruncon
wundum wērige, wæl fēol on eorþan.

An English army, arriving at the spot chosen to meet the foe, would first dismount. (Norse evidence suggests that the battlefield would have been marked out previously with wands of hazelwood.) Identification of actual battlegrounds from the period is fraught with difficulty, hence there is little evidence for the type of terrain preferred. However, the evidence of *Egilssaga Skállagrímsonar* for Egil's involvement in Athelstan's victory[18] over a combined force of Norsemen, Irish, Welsh and Scots describes the site as an open heath bounded on its west side by a stream and on its higher, eastern side by dense woodland. The heath sloped gently down from the north. The English force was encamped at what the saga calls a *borg* (i.e. a *burh* or fortress) while the invaders had their own *borg* some miles away (they exchanged messages by horsemen, so the distance should have been greater than one would choose to walk). The site of the battle had been nominated by Athelstan himself, if we trust the saga, and he would presumably have selected the higher ground for his army,[19] and he drew

---

[16] Or possibly Ashdon, Essex.

[17] This folk was based in the Herefordshire – Gloucestershire region.

[18] The battle is called in the Norse saga *Vinheiðr* 'meadow-heath' but has been identified with the *Brunanburh* of the English sources. The coincidental evidence suggests the two must probably be the same engagement, although the overenthusiastic use of the detail of the saga's evidence to locate the site is unwise given that it was written down some 300 years after the events it describes.

[19] Higher ground is usually desirable because it gives a better view of the enemy's movements; it makes a downhill charge both easier to undertake and harder for the attacker to stop, while an

up his forces where the gap between the river and the wood was narrowest (i.e. where the shieldwall could most easily be arrayed to take full advantage of the cover these features provided).

Figure 36 King and companion from an Anglo-Saxon manuscript. The youth is unarmed and appears to be providing additional protection for his lord with the ornate shield he carries.

Once the men had all arrived and found their respective groupings, their horses and waggons would be taken to the rear, and they would choose their weapons and form up in the shieldwall (it is at this moment that the poem *The Battle of Maldon*[20] opens).

---

uphill one is more tiring and harder to maintain. There are also psychological advantages in looking down on the enemy.

[20] The poem *The Battle of Maldon* is not an eye-witness account of a battle retold as a front-line despatch by a war correspondent. The poet may or may not have been present at the battle, but the poem itself is an 'interpretation' of the events described, not an attempt to give a scientific analysis or journalistic description of them. Poetry operates at a greater remove from empirical reality than does straight narrative; nevertheless, an Anglo-Saxon poet's account of a battle ought to be generally reliable since one of the things OE verse was designed to do was record military victories. Futhermore, the poem was presumably to be read among an audience who either had been at the battle or whose relatives were there: to deliver something plainly untrue would have been insulting to the men and their families.

Since English forces operated in territorial units, a certain amount of time would elapse as the various groups formed up.

The shieldwall would probably be long enough to take advantage of any helpful features of the terrain and to prevent the enemy encircling them, but obviously not so long that there were not enough men to withstand a charge by the foe. The precise form of the wall is disputed: some argue for a close-knit formation with touching or overlapping shields from between which protrudes a thicket of spearshafts; others suggest that a looser, more flexible array would be more in keeping with the nature of Anglo-Saxon and Scandinavian warfare traditions. Unfortunately there is no precise and unambiguous description of a shieldwall from which to judge. The only clear pictorial evidence (the Bayeux tapestry) shows overlapping shields[21] (Fig.1, p.21) used by the heavily-armed warriors, but later a small group of lightly-armed men who are in 'open order' (Fig.34, p.169). Common sense (in the absence of any better evidence) suggests that there was nothing to prevent the English or their foes from having adopted whichever tactic best suited the situation, nor from having been able to re-form in either way at need – the vikings were apparently able to move through woodland quickly in 'open order' but emerge in fighting formation. One might suggest that, in the pre-combat shieldwall, the maximum benefit would be gained from standing in a fairly dense mass, to present as impenetrable a frontage as possible to the foe, but that once it came to the point where swords were unsheathed, the front-line men would stand a little spaced out, with enough room to wield their weapons effectively. Staying in close order with their shields overlapping would be a useful tactic if being attacked by greatly superior numbers, or by heavy cavalry (exactly the Bayeux situation illustrated) where mutual defence is paramount. Standing in 'close order' for any length of time would, however, leave the men unnecessarily vulnerable to missile attack. One of the Old English poetic variant words for the shield formation is *wīhaga* 'war-hedge', but here the word probably has more the sense of 'limit, boundary' than any reference to a bristling hedge of spear-points.

The plan of the battle line given opposite shows a suggested formal battle-array, with the leader centrally placed to oversee his men but not in the front line where he would be perilously exposed. The fall of a leader was often the crucial and deciding factor in early battles (e.g. Byrhtnōð's death is a case in point). The term 'shieldwall' (OE *bordweall*) – a line of men abreast each with his shield in front of him – is of course only one of the possible formations open to an Anglo-Saxon army, and is a naturally defensive position. There is also evidence for a wedge-shaped battle line (called in Latin sources *cuneus* and in Norse *svínfylking*) which could be used to force a breach in the opposing defensive line by concentrating all the striking power at one point; the disadvantage of the 'wedge' is obviously that it is narrower and so much easier for the enemy to surround.

---

[21] This may be put down to artistic licence (or an attempt at perspective illustration) since in such a formation there would not be room to swing a sword or axe.

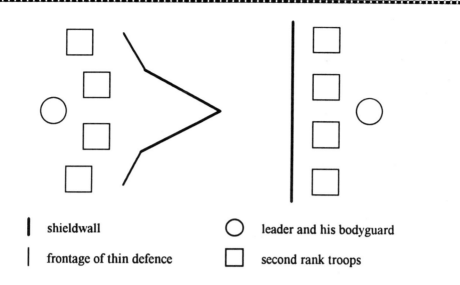

| | shieldwall | ◯ | leader and his bodyguard |
| | frontage of thin defence | ◻ | second rank troops |

Figure 37 Schematic representation of 'svínfylking' shieldwall formation

Viking armies generally avoided battle if at all possible, preferring raids and expeditions against unprepared targets. A battle-plan consisting of a quick strike with the prospect of some booty, followed by a rapid and orderly withdrawal, had much to recommend itself to men whose principal strategic advantage was speed. They often massed and launched their attacks from within wooded areas, making observation of their numbers and movements almost impossible. Yet when they did take to the field in earnest, there was no question of their being at a disadvantage.

The proceedings usually opened with preliminary talks, the offer of peace or safe passage in exchange for a price; where matters plainly were not going to end peacefully, taunting and insults ensued. The heralds (OE *ār*) withdrew to their respective battle lines and the two armies stood ready. At this point, according to *The Battle of Maldon, þær wearð hrēam āhafen* "there a shout was raised up"(line 106), the two armies yelling their battle-cries. The importance of the shout was in its psychological effect: on the one hand, it involved taking a deep breath, which has a naturally calming effect; it also allowed for the release of some of the pent-up emotions (anger or fear), steadying their nerves. Conversely, a loud and bellicose roar could have an unnerving effect on the opponent. Germanic armies of the 1st century AD could, according to Tacitus, tell the mettle of their opponents from their *baritus* or battle-cry, perhaps being able to catch a wavering quality or the strangulated timbre of frightened men. A battle-cry can, of course, serve as a unifying factor also (like a 'Mexican wave' at a football match), drawing the various elements of the army together for a moment in one concerted act in which all can take part. No reliable record of an early English battle-cry is known, although Harold's cry at Hastings is said to have been 'Holy Cross', the name of the Essex religious house he endowed and where his body was finally buried.

There followed an exchange of missiles – throwing-spears[22] and arrows – with the aim of softening up the opposition, creating gaps in the shieldwall, demoralizing the opposing troops with heavy early losses. The bowmen were perhaps not expected to do more than harass the enemy and break up the opposing forces' initial cohesion – battles were won and lost by the big men in armour, hacking and slashing toe to toe with their opposite numbers.

After the initial exchange of missiles, the two armies locked together: one side must have deliberately moved forward from its starting position to engage the other, sacrificing something of the shieldwall's protection in order to have the advantage of momentum in 'shock combat'. The shieldwall (particularly the 'tightly-packed' form) could hardly have been held over anything but a perfectly flat meadow for more than a few paces without partly breaking up, but disciplined and well-practised troops could have slowed and drawn back into line as they neared the enemy's position. The first clash as the advancing troops thudded into the defensive line was crucial: a shieldwall successfully held would leave the enemy at a disadvantage, exposed and without the possibility of orderly withdrawal; a shieldwall broken would leave the defending troops in pockets which the attackers could surround and pick off one by one.

Generally it must be presumed, neither side scored a decisive victory so early in the contest: the shieldwall held for most of its length, and those hardy few who managed to fight their way through it were picked off by the second ranks behind. Then began the second phase of battle: the traditional Germanic hacking-match, where the grit and muscle of the trained warriors came into play. Here reputations were won and lost, as men stood shoulder to shoulder in the thick of a furious and bloody mêlée; here sworn brothers tested the bonds of friendship, kings found out which of their men were as good as their boastful words of loyalty, and which had taken their bounty fraudulently; here death and wounds abounded amid the flashing steel of axe, sword and spear. It was in this mêlée that the forces of attrition came into play – vulnerable shields would be hacked down to the metal bosses, which were nevertheless still usable for parrying and even in an offensive role as a spike. Spearshafts would be lopped or splintered, sword blades bent under the force of the blows they dealt, axes lose their heads. Cutting edges were blunted through hard use, the metal twisted and cracked and its edges burred. Weapons were tested every bit as much as their wielders.

No-one could keep fighting with shield and spear for very long without feeling the effects of fatigue. Men could disengage temporarily, as if by common consent, to retrieve arrows and spears, to clear away the dead and help the wounded, to carry out running repairs to weapons and to re-form for the next clash. If later saga evidence is to be trusted, warriors could retire to prepared positions for a drink and to have their wounds dressed, to bend their sword-blades back straight and to report to their leaders. Certainly, the impression given in *The Battle of Maldon* is that there were lulls in the fighting during which the English warriors spoke together, reminding each

---

[22] The early types of throwing spear (e.g. Type'A' on p.121) had soft iron necks which would deform on impact and prevent re-use. If the head lodged in a shield, it weighed down the bearer's arm and would leave his body unprotected; if it stuck in his body itself, it would be difficult to remove.

other of their duty of vengeance for their fallen lord and encouraging each other to deeds of glory. The scenario presented in that poem suggests that both entire armies withdrew briefly before stepping forward for another attempt; this may explain the constant repetition of *forð* 'forward' in the poem, as the various warriors are urged onwards from the beleaguered English enclave to the front line.

Even when the assault had failed, all was not necessarily lost. If the men in the intact shieldwall did not act in unison, it could disintegrate even after repelling an attack. There were two great temptations: first, the desire to pursue a fleeing foe, which could dissolve the defensive line more effectively than any frontal assault; and secondly, the desire to get some booty, particularly if it looked likely that somebody else might get it first. Only training, internal cohesion and high morale could overcome these dangerously disruptive factors. It is not surprising, then, to discover in Old English military poetry that leaders kept up a more-or-less constant stream of encouraging words to spur on their supporters and raise their spirits. The corollary to this was that, if the leader fell, the men lost heart quickly and their morale crumbled; this happened to the English at Maldon and at Hastings, and seemingly nearly happened to the Norman army there, which was on the point of retreating as rumours of William's death spread through the lines. It is hardly surprising that the *Maldon* poet cursed the faithless Godric and his brothers for fleeing, since they were the first tumbling pebbles that launched an avalanche.

And finally one side broke. It might be the death of a leader which made them lose heart, or the capture of a banner, or the fall of some prominent man, or simply the increasing feeling that they just weren't going to win this time. Whatever the reason, the exhilaration of their spirits turned to a knot of fear which spread quickly among their ranks. In some cases, they probably retreated into a defensive stance and tried to fight their way out; in others, they just pulled back and as they did so the foe advanced to stay within reach, and before long the staged withdrawal had turned to all-out flight.

With the rout or panicked retreat in flight (OE *flēam*) of one side, the other had two options: to stay put and consolidate the gains, or to pursue the foe. The obvious course in most cases was to pursue the fugitives with a view to catching as many as possible and then ransom, enslave or kill them. After the English victory at *Brunanburh*, the West Saxon and Mercian forces took to their horses and rode down all the invaders they could find; clearly, the duty of revenge for the killing of comrades and kinsmen was uppermost in their minds. However, the prudent commander might prefer to keep his men together and under control rather than giving in to their natural desire to press home their advantage to the maximum extent. Victory in Old English texts is described in terms of *wælstōwe geweald habban* "to have control of the slaughter-place", which rather suggests a mopping-up exercise, finishing off any last pockets of resistance and taking charge of any captives and survivors. It also afforded the victor the opportunity to despoil the dead, taking away costly weapons and war-gear to be redistributed by the lord among his own men at the appropriate time. Flight from the battlefield meant abandoning not only material goods but also the bodies of fallen comrades – often to an ignominious fate, hence the constant poetic references to wolves and ravens devouring the corpses of warriors.

Very occasionally, though, when the battle was lost something else happened: instead of running, men chose to stay and fight it out. While it must have been clear that their position was hopeless and that they could not fight on and expect to escape with their lives, nevertheless warriors sometimes did choose to stand together to the last man and die fighting rather than give up. The phrase "death before dishonour" would not have been just empty words to such men.

This 'ideal' of men dying with their lord has been studied by Rosemary Woolf, who concludes that the decision to fight on after the death of the leader at Maldon cannot be considered a mere echo of the literary motif recorded in Tacitus's *Germania,* and must represent a conscious act of will by the men present on the day. Indeed, I have suggested elsewhere that once the leader was down at Maldon and the half-hearted English force fled, the only choices left to the remnant were total surrender (they had no bargaining power) to the mercy of their foes; trying to flee; or fighting on in the face of the inevitable war-death. Given these choices, and the fact that wounded men could not often expect to survive anyway, it must have seemed preferable to die quickly in battle rather than to die slowly of blood-poisoning from their wounds, or be tortured to death by the vikings for sport.

Retreat generally seems to have meant finding a place of refuge, and in well-wooded Anglo-Saxon England this was not difficult. Withdrawal into the safety of tree cover was a well-practised technique which could save the lives of a defeated army:

> and then the deadly foes followed
> until they went with much difficulty
> into Raven's Wood, deprived of their lord
> Then the great army surrounded those the sword had spared,
> weary with wounds…
>
> (*Beowulf,* lines 2933–7)

> *ond ðā folgode feorhgenīðlan*
> *oððæt hī oðēodon earfoðlīce*
> *in Hrefnesholt hlāfordlēase.*
> *Besæt ðā sinherge sweorda lāfe*
> *wundum wērge…*

Defensible structures such as stone buildings or churches were a favourite retreat for viking troops, although they could make use of woods as well as the English. The later Scandinavian armies are reported to have carried on board their ships sufficient timbers and tools to erect field fortifications in a very short time.

The Anglo-Saxon infantry army was hampered to some extent by its lack of mobility. The Norman army, with its horsemen using lances and its massed archers, held a crucial advantage: the combination of mobility and firepower. Nevertheless, against its traditional enemies – vikings, Welsh, Scots, other English armies – it was

186

remarkably effective and Hastings was no walkover. The Norman cavalry made little headway against the well-defended infantry block, and the Breton archers do not seem to have had the devastating effect one would expect (in marked contrast to later English and Welsh forces armed with longbows). One determined English counter-attack, one more failed Norman cavalry charge, and the day could have been Harold's – yet his death sealed the outcome of the battle, and effective English resistance crumbled around his mutilated corpse.

Wounds

In early mediaeval warfare, the effects of wounds were not always immediately apparent – the quick, clean kill was the exception rather than the rule. Could those who underwent a stab or thrust expect to live, or were they as good as dead? Anglo-Saxon medical literature, and the knowledge which it represents, has been regularly belittled as the blind but hopeful gropings of savages towards cures by sympathetic magic. The standard reference works[23] tend to adopt a slightly superior tone, and generally imply that most early English medical practice was nothing more than superstition, while in the few cases where the remedies actually worked they must have been learnt from the Greeks, the Romans or the Arabs. A recent re-evaluation of Anglo-Saxon medicine by M. L. Cameron suggests that there were certainly works of questionable value in circulation among the literate – these were those very works copied from the classical sources of antiquity, while the 'native' (English, probably supplemented by Irish) traditions mostly seem to have had a sound pharmacological basis.

S. J. Wenham has studied the skeletal evidence for weapon-inflicted injuries on six male interments from the early Anglo-Saxon cemetery at Eccles, Kent, all with cranial evidence of blows to the head. Obviously, any soft tissue injuries which do not affect the underlying bone will not show up in such a study, but the skulls themselves reveal quite a lot of information. Wenham took care to exclude, as far as possible, bone damage which could have taken place after the bodies were laid in their graves, due to the decomposition of flesh which would hold the bone in place – which is to say that the damage occurred while the men were still alive or only recently killed. He also tried to determine whether there was any fresh growth on the injuries, which would be caused by the bone growing back together as the wound healed – a sign that the warrior had survived the wound for at least five days or more (the usual length of time taken for fresh growth to begin). There was no evidence of such healing on any of the skeletons – all the cuts were clean – so the likelihood is that these injuries were mortal wounds to the men buried here.

The skeletons were of men aged between 20 and 35 years old (one was apparently older than 35), between 5ft 8ins to 6ft 3ins (163cm and 179cm) tall; the skulls had damage in the form of linear injuries to the brow, temple and crown (mostly to the left). Many seem to have been the result of a downward (vertical or angled) chop. One

---

[23] For example, Grattan and Singer.

man (Victim II) had suffered as many as eleven blows to the head and a further five to the neck, ten to the back and three to the arms, which were such as to make him unable to hold any weapon or shield. Another (Victim III) had a projectile point lodged in his spine, which had entered from his right side.

The head wounds, of which the detected cranial damage is the evidence, were all of a kind which would have caused concussion and profuse bleeding from the scalp. There was not only the incision itself, but also the flaking and cracking of the skull, parts of which would have entered the brain, driven deeper into the soft tissue by the thrust of the weapon's edge. Shock to the brain may have caused a quick death in some cases; Victim II would have died from the first of the neck-blows to sever his brain stem, while for the others a maximum few hours of life could be expected, unconscious and bleeding to death, prey to infection of the open wounds. If any of the men buried here had survived, they could have expected to experience a long and painful period of recovery and possible after-effects such as epilepsy, progressive blindness, and so on.

The lengths of the cuts on the skulls suggests that they were nearly all caused by blows from swords (up to 6½ins, 16cm) while one could have been caused by an axe, being shorter (up to 3ins, 7cm) and having crushed and split (the thicker axe blade acts as a wedge) the surrounding area of bone more – even a light blow from an axe can cause compression injuries, due to the relatively heavier blade.

The injuries suggest that the fighting in which some of these men died was probably that of swordsman versus swordsman, possibly even duelling. Right-handed men holding their shields at chest height in their left hands can most easily attack the left side of their opponents' heads, shoulders and arms. Cutting strokes would be the most effective, though well-aimed thrusts could be deadly if they were to land properly. Three of the six skulls examined had cuts to the mid-left brow or pate, consistent with fatal duelling wounds, although they could just as easily have been sustained in battle. The multiple wounds on the body of Victim II suggest either a man disabled in battle by a powerful blow from behind, then hacked to death, or possibly a fallen warrior unable to defend himself from an enemy who comprehensively finished him off, almost beheading him in the process. Whether all these men died at one time (in one battle) or over a longish time span (a generation or two) has not been determined.

Horses and Waggons

Loud were they, Lo! loud when they rode over the barrow,
they were determined when they rode across the land.
Shield thyself now that thou may escape this attack...

(*Wið færstice*, metrical charm lines 3–5)

188

Hlūde wǣran hȳ lā hlūde ðā hȳ ofer þone hlǣw ridan,
wǣran ānmōde ðā hȳ ofer land ridan.
Scyld ðū ðē nū þ þū ðysne nīð genēsan mōte...

It is well known that the Anglo-Saxon army consisted of infantry men (OE *fēðan*), some of whom travelled by foot (at least in the earlier period, before the Danish wars) and others by horse. We have the testimony of various OE poems that the saddle was part of the warrior's normal equipment and that warriors arrived at the field of battle on horseback, drove off their mounts and formed up on foot – presumably the men whose task it was to keep the supply waggons also had to look after the horses during fighting. But, though Byrhtnōð, the English commander at Maldon, kept his horse by him for mobility, to what extent was the horse generally used in warfare? To be of service, horses have to be trained not to rear and flee at the commotion of battle; they have to be quite large – taller than a man's shoulder if the rider is to have a real advantage of height; and they should be strong, with enough staying-power to keep going when the opposition has begun to flag. All these qualities are present, to varying degrees, in the later mediaeval destrier but the native northern European horse is seldom larger than a Shetland pony (say, 10 hands) and leaves much to be desired in its military usefulness.

R. H. C. Davies has studied the background to Anglo-Saxon horsemanship and points out that horses of a size to be used for cavalry purposes are expensive to produce – they have to be selectively bred over several generations, involving rigorous segregation of the selected breeding stock on stud farms – and naturally eat and drink more than their smaller unselected counterparts. One factor is the diet of the mare while she is carrying the foal during the winter months, a period when food will be harder to find, producing a smaller and weaker animal – the breeder who provides hay and oats is rewarded with better stock in the spring. The Anglo-Saxons certainly had such breeding places (OE *stōd* 'stud') with separate areas (*stōdfaldas* 'stud-folds, paddocks) set aside for the mares (*stōdmyra*) and stallions (*stōdhors*) to prevent uncontrolled procreation and keep out horse rustlers (*stōdðēofas*).

Old English poetry recognizes the heroic warrior as a 'rider', as for example in *Beowulf*:

> ... the rider sleeps,
> the hero in [his] grave...

(lines 2457–8)

> ....*rīdend swefað,*
> *hæleð in hoðman* ...

and the *Maxims*:

> A nobleman should be on a horse's back

(I, line 62)

> *Eorl sceal on ēos bōge*

and the language has a number of other terms for mounted warriors, including *ridda* and *rīdere* 'rider', *rīdehere* 'mounted raiding force' and *rīdwiga* 'one who fights on horseback'. A common term is *ēored* 'mounted troop', transparently derived from *ēoh* 'horse' and *rād* 'riding'; this word occurs in compounds such as *ēoredgeatwe* 'military apparel'.

Leather bridle-reins and tack (OE *bridelþwancgas ⁊ gerǣde*) are among the items made by the *scōwyrhta* 'shoemaker' in Ælfric's *Colloquy* and these could be quite ornate. Gale Owen-Crocker has argued that the word *gerǣdu* should be translated 'trappings' as it may refer to more than the simple harness, sometimes to horse furniture with evident overtones of high social status. Even so, warriors seem consistently to have dismounted to fight, so the horse itself would not have been armoured.

The 7th century Sutton Hoo helmet has a reconstructed decorative plate showing a bare-headed warrior riding down an armoured footman: the rider's harness consists of a bridle and bit, reins (which the rider is not holding) a crupper and girth; the saddle is hidden by the warrior's shield. There is no suggestion of a stirrup on this early representation, which may derive from a Scandinavian original design. The stirrup's introduction to Europe took place in the 600s and Anglo-Saxon horsemen must have begun to use them – the word 'stirrup' itself is of Old English origin: *stigrāp* 'climbing-rope' – as these items evidently were made of organic fibre (or possibly wood?), they do not survive well archaeologically, although there are metal examples from later in the period e.g. the Seagry Anglo-Scandinavian example made of gilded iron.

The saddle could be splendidly ornamented, if we accept the *Beowulf* poet's reference to the *hildesetl* 'war-seat' of the Danish king at face value. Occasional examples of saddle fittings have survived which attest to the use of decorated metal plates. The horse harness shown on the Bayeux tapestry is not illustrated consistently enough for safe assumptions to be made, but it seems that curved bits and breast straps were in use by that time, and there is a suggestion of padding on the saddle seats.

The distances over which Anglo-Saxon armies travelled to meet each other, or the Danes, in battle clearly show that they had to ride to war. The Danes certainly knew where to obtain horses when they raided inland and had to keep their ships available at the coast while needing speed and mobility, since they were often *gehorsod* 'provided with horses' from English studs. Yet for the year 893, the ASC records:

Here in this year the great army of which we previously spoke went back from the Eastern Kingdom westwards to Boulogne and there they were put on ships so that they all crossed over at one time with their horses...

Hēr on þysum gēare fōr se micla here þe wē gefyrn ymbe sprǣcon eft of þǣm ēastrīce westweard tō Bunnan ond þǣr wurdon gescipode swā þæt hīe āsettan him on ānne sīþ ofer mid horsum mid ealle...

Figure 38 Mounted warrior based on detail of a helmet plate from Mound 1 at Vendel, Sweden. The warrior is accompanied by two birds of prey (eagle and raven?) and has a helmet surmounted by an eagle crest on the 'wala'.

Remarkably, the Danes found it necessary to bring horses with them from the Continent because Alfred had seized all they had captured the previous year. Indeed, at this time the English seem to have generally pursued and harried their enemy on horseback, making warfare a pursuit which relied to a large extent on supplies of horses. In 894, the Danes came to depend on their mounts for more than just transport:

...When they were all gathered [i.e. the English and their allies] they caught up with the raiding-army from behind at Buttington on the bank of the Severn, and besieged it there on both sides in a stronghold. When they had remained there on both sides of the river for many weeks and the king was away west in Devon [acting] against the ship-borne army, they [the Danes] were then afflicted with longing for food and had eaten the greater part of their horses, and the others had died from hunger...

...Þā hīe þā ealle gegaderode wǣron þā offōron hīe þone here hindan æt Buttingtūne on Sǣferne staþe ond hine þǣr ūtan besǣton on ǣlce healfe on ānum fæstenne. Þā hīe ðā fela wucena sǣton on twā healfe þǣre ēa ond se cyng wæs west on Defnum wiþ þone sciphere þā wǣron hīe mid metelīeste gewǣgde ond hæfdon micelne dǣl þāra horsa freten ond þā ōþre wǣron mid hungre ācwolen....

It is clear that, though the English used their horsemanship to overtake their foes, there is no suggestion that they intended to fight them on horseback: the Danes had managed to get to safety in a defensive position, and the English decided to starve them out. Had they caught them in the open, it is unlikely that their horses would have been in any condition to give chase after the long, hard ride in pursuit. There can be little doubt that both armies were encumbered by pack animals which would be unable to maintain a swift pace over any distance, and the *fyrd* evidently had enough supplies to make their siege a viable proposition, though naturally they could expect to be re-supplied from the surrounding area. Pack-horses and carts were used to carry supplies which would have been necessary for a campaign of any length; Bede's story of the thane Imma suggests that he deliberately passed himself off as a poor, menial non-combatant whose task it was to bring food to the army.

Living off the land is one option for an army, but not a very attractive one when one can't be sure of the supply situation or the availability of usable foodstuffs in the region, so the prudent military commander would want to satisfy himself that his troops' health and morale could be sustained in the field by bringing supplies along. In order to keep a large force supplied, it would be necessary to disperse the men in smaller units across the country, which would mean losing any advantage of numbers. In fact, the surprise Danish attack on Alfred over Christmas at Chippenham would have been total folly had they not known that the king was there for the winter: where the king stayed there would certainly be stores of food and drink. For a defensive force on home territory, living off the land means taking whatever generosity is offered by landowners, since plundering one's own people is not good practice. Nevertheless, despoliation (OE *herehūð*) was an important factor in early warfare since it enriched those who undertook it and defamed the military power of those who were plundered. The threat of unchecked plundering was enough to make successive English kings pay the Danes to leave, the so-called *Danegeld*; when the Danes attacked from bases on mainland Britain it is likely that as their supplies of food and drink were used up, the horses could be sent back to the homeland laden with booty.

Two years after Buttington saw the death of one of Alfred's most illustrious followers called *Ecgulf cynges horsþegn* "Ecgwulf, the king's horse-thane". Perhaps this warrior official had the duty of looking after the king's horses on campaign: the titles 'marshall' and 'constable' have a similar origin in Frankish *marhaskalkaz* 'horse-servant' and Old French *conestable* 'officer of the stable' respectively, suggesting that the West Saxon *horsþegn* may have been directly modelled on the Frankish office. Supporting this assumption is the later ruling of King Athelstan that horses could only be sent overseas as gifts, and that every landowner should provide two mounted men for each plough he owned.

In c.1023, the Laws of King Cnut stipulated that the heriot (military death duties) of an earl included eight horses, four with saddles and four without, as well as four helmets, four mailcoats, four swords, eight spears and eight shields. This suggests that the earl was accompanied by three men armed with helmet, sword, shield, spear and mailcoat (like the earl himself), while another four men, armed only with spear and shield, led the remaining horses. A king's thane's heriot was of four horses (two with and two without saddles), two swords, a helmet, a mailcoat and four spears and shields: again, the thane may be presumed to have had a saddled horse, the mailcoat and helmet, a sword, spear and shield, while a companion took the other saddled horse, a sword, spear and shield and the other two horses were led by men with just spears and shields. There is little doubt that the horses without saddles were used to transport the provisions and spare weapons and equipment of the warriors who rode, led by attendants or retainers whose duty it was to protect the lord's property and person.

The office of *steallere*, which corresponds rather closely to the Franco-Norman *comes stabuli* 'constable', was apparently introduced to England by Edward the Confessor after his stay at the Norman court. There were up to three men of this title at any one time, all with at least some military responsibility, suggesting that horses may have come to play a more important role in late Anglo-Saxon military affairs than previously – unless we are misled by the invention of a new title into assuming that a new office has been created, and we should rather see continuity of earlier practice.[24]

Earthworks and Strongholds

> ...Fortresses are seen from afar,
> marvellous work of giants, those which are on this earth
> splendid work of wall-stones...
>
> (Exeter Book *Gnomic Verses*, lines 1–3)

> ... *ceastra bēoð feorran gesȳne,*
> *orðanc enta geweorc þā þe on þysse eorðan syndon*
> *wrǣtlic weallstāna geweorc...*

Linear Earthworks

Earthworks are large-scale construction and civil engineering projects which require immense organization in non-urban communities. They were part of the English tradition of defensive measures long before the nation transferred its seat of power to

---

[24] There are early West Saxon references to an officer called *horswealh* 'horse-servant', who may have been the king's personal groom or equerry; however, since the second element of the word (*wealh*) means 'Welshman', it is at least theoretically possible that the West Saxons required riding service of their Celtic subjects.

Britannia, as can be seen from the construction called *Olgerdiget* in southern Jutland, constructed in the early Roman Iron Age and almost certainly inspired by contact with the Roman fortified *vallum* or Gaulish walled blockades. No doubt the communities which were persuaded to undertake such public works believed that one large effort of construction could save a great deal of regret later; equally, the leader whose people could boast such a powerful symbol of territorial boundary-marking would be several jumps ahead of his rivals. Earthworks like these clearly show that territory was becoming important and worth fighting for – they were not erected to keep out small-scale cattle-raiders but to halt entire armies.

If the construction of earthworks shows that territory was rising in importance, there must have been sufficient incentive for scattered communities to combine forces for the construction project, and there must also have been acknowledged leadership to mastermind the undertaking. Where the ditch and bank delimit a territory, the boundary marked so permanently had to be a commonly agreed (or enforced) one, presumably, since otherwise the effort of construction would not be worthwhile. All these factors suggest a trend towards central authority and the concept of the 'nation' standing behind one leader; they also suggest that these nations felt sufficiently threatened to agree to undertake the vast amount of work involved, both in the physical construction itself and in the feeding and billeting of the labour force.

In England, earthwork boundaries are a notable feature of the early period of Germanic settlement. Many are in direct relation to late Roman roads and centres, suggesting that their origins lie in the period of strife and uncertainty following the collapse of direct Roman rule during which the main Anglo-Saxon political boundaries were established, and so sometime before the rise of the settled kingdoms and provinces of the early Christian era. Unfortunately, dating earthworks is notoriously difficult and often based on slender evidence. Nonetheless, an early Saxon date is quite well established for many of the ditch-and-bank structures, but seldom any convincing context. We simply do not know which folk built them and what part they played in the military campaigns which they were built to further or prevent.

Perhaps the best known of these early features is the Wansdyke, which is in two parts: the West Wansdyke runs parallel to the Somerset Avon in northern Somerset, while the East Wansdyke lies across the uplands by the River Kennett. Both sections face north, which suggests that they were erected to keep out invaders from the Thames Valley where a strong Saxon enclave came to early prominence and eventually seized the throne of the West Saxons. The name 'Wansdyke' is presumed to be based on an earlier *Wōdnes dīc* 'Woden's ditch', which commemorates the heathen war-god; it is unlikely such a name would have been given in Christian times, so this supports an early date for the feature – but Roman pottery in undisturbed layers *beneath* the ditch puts it firmly in the post-Roman Anglo-Saxon period. In fact many such linear boundaries are called Grim's Ditch, Grimsdyke, and so on, where 'Grim' (OE *grīma* 'mask') is a byname for Woden, the 'hooded god'. Perhaps those cases where the name has been changed to 'Devil's Ditch' or similar represent a later Christian unwillingness to mention the ancient god by name.

194

The Fenland has its share of these early ramparts – Cambridgeshire alone has a Devil's Dyke (perhaps a re-named *Grim's Ditch*?), Fleam Dyke (OE *flēam* 'rout'), Heydon Ditch and Brent Ditch. The first was 7·5 miles long, accurately surveyed and laid out in straight lines, and it stretched from the marshy Fens to the Essex clay at the county's southern border. It may once have extended to the Cam. It still stands up to 15ft tall and up to 70ft wide, with the ditch 17ft deep and 65ft wide on its southwestern face; originally there had been a low outer bank also. The chalk soil from the ditch had been hauled or hoisted to the top of the bank, where it lay in longitudinal strips. The whole structure had been built in a short space of time, perhaps one summer, and once erected, the bank had never been altered or enlarged. The Fleam Dyke is a little over 3 miles long, its southern section erected in the same manner and perhaps at the same time as the Devil's Dyke, to which it runs parallel. It is now an 11ft high bank with an 11ft deep ditch, and 85ft wide overall, though it had been built over an earlier 7ft high bank; again there was a low outer bank. Brent (or Pampisford) Ditch is 1·5 miles long running from Abington to Pampisford; no bank survives, though its ditch is still 7ft deep. The Heydon (or Bran) Ditch extends from Heydon to Fowlmere, less than 3 miles, and is again of a similar type of construction to the previous dykes, although it has now been almost completely ploughed out. Its ditch's dimensions are said to have been 8ft deep and 22ft wide, and there were traces of a previous structure consisting of two shallow ditches with a wooden palisade between them, which the dyke replaced. Significantly, a burial ground was found next to the bank containing over fifty human skeletons, nearly all mature males showing signs of violent death such as beheading, hanging, and throat-cutting. It was immediately thought that this represented the mass-grave of the dead from a battle at the ditch, though subsequent research has shown that some of the corpses' bones were in advanced stages of decay before they were buried, and from this it has been argued that the site was a place of legal, ritual execution (OE *cwealmstōw*) where criminals were executed and their bodies left, hanging, to rot before finally being buried; the east-west alignment of the bodies points to a date in Christian times.

The best known linear earthwork in Britain from the Anglo-Saxon period must surely be Offa's Dyke, which marked off the English Midlands from the Welsh polities to the west. It was constructed in the late 780s under the Mercian king, Offa,[25] as a showpiece of civil engineering and a flagrant and intimidating demonstration of Mercian power. The dyke consisted of a ditch and bank some 25 feet high (ditch bottom to bank top), with a sheer western face to the bank which was surmounted by a wooden fence with stone reinforcements at certain points, perhaps the foundations for wooden towers. The wall was seemingly never permanently 'manned' but presumably patrolled by horsemen; the provision of towers would allow for beacons to summon assistance if an attack was expected. The ditch and its bank were built in sections by

---

[25] It is presumably no accident that this Offa traced his direct paternal descent from the famous Offa of Angeln, whose most remarkable and lasting achievement was the establishment of a boundary against the foe – evidently the latterday Offa wanted to be remembered for similar successes among his people.

many different 'gangs', possibly in just one season (if the many peoples subject to the powerful King Offa had their tribute payments[26] commuted to construction labour) and stretched from the Irish Sea to the Bristol Channel, sealing off the English heartlands against military incursions from Wales. The sheer amount of labour involved in such a task as erecting this boundary in Offa's day defies the imagination, and argues for an administration of unsuspected efficiency and remarkable organizational skill.

Strongholds

Strongholds played an important part in early warfare in Britain as centres of defence and attack. The early fortifications of the English on the Continent and their foes rarely seem to have been more substantial than a raised mound with a wooden palisade around its perimeter, useful for keeping cattle and livestock in, and predators out, but not likely to deter a warband or raiding party.

With the transfer to Britain, the Germanic incomers came up against some very substantial fortifications in the walled towns of the later Roman period. The *Chronicle* records one early victory over the inhabitants of a fortress:

491. Here Ælle and Cissa besieged the fortress of Anderida and slew all those who lived within it, whereby there was not one Briton left alive.   (*ASC 'A'* s.a. 491)

Her Ælle ⁊ Cissa ymb sæton Andredes cester ⁊ ofslogon alle þa þe þær inne eardedon ne wearþ forþon an Bret to lafe

It is not clear how Ælle and Cissa managed to overcome the resistance of the inhabitants of *Anderida*, the Roman coastal fort at Pevensey, as the *Chronicle* simply says that they 'surrounded, sat around' (*ymb sæton*) it. Nor is it known whether those living inside were peasant farmers holed up within the massive walls for safety, or some kind of garrison. The decision not to spare them argues for the latter, as this wholesale destruction of the foe is typical of the tribute due to the war-god, Woden, rather than an act of bad-tempered savagery after a long and frustrating siege. It would be illuminating to discover whether the South Saxon leaders starved the inhabitants out over a period of weeks, or took the stronghold by storm – despite the strength of the walls, which survive to this day as an impressive construction, the very length of the perimeter would be difficult to defend adequately against a determined foe.

The ASC also records the construction of an English fortress *de novo*:

547. Here Ida came to power from whom the Northumbrians' royal family sprang, and he reigned for 12 years and he built Bebba's fortress [Bamborough] which was first enclosed with a fence and afterwards with a wall.   (*ASC 'E'* s.a. 547)

---

[26] It has been suggested that the *Tribal Hideage* document represents the liabilities of Offa's subject and satellite territories which were used for this purpose.

Hēr Ida fēng tō rīce þanon Norðhymbra cyne kyn ǣrost āwōc ꝥ rīxade .xii. gēar ꝥ hē ge timbrade Bebban burh sy wæs ǣrost mid hegge betīned ꝥ þǣr æfter mid wealle.

It seems clear that the preliminary fortification, inside which Ida and his men sheltered at first, was perhaps no more than a palisade,[27] which was then replaced with more substantial defences (bank-and-ditch) under cover of this. It is possible that Ida's troops lived 'under canvas' while the walls were being thrown up, as King Edward the Elder did later when he came to supervise the construction of a *burh* in Essex:

… then King Edward travelled with some of his reinforcements to the East Saxons, to Maldon, and camped there for the time that the *burh* was being constructed and built at Witham … (*ASC 'A'* s.a.912)

… þā fōr Eadweard cyning mid sumum his fultume on ēast Seaxe tō Mældūne ꝥ wīcode þǣr þā hwīle þe man þā burg worhte ꝥ getimbrode æt Withām…

The Old English word *burh*[28] originally meant any place of safety or refuge; it is derived from the verb *beorgan*[29] 'protect' and simply means 'that which is protected, haven, refuge'. In common with its counterparts in Continental Germanic languages, it came to be used especially of fortified sites, of forts and military strongholds but curiously not of Roman defences which were called *ceastra*,[30] modern '-chester, -cester' in place names.

What form these early *byrig* took is not clear, although the eighth century Mercian royal sites at Hereford and Tamworth both featured extensive ditch-and-bank defences, the former enclosing 33 acres with its internal structures sited according to a strict ground plan. These were, however, royal centres associated with a powerful and ostentatious dynasty and probably had time and labour lavished on them on a scale which more modest kingdoms could not contemplate.

The catalyst in the further development of English fortifications was the Danish wars of the mid-800s, during which the ability of the raiders to strike quickly and in force demonstrated quite clearly the deficiencies of the defence systems which had

---

[27] The phrase *mid hegge* could mean 'with a fence' or even 'with a hedge' but this seems an unnecessarily pessimistic view of English military fieldwork capabilities.

[28] Also spelt *burg* as in the extract just quoted, both with the plural *byrig*.

[29] There are, incidentally, some interesting words based on *beorgan* and its root forms. One such in OE is *hereburh* 'raiders-fortress' which by a convoluted development of meaning becomes the modern word 'harbour', while the word *burh* itself developed the meaning 'township', whence our 'borough'; town-dwellers came in mediaeval times to be called 'burghers' (as in 'the Burghers of Calais'), and, through this word's adoption into French, the town-dwelling professional and middle-classes came to be known as the *bourgeoisie* (*bourg* is *burg*). Finally, the OE word *healsbeorg* 'neck-protection' or its Frankish counterpart *halsberg*, gave rise to the word 'hauberk' for a coat of mail.

[30] Singular *ceaster* from the Latin *castra* 'camp'.

evolved during the previous centuries. As kingdom after kingdom toppled before the viking onslaught, it must have seemed that there was no means of resisting the Scandinavian forces. Alfred of Wessex's experiences – and especially the near-disastrous attack on his residence at Chippenham over Christmas 878   led to a re-evaluation of priorities. His most pressing need was to keep the Danes out while the West Saxons re-armed and prepared for further struggles. We know Alfred had visited the Continent as a boy and no doubt had seen or heard of the system of fortified bridges which Charles the Bald had instituted in order to deny the foe free access to the interior via the rivers. Alfred also knew that the vikings themselves regularly carried the materials to construct makeshift yet serviceable defences in their ships. It would be natural that his thinking should turn first to the possibilities for strengthening his kingdom's land-based defences as a means of stopping the terrible, demoralizing effect on his people of not being able to find any refuge from the enemy – he had himself had to skulk in the Somerset swamps for some time – who could roam unchecked across the land. If the king was at that time also reflecting on the possible re-organization of the *fyrd* then he had the perfect opportunity to kill two birds with one stone: by dividing the *fyrd*, the mobile army, into two he could provide mobile attack and mobile defence forces, but he still needed permanent defence measures which would not 'stand down' after so many months' service. This meant static fortifications which could be permanently manned because those responsible for defending them would be living inside them.

Alfred's overall plan was presumably to combine the mobile *fyrd* with the static *burhwaran* ('stronghold-dwellers') into a network of defences. The strongholds were not to be sterile military outposts in an agricultural setting, however; Alfred's depth of vision carried him beyond the manifest disadvantages and burdensome expense of such a scheme. Rather, he foresaw a system of strategically-sited strongpoints which could be used to protect whole regions, but chosen so as to be linked into a network and not too far apart to give each other assistance at need.[31] These new fortified sites would both deny the enemy his power of unchecked movement and spread the economic revival (for towns meant power and money) across the whole West Saxon-controlled territory. Despite much local opposition and reluctance to comply with the king's wishes, Alfred's vision was achieved with the establishment of the so-called 'burghal' system across southern England, whereby the new fortifications were constituted as embryonic towns with an economic, governmental and political role. They served to hold territory for the West Saxon kings and, once the wars of re-conquest got underway under Alfred's son Edward the Elder, to consolidate the territory won from the Danes. The network is described in a document known as *The Burghal Hidage* which sets out the number of households contributing through taxation to each *burh*:

---

[31] The system was supplemented by groups of beacons and watchpoints, called *tōthyll* in Old English. These enabled the home forces to maintain a vigilant presence across the land, and to alert the nearest garrison if raiders were detected. The 'tothills' were sited on the military roads (*herestrœtas*).

... and to Exeter belong four and thirty hides and seven hundred hides ... and twelve hundred hides belong to Malmesbury and to Cricklade belong 14 hundred hides and 15 hundred hides to Oxford ...

... ꝺ tō Eaxanceastre hyrþ fēower ꝺ xxx hīda ꝺ .vii. hund hīda ... ꝺ twelf hund hīda hyrþ tō Mealdmesbyring ꝺ tō Crecgelāde hyrþ .xiiii. hund hīda ꝺ xv. hund hīda tō Oxna forda...

The principle by which the size of the hide contribution was measured was the length of the *burh*'s ramparts. Briefly, the statutes require that each *pole* of the wall be manned by four men.[32] A *pole* was a unit of length equal to five and a half yards or 16ft 6ins (about 5m) hence each man was responsible for about 4ft (or about 1·25m) of wall, a distance great enough for him to stand armed and defend without undue difficulty. The detail of how the ramparts came to be manned in emergency is not clear, since many *byrig* were built on too grand a scale and never fully settled, while others were tiny and could not have held a resident population sufficient to man them properly. In all likelihood, the hidage was a taxation requirement for the support of the stronghold – money and services and food rents paid to the thane in the *burh* rather than to the king direct – on the principle that the military establishments were not meant to be economically self-supporting. However, with permanent residents moving into their relative safety, they quickly took on an important economic aspect as centres of administration. Some measure of the success of the system can be gleaned from the fact that nearly all the thirty sites chosen for development remain in use as prominent towns to this day (though a few were later replaced by nearby locations which were better sited for trading purposes, such as Pilton by Barnstaple).

The first phase of the system – Alfred's vision, one might say – encompassed thirty strongholds spread across West Saxondom at intervals of around twenty miles and mainly on navigable rivers or major land routes, which would allow the *fyrd* to march from one to the next in a day, avoiding difficult and dangerous night marches. Also, logically, no farm or village was more than ten miles from the protection of the king's troops at the nearest *burh*. The location of each fort was carefully chosen to benefit from advantages of terrain, as well as being near a royal estate; where possible, existing Roman or Iron Age walls or earthworks were re-used (they had been sited for similar reasons of defence, after all) but the king did not hesitate to order building to begin at 'greenfield' sites if necessary. Richard Abels notes, in his perceptive survey[33] of Alfred's establishment, based on the earlier work of David Hinton, that the major river mouths, the inland waterways and the best south coast natural harbours were all secured while the Thames (the West Saxons' northern border for much of its length) was protected by forts at Southwark, Sashes, Wallingford and Cricklade. Dorset's

---

[32] The size of garrison necessary to man the average *burh* was 900 men, according to Abels.

[33] In *Lordship and Military Obligation in Anglo-Saxon England.*

interior was guarded by the *burh* at Wareham,[34] overlooking the Rivers Frome and Piddle, while Lydford, Wallingford and many of the other sites were presumably strategically important river crossings which it was essential to protect if the interior of Wessex was to be adequately defended. The vikings had to be denied their twin advantages – surprise and mobility – and Alfred's burghal system could do that. But it could do more, of course; each *burh* held a garrison which was in itself a potentially active task-force: raiders who slipped past the strongholds on their way inland in search of plunder still had to travel along roads which were controlled by the *byrig*; travelling across country with quantities of booty and slaves was too slow and dangerous, but many such viking troops found that the roads themselves were not safe, as the English forces gathered from the nearest strongholds and fought them off or closed off their escape routes so that they often had to abandon all they had taken just to get away. The great cost of manning the *byrig* was more than repaid by the advantages it offered the English at a time when they needed all the help they could get; strongholds left unmanned were potential bases for the enemy, of course, so Alfred's scheme had to take into account the need for permanent garrisons.

The *Chronicle* entries for 893 and 894 show that the Danes appreciated the possibilities of good defensive positions, though Alfred was resourceful enough to counter their efforts:

893. Here in this year the great army of which we previously spoke travelled back from the east-kingdom [France] westwards to Boulogne and were provided with ships there so that they transported themselves in one go with horses and everything [else] and then came up to the mouth of the Lymn with 250 ships. That river mouth is in the eastern part of Kent at the eastern end of the great wood which we call *Andred* [the Weald]; that wood is 120 miles long eastwards and westwards or longer, and thirty miles wide. The river which we previously spoke about runs out of the wood. On this river they drew up their ships as far as the wood 4 miles from the estuary and there they broke into a fortification; in the stronghold a few yeomen were dwelling and it was half-built.

Then soon after Hæsten came with 80 ships into the Thames estuary and built himself a fortification at Milton, and the other *here* [did likewise] at Appledore.

894. In this year which was twelve months since they had constructed a fortification in the eastern kingdom [Kent] the Northumbrians and East Angles had given oaths to King Alfred, and the East Angles 6 preliminary hostages, yet despite the promise as often as the other raiding troops went out in full force, then they went [also] either with [the *here*] or on their own account. Then King Alfred gathered his *fierd* and passed so that he camped between the two raiding troops at

---

[34] Abels notes with a touch of admiration that the defensive possibilities of Wareham were so good that it was refortified against possible invasion in 1940.

the place where he had room closest to the woodland fort and to the river fort, so that he could reach either if they sought open country…

(*ASC 'A'* s.a. 893–4)

Hēr on þysum gēare fōr se micla here þe wē gefyrn ymbe sprǣcon eft of þǣm ēast rīce west weard tō Bunnan ⁊ þǣr wurdon gescipode swā þæt hīe āsettan him on ānne sīþ ofer mid horsum mid ealle ⁊ þā cōmon ūp on Limene mūþan mid ccl. hunde scipa. Se mūþa is on ēaste weardre Cent æt þæs miclan wuda ēastende þe wē Andred hātað; se wudu is ēast lang ⁊ west lang hund twelftīges mīla lang oþþe lengra ⁊ þrītiges mīla brād. Sēo ēa þe wē ǣr ymbe sprǣcon līð ūt of þǣm wealda. On þā ēa hī tugon ūp hiora scipu oþ þone weald .iiii. mīla fram þǣm mūþan ūteweardum ⁊ þǣr ābrǣcon ān geweorc inne on þǣm fæstenne sǣton fēawa cirlisce men on ⁊ wæs samworht.

Þā sōna æfter þǣm cōm Hæsten mid lxxx. scipa ūp on Temese mūðan ⁊ worhte him geweorc æt Middeltūne ⁊ se ōþer here æt Apuldre.

On þȳs gēare þæt wæs ymb twelf mōnað þæs þe hīe on þǣm ēastrīce geweorc geworht hæfdon Norþ hymbre ⁊ ēast Engle hæfdon Ælfrede cyninge āþas geseald ⁊ ēast Engle foregīsla .vi. ⁊ þēh ofer þā trēowa swā oft swā þā ōþre hergas mid herige ūt fōron þonne fōron hīe oþþe mid oþþe on heora healfe on. Þā gegaderade Ælfred cyning his fierd ⁊ fōr þæt hē gewīcode betwuh þām twām hergum þǣr þǣr hē nīehst rymet hæfde for wudu fæstenne ond for wæter fæstenne swā þæt hē mehte ǣgþerne gerǣcan gif hīe ǣnigne feld sēcan wolden…

The Danes retrieved the initiative and moved in 895 to a base at Mersea Island, Essex, from which they began to threaten London by constructing a fortification on the River Lea:

Then that same year before winter the Danes who had settled on Mersea drew their ships up along the Thames and then up the Lea; that was then two years since they came here from over the sea.

896. In the same year the above-mentioned raiding force constructed a fortification on the Lea, 20 miles above London. And in the summer after a large part of the city folk and also of other people travelled so that they reached the fortification of the Danes, and they were put to flight, and four of the king's thanes were slain there. Then after that in harvest-time the king camped in the neighbourhood of the stronghold while they reaped their corn in order that the Danes might not deprive them of the harvest. Then one day the king was riding along by the river, and noticed where the river could be obstructed so that they could not bring their ships back out, and they did [as he decided], they constructed two strongholds [one each] on the two sides of the river. When they had first begun the fortress and were camped out in that place, the *here* realized that they could not bring the ships out.

Then they abandoned them, and travelled across country so that they reached Bridgenorth beside the Severn, and made a fortification there. The *fierd* then rode west after the *here*, and the men from London fetched the ships, and all those they could not take away they broke up, and those which were serviceable they brought into the city of London...

(*ASC 'A'* s.a. 895–6)

...Đā þȳ ylcan gēre on foran winter þā Deniscan þe on Meresīge sǣton tugon hira scipu ūp on Temese ⁊ þā ūp on Lygan, þæt wæs ymb twā gēr þæs þe hīe hider ofer sǣ cōmon.

On þȳ ylcan gēre worhte se foresprecena here geweorc be Lygan .xx. mīla būfan Lunden byrig. Þā þæs on sumera fōron micel dǣl þāra burgwara ⁊ ēac swā ōþres folces þæt hīe gedydon æt þāra Deniscana geweorce ⁊ þǣr wurdon geflīemde ⁊ sume fēower cyninges þegnas ofslǣgene. Þā þæs on hærfæste þā wīcode se cyng on nēaweste þāre byrig þā hwīle þe hīe hira corn gerȳpon þæt þā Deniscan him ne mehton þæs rīpes forwiernan. Þā sume dæge rād se cyng ūp be þǣre ēæ ⁊ gehāwade hwǣr mon mehte þā ēa forwyrcan þæt hīe ne mehton þā scipu ūt brengan. ⁊ hīe swā dydon, worhton ðā tū geweorc on twā healfe þǣre ēas. Þā hīe ðā þæt geweorc furþum ongunnen hæfdon ⁊ þǣr tōgewīcod hæfdon, þā ongēt se here þæt hīe ne mehton þā scypu ūt brengan. Þā forlēton hīe hīe ⁊ ēodon ofer land þæt hīe gedydon æt Cwatbrycge be Sæfern ⁊ þǣr geweorc worhton. Þā rād sēo fird west æfter þōm herige ⁊ þā men of Lundenbyrig gefetodon þā scipu ⁊ þā ealle þe hīe ālǣdan ne mehton tōbrǣcon ⁊ þā þe þǣr stælwyrðe wǣron binnan Lundenbyrig gebrōhton...

Evidently Alfred's campaign had a cat-and-mouse element at this time – after the attack from London was repulsed he brought his forces into the area of the Danes' base to protect the gathering of the crop, then rather than risk an all-out assault or a protracted siege, he simply cut off their escape route back to the river, so that their ships were trapped, and the *here*'s mobility impaired. To ensure there was no possibility of the ships' recapture, he wisely had the serviceable ones brought into a place of (English-held) safety, and the rest destroyed.

It is interesting that the Danes did not try to impede the building of the forts on the Lea (at modern Hertford, apparently), since that would have been a less costly exercise than simply leaving the ships behind. They seemingly did not trust to their strength to risk a stand-up fight with Alfred's forces by this time. When they came up against *byrig* the vikings generally seem to have fought shy of them, having no means of taking them by storm and insufficient patience or supplies to undertake a siege, and the garrisons were able to drive off attackers on several occasions. In any event, a siege would have been risky for a force whose main weapons were mobility and surprise, since to stay too long in one place was to invite attack by a massed army.

Despite the later running down of the burghal system, Æþelred did build more strongholds, however. From his reign dates the refurbishment of the Iron Age hill-fort of South Cadbury with massive stone facings and mortared walls. Cadbury was the site of a mint but was abandoned within a very short time of completion, suggesting that it was one of the temporary centres to which normal *burh* activity was transferred during the upheavals of renewed viking activity. However, despite such sporadic fortification work, the strongholds were not part of a network, just stand-alone fastnesses; they contributed little to the general security of the population and were themselves vulnerable, since they did not form part of an overall planned strategy for defence. Æþelred seems to have relied much more on his naval forces (*scipfyrd*) to prevent viking raiders from landing, and concentrated his efforts towards raising taxes to cover the expense of ship-building.

The *byrig* were to some extent victims of their own success. Their acquired economic and administrative roles grew in importance as the threat of hostilities faded in the mid 10th century, and they became centres of royal power by which the king and his followers were able to control the surrounding countryside (not unlike later Norman castles in this respect). One *burh*, that at Goltho Manor, Lincolnshire, is strongly reminiscent of the earliest Norman motte-and-bailey creations with massive ramparts, even though it is dated to about 1000 AD; it is likely enough that there are many more such strongholds beneath the streets of modern English towns.

Figure 39 English warrior with drawn sword and circular shield with what appears to be a 'sugar-loaf' boss, based on a detail from an Anglo-Saxon manuscript illustration.

Hall Attacks

Traditionally, battles took place out in the open (*on middan felda*, 'in open country') in prepared locations under the eyes of the gods who would decide the outcome. However, not all fighting was of this nature and there are many references in northern literature to what we might call 'surprise attacks'. These were prepared under cover of darkness and launched at dawn for maximum effect. They are always attacks against buildings, whether domestic dwellings or military strongholds, which meant that the warriors who bedded down in the hall could never be sure that they would be woken by their womenfolk calling them to breakfast and not the trumpet alarms signalling an assault. Speaking of his presage of doom for his people now their lord is dead, Bēowulf's loyal thane Wīglāf says:

> … Now haste is best
> that we look upon our folk-king there
> and bring him who gave us rings
> to the balefire. Nor shall only part
> melt with the brave man for there is a hoard of treasures,
> countless gold, grimly won,
> and now at the last with his own life
> he bought the rings; then flame must devour him,
> fire enfold him, not a warrior carry
> the treasures as his memorial, nor a pretty girl
> have at her neck the ring-adornments,
> rather she must in sorrowful mood, bereft of her gold,
> often, not only once, tread a foreign land
> now that the wise-in-warcraft has laid aside laughter,
> play and joy. Therefore shall be
> many a morning-cold spear grasped with fists,
> held in the hand, not the sound of the harp
> wake the warrior but the dark raven
> croaking eager over the doomed men,
> telling the eagle how he fared at the eating
> while he robbed the slaughtered with the wolf.

(*Beowulf*, lines 3007–27)

> "….*Nū is ofost betost,*
> *þæt wē þēodcyning þǣr scēawian*
> *ond þone gebringan þe ūs bēagas geaf*
> *on ādfǣre. Ne scel ānes hwæt*
> *meltan mid þām mōdigan ac þǣr is māþma hord,*
> *gold unrīme, grimme gecēapod*
> *ond nū æt sīðestan sylfes fēore*
> *bēagas gebohte; þā sceall brond fretan,*
> *ǣled þeccean nalles eorl wegan*

māððum tō gemyndum ne mægð scȳne
habban on healse hringweorðunge
ac sceal geōmormōd, golde berēafod
oft, nalles ǣne, elland tredan
nū se herewīsa hleahtor ālegde,
gamen ond glēodrēam. Forðon sceall gār wesan
monig morgenceald mundum bewunden,
hæfen on handa, nalles hearpan swēg
wīgend weccean ac se wonna refn
fūs ofer fǣgum fela reordian,
earne secgan hū him æt ǣte spēow
þenden hē wið wulfe wæl rēafode."

The association of the early morning with the 'dawn raid' is clear in this example, as also one of the most feared fates: the capture of the womenfolk by enemies,[35] who would presumably rob and rape them before selling them on into slavery (hence the reference to treading a foreign land 'often, not only once'). The contrast between the normal association of the hall with all that is good and desirable in warrior life,[36] with the present example of the worst possible turn of events is a powerful role-reversal in the poem. Indeed, the custom at *Heorot*, the hall of the Danish king Hrōþgār, is specifically in reaction to the possibility of unexpected attack:

> they cleared the benches; [the floor] was bestrewn
> with beds and bolsters. One of the beer-drinkers,
> eager and doomed, bent to his floor-rest.
> They set beside their heads their battle-shields,
> bright wood-boards; on the bench was
> evident above the nobleman
> a helm high-in-battle, a ring-mail coat,
> a stout spear. It was their custom
> that they were always ready for battle
> both at home and on campaign....

(*Beowulf*, lines 1239–48)

Benc-þelu beredon; hit geondbrǣded wearð
beddum ond bolstrum. Beōrscealca sum
fūs ond fǣge fletreste gebēag.
Setton him tō hēafdon hilde-randas,
bord-wudu beorhtan; þǣr on bence wæs
ofer æþelinge ȳþgesēne

---

[35] Tacitus says (*Germania*, ch.8) that the early Germanic warriors feared slavery greatly, but more for their women than for themselves.

[36] The 'hall' was essentially a male-dominated and public building in which bachelor-warriors could indulge their appetites in direct contrast to the female-dominated household of the married man.

heaþostēapa helm, hringed byrne,
þrecwudu þrymlīc. Wæs þēaw hyra
þæt hīe oft wæron ānwīg gearwe
ge æt hām ge on herge ....

Probably the classic example of a surprise attack is in the fragment known as *The Battle of Finnsburg* which relates to events at the Frisian court, where a party of Danes and Jutes are spending winter with Hildeburh, the sister of their leader, Hnæf, and her husband Finn, king of the Frisians. At Finn's court were other Jutes, probably exiles from their homeland who had taken service with him, and inevitably the proximity of old enemies led to thoughts of revenge. While Hnæf and his men are asleep in the guest-hall, the attackers are gathering at the doors to kill any who come out. The fragment, which I quote in full in Appendix II,[37] begins with one of the men seeing the glint of weapons outside in the darkness and Hnæf's exhortation to his men to take up arms.

The reference to the *wreccea* 'adventurer' in the poem is probably a commonplace, as Sigeferþ is there presented as the type of hard-fighting man who would be expected to carve out a career in the service of a foreign lord. The opening remarks about the possibility of the burning gables reflects a more direct approach to killing men in a house, as narrated in the Icelandic *Brennu Njáls saga,* where the attackers simply set fire to the thatch and prevent any of those they want to kill from escaping. In this tale, the ploy backfires as one of the intended victims manages to climb out on a fallen roof timber, and get away under cover of the smoke; he undertakes a campaign of vengeance which results in the deaths of almost all the burners. A similar fate awaited the great hall of the Danish kings, *Heorot*:

> ... The hall towered,
> high and wide-gabled; it awaited the war-waves
> of hateful flame
>
> (Beowulf, lines 81–3)

> ... *Sele hlīfade,*
> *hēah ond horngēap; heaðowylma bād*
> *lāðan līges ...*

The archaeological evidence of early English dwellings is inconclusive as to whether they were fortified or not. Logic suggests that settlements would have some form of perimeter marker which might be a flimsy fence just sufficient to stop livestock straying, but could sometimes have been more substantial. Nevertheless, there is no real evidence for the houses of ordinary folk having been protected at all, perhaps because under normal circumstances warfare was not their concern and they would generally not be attacked: the targets for raiding parties were halls and kingly

---

[37] I follow Professor Tolkien's emendations to Chambers's edition of the text as set out in *Finn and Hengest* and elsewhere.

dwellings (e.g. the Danish attack on Chippenham where they knew King Alfred to be in residence), where there would be gold and riches and the profits of war and taxation, not farmers' huts.

There were fortified places in the landscape, but under the West Saxon regime of resistance and reconquest the idea of a central place which would be both a refuge at need and a base for counter-attacks took root and flourished with the establishment of such places across the south and Midlands. Towards the end of the Anglo-Saxon period it was the right of every thane to have a *burhgeat* 'stronghold-gate', suggesting that his residence was itself fortified also, a rallying point and a defensive position.

The *Chronicle*, in its first long (and most confusing) entry, records the aggression of the brother of a former ruler towards the new king:

> and then he learnt of the king [being] with a small company on a visit to a woman at Merton, and rode to him there and surrounded the farmhouse before the men who were with the king were aware of him. Then the king found out about it and he went to the door and they defended him valiantly until he spotted the nobleman, and they rushed out against him and mightily wounded him, and they were all attacking against the king until they had slain him.   (*ASC 'A'* s.a.755)

> *ond þā geāscode hē þone cyning lȳtle werode on wīfcȳþþe on Merantūne ond hine þær berād ond þone būr ūtan beēode ǣr hine þā men onfunden þe mid þām kyinge wǣrun. Ond þā ongeat se cyning þæt ond hē on þā duru ēode ond þā unhēanlīce hine werede oþ hē on þone æþeling lōcude ond þā ūt rǣsde on hine ond hine miclum gewundode, ond hīe alle on þone cyning wǣrum feohtende oþþæt hīe hine ofslægenne hæfdon.*

What the king was doing *on wīfcȳþþe* (probably 'in intimacy with a woman') with only his closest personal followers the *Chronicle* does not record, but if he were staying on a small farm then the billeting of a large troop of warriors would not have contributed to the romantic atmosphere. The numbers involved must have been small, however, since the fighting all took place around the gates of what is later called a *burh* 'stronghold':

> When in the morning the king's thanes who were behind him heard of that, that the king had been slain, then they all rode there, and Ōsrīc his governor and Wīferþ his thane and the men whom he had previously left behind him, and they met the nobleman in the stronghold where the king lay dead, and they had fastened the gates against them .... and then they began fighting around the gates until they could get inside there and they slew the nobleman and the men who were with him....

> *Þā on morgenne gehīerdun þæt þæs cyninges þegnas þe him beæftan wǣrun þæt se cyning ofslægen wæs, þā ridon hīe þider ond his aldormon Ōsrīc ond Wīferþ his þegn, ond þā men þe hē beæftan him lǣfde ǣr ond þone æþeling on þǣre byrig mētton þǣr se cyning ofslægen læg ond þā gatu him tō belocen*

hæfdon....ond hīe þā ymb þā gatu feohtende wǣron oþ þæt hīe þǣrinne fulgon ond þone æþeling ofslōgon ond þā men þe mid him wǣrun ....

There seems to be a pattern of attacking a house or stronghold, whereby the gates and doors are the focus for all the action, both at Merton and at Finnsburg, and there is apparently no thought of storming the walls or any of the other tactics of Roman and mediaeval siege warfare. Probably these English warriors did not think in terms of stratagems and measured harassing actions, preferring to do what warriors were used to: launching powerful frontal attacks against other infantrymen – significantly, the king did not sit back in his *burh* and wait for help from outside, but rather formed up his *werod* around him and took the fight to the enemy. Whether this was because he feared death in battle less than being burnt to death with his mistress, or whether he was impetuous by nature and wouldn't wait to get at his adversary, the *Chronicle* does not record.

After the Battle

> Before that unavoidable journey none of us becomes
> so wise in thought, that he need not
> reflect before his going forth
> what of good or of evil to his soul
> may be deemed after the day of his death.
>
> (Bede's Death Song, Northumbrian version)
>
> *Fore thaem neidfaerae naenig uuiurthit*
> *thoncsnotturra than him tharf sie*
> *to ymbhycggannae aer his hiniongae*
> *huaet his gastae godaes aeththa yflaes*
> *aefter deothdaege doemid uueorthae.*

What happened to the dead after a battle? What, for that matter, happened to the sick and the wounded? There is naturally little evidence for funerary practice since it is not usually in keeping with the heroic tone of verse, nor the terse concision of prose, to record how the corpses were disposed of.

Yet there are occasional clues in the literature to show how others reacted to the deaths of warriors. A telling example is in *Beowulf* referring to events at the royal court of Finn in Frisia (See Appendix 1) where a great attack has taken place on some of the king's Danish and Jutish guests in their lodgings by exiled members of the same folk,[38] with much loss of life on the attackers' side. Those who attacked the guest-hall had relatives among those who were defending, and there was a terrible sense of divided loyalties (that to kinsfolk versus that to leader and friends) on both sides. The

---

[38] Here again I follow Professor Tolkien's emendations to Chambers's edition of the text as set out in *Finn and Hengest* and elsewhere.

poet tells of the uneasy truce which held the various emotions in check for the time being, and communal funeral ceremony for the fallen of both sides:

> A balefire was built and bright gold
> lifted from the hoard. The Here-Scyldings'
> best of warriors was ready on the pyre,
> by the balefire was clearly visible
> a bloody mailcoat, a swine all of gold,
> – an iron-hard boar – and many a nobleman
> doomed by his wounds; some of them fell in the slaughter.
> Then at Hnæf's balefire, Hildeburh bade
> the flames engulf her own son,
> burn his bones' covering, and be put on the pyre
> at his uncle's shoulder; the lady wailed,
> sorrowed with songs; the warriors' smoke rose up,
> the greatest burning of the slain wound up to the clouds,
> blazed before the burial mound; heads melted,
> wounds burst, then blood sprang forth,
> terrible bites on the body. Flame swallowed up all
> – greediest of spirits – of those whom war carried off
> from both sides of the people; their fame went forth.

(lines 1107–24)

> _ād wæs geæfned ond icge gold_
> _āhafen of horde. Here Scyldinga_
> _betst beadorinca wæs on bǣl gearu,_
> _æt þǣm āde wæs ēþgesȳne_
> _swātfāh syrce, swȳn ealgylden,_
> _eofer īrenheard, æþeling manig_
> _wundum āwyrded; sume on wæle crungon._
> _Hēt ðā Hildeburh æt Hnæfes āde_
> _hire selfre sunu sweoloðe befæstan,_
> _bānfatu bærnan ond on bǣl dōn,_
> _eame on eaxle; ides gnornode_
> _geōmrode giddum; gūðrēc āstāh,_
> _wand tō wolcnum wælfȳra mǣst_
> _hlynode for hlǣwe; hafelan multon,_
> _bengeato burston, ðonne blōd ætspranc_
> _lāðbite līces. Līg ealle forswealg_
> _gǣsta gīfrost þāra ðe þǣr gūð fornam_
> _bega folces; wæs hira blǣd scacen_

The funeral pyre was made ready and decorated with 'tributes' of gold from the royal hoard, and the warriors laid out in (or, at least, with) their armour. The 'swine' is presumed to be a boar-crested helmet of Benty Grange type. The public show of grief

209

by Hildeburh is doubly poignant since she is the mother of one of the warriors and sister of the other (who was thus the youth's *ēam*,[39] a very important relationship in Germanic society); the fact that they fought on opposing sides in the fight and both lost their lives meant that the normal way of dealing with such loss – turning it outward, into a hatred which would result in a vengeance killing – was not open to her.

A comparable set of funeral rites took place when the aged king Bēowulf himself fell in his last great fight against the fire-drake.

> Then the people of the Geats made ready for him
> a balefire on earth by no means feeble,
> hung about with helmets, with battle-shields,
> with bright mailcoats, as he had asked;
> [they] set down in the middle the renowned leader –
> those mourning heroes – their dear lord.
> Then, on the mountain, the greatest of balefires
> the warriors lit, the woodsmoke rose up
> dark above the flame, the swallowing fire
> wound about with weeping – the tossing wind subsided
> – until it had broken the house of bones,
> hot in its heart. With sorrowing minds
> [they] mourned the grief of the lord's death;
> such a sorrowful song, the former wife .....
>
> .....Heaven swallowed the smoke.
> Then the folk of the Wederas made
> a mound on the cliff, which was high and wide,
> widely seen by seafarers,
> and built within ten days
> the beacon of the battle-strong [man]; the men spared by flames
> made a wall, just as most honourably
> the cleverest men could devise it.
> Into the mound they put ring and jewels,
> all such trappings as previously from the hoard
> war-minded men had taken out;
> they abandoned the noble treasures, let the earth hold it,
> gold in the ground, where it still remains
> as useless to men as it formerly was.
> Then the battle-brave rode around the gravemound,
> noblemen's sons, twelve in all,
> they wished to lament their worries, mourn their king,
> wreak a song of words and speak about the man;

---

[39] See p.65 for more on the special relationship between maternal uncle and nephew.

they praised his chivalry, and his deeds of courage
they doughtily judged, as it is fitting
that a man praise his friendly-leader in words,
cherish his spirit, when he must be
led forth from his body.

(lines 3137–77)

Him ðā gegiredan Gēata lēode
ād on eorðan unwāclīcne
helmum behongen, hildebordum,
beorhtum byrnum, swā hē bēna wæs,
ālegdon ðā tōmiddes mærne þēoden
hæleð hīofende, hlāford lēofne.
Ongunnon þā on beorhe bælfȳra mǣst
wīgend weccan, wudurēc āstāh
sweart ofer swioðole, swōgende lēg
wōpe bewunden – windblond gelǣg
– ðþæt hē ðā bānhūs gebrocen hæfde,
hāt on hrēðre. Higum unrōte
mōdceare mǣndon mondryhtnes cwealm;
swylce giōmor gyd sīa geōmēowle
...... (lines too corrupt to interpret)
... Heofon rēce swealg.
Geworhton ðā Wedra lēode
hlǣw on hliðe se wæs hēah ond brād,
wǣglīðendum wīde gesȳne
ond betimbrodon on tȳn dagum
beadurōfes bēcn; bronda lāfe
wealle beworhton swā hyt weorðlīcost
foresnotre men findan mihton.
Hī on beorg dydon bēg ond siglu
eall swylce hyrsta, swylce on horde ǣr
nīðhēdige men genumen hæfdon;
forlēton eorla gestrēon eorðan healdan,
gold on grēote þǣr hit nū gēn lifað
eldum swā unnyt swā hit ǣror wæs.
Þā ymbe hlǣw riodan hildedēore
æþelinga bearn ealra twelfa,
woldon ceare cwīðan, kyning mǣnan,
wordgid wrecan ond ymb wer sprecan:
eahtodan eorlscipe ond his ellenweorc
duguðum dēmdon, swā hit gedēfe bið
þæt mon his winedryhten wordum herge,

211

ferhðum freoge, þonne hē forð scile
of lichaman læded weorðan.

Mounds such as the one raised over Bēowulf still survive from Anglo-Saxon times, some (though few now, and increasingly fewer) with their hoard of treasures still intact.[40] A parallel custom to mound-burial with a ship was that ascribed to King Haki in the Scandinavian *Ynglinga saga*:

> King Haki received so great a wound that he saw that his life's days could not continue much longer. Then he bade a warship which he owned be taken, and had it laden with dead men and weapons, and floated out to sea, and the steering-oar laid in position and the sail raised, and had flame set to tarwood and a funeral pyre made on the ship. A wind blew away from the land. Haki was then on the point of dying or already dead, when he was lain on the balefire. The ship sailed blazing out to sea, and that was much talked about long afterwards.

(*Ynglinga saga*, Chapter 27)

Haki konungr fekk svá stór sár at hann sá at hans lífdagar mundu eigi langir verða. Þá lét hann taka skeið er hann átti, ok lét hlaða dauðum mönnum ok vapnum, lét þá flytja út til hafs, ok leggja stýri í lag ok draga upp segl, en leggja eld í tyrvið ok gera bál á skipinu. Veðr stóð af landi. Haki var þá atkominn dauða eða dauðr, er hann var lagiðr á bálit. Sigldi skipit síðan loganda út í haf ok var þetta allfrægt lengi síðan.

Naturally, there is no archaeological evidence for such practices.

A gold- and weapon-bedecked balefire was appropriate in heathen times but Christian warriors had to hope for Christian burial. While it is likely enough that other Christian folk would release the bodies of the slain to relatives or to the church for normal burial rites, there was apparently no such moral duty on the heathens. It is related that the monks of Ely asked for the body of Byrhtnōþ after his death at Maldon, and managed to find his corpse but not his head which the vikings had taken away as a kind of grizzly trophy. That this is not mere mediaeval hagiographic fantasy is confirmed by the evidence of an eye-witness to the opening of his tomb in the 1700s, who found the bones of a large man, but no skull – and the collarbone had been split right through as if by a powerful blow. We also have the evidence that after Hastings, Ēadgyþ, Harold's mistress, had to be called in to identify his body, so violently had it been abused. The account of the death of King (later Saint) Edmund of the East Angles, related by Ælfric, tells how the king refused to bow down to the viking army

---

[40] The barrowground at Sutton Hoo is a case in point, with many of the mounds partly or completely robbed in previous centuries. The cemetery is interesting, quite apart from the magnificence of some of the finds made there, because of the great variety of burial practice in evidence – no two mounds seem to have held bodies disposed of in quite the same way, while there are ancillary burials of a fairly bizarre nature.

which effectively had control of eastern England at that time, and defied the Danes and their heathen gods even after they had taken him captive:

Then they shot at him with spears as if it were a game for them, until he was totally covered with their missiles like a hedgehog's bristles, just as St. Sebastian was. Then Ingvarr, the merciless seaman, saw that the noble king did not intend to forsake Christ, but rather with firm belief he called out to him continually; he bade him be beheaded and the heathens did so. While he was still calling to Christ, the heathens dragged that holy man away to the slaughter, and with a single blow struck off his head...

Hī scuton þā mid gafelucum swilces him tō gamenes tō oðþæt hē eall wæs besett mid heora scotungum swilce igles byrsta, swā swā Sebastianus wæs. Þā gesēah Hingwar, se ārlēase flotman, þæt se æþela cyning nolde Crīste wiðsacan ac mid ānrædum gelēafan hine æfre clypode, hēt hine þā behēafdian and þā hæðenan swā dydon. Betwux þām þe hē clypode tō Crīste þāgit, þā tugon þā hæþenan þone halgan tō slæge and mid ānum swencge slōgon him of þæt hēafod...

The death of this king is comparable to that of Ælfhēah (St. Alphege) at Greenwich, where he was first tortured, then, when he offered no more sport, he was quickly despatched by a powerful blow.[41]

It is appropriate that the funerals of Hnæf and Bēowulf are accompanied by expressions of grief which are said to take the form of 'songs' or 'verses' (OE *giedd*) since verse was the only form of record among the Germanic peoples, according to Tacitus. Rather than simply weeping and wailing at the funeral, in both instances there is a woman present who must mourn publicly the passing of the warrior(s), in a poetic declamation before the assembled folk. This is not like singing a hymn or favourite song at a modern funeral, however: the poem was probably composed on the spot, in the traditional Germanic alliterative verse metre, and was thus delivered 'off the cuff' but in the largely fixed and formal phrasing of the technique. By this means, the dead man's life was converted to song and consequently went to make up a (smaller or larger) part of the folklore and tradition of his people. It is not stretching the evidence too far to suggest that a poem like *The Battle of Maldon* represents a later descendant form of this practice, which had by then become a kind of 'occasional verse' for the commemoration of momentous events. There are a few other such verses, among them *The Battle of Brunanburh* and other short poetic sections of the *Chronicle* recording the deaths of kings and other notable matters. Here is how the capture of the Five Boroughs from the Danes is recorded under the year 942:

Here King Edmund, lord of the English,
protector of men, went into Mercia,
the brave accomplisher of deeds, as the Dore separates it,

---

[41] For Ælfhēah's death, see p.166.

the gate of the Whitewell and the Humber river,
the broad water which flows into the sea. Five strongholds,
Leicester and Lincoln
and Nottingham, as also Stamford
and Derby. The dales were formerly
subject by force to the Northmen,
in the fetters of the heathens
for a long time, until [he] set them loose again
because of his renown, the warriors' defender,
Edward's heir, Edmund the king.

Hēr Eadmund cyning Engla þēoden,
mæcgea mundbora Myrce geēode,
dyre dædfruma, swā Dor scadeþ
Hwitanwyllesgeat ond Humbra ēa,
brāda brimstrēam. Burga fife,
Ligoraceaster and Lincylene
and Snotingahām, swylce Stānford ēac
and Deoraby. Dæne wæran æror
under Norðmannum nȳde gebegde
on hæþenra hæfteclommum
lange þrage oþ hīe ālysde eft
for his weorþscipe wiggendra hlēo,
afera Eadweardes, Eadmund cyning.

Such formulaic phrasing is characteristic of Old English verse, which is seen here doing one of the jobs it was intended for – the recording (and glorification) of a military victory.

Afterword

The subject presented in this book, the background of the earliest English warriors, is one of courage and treachery, naked will and passion, cunning and careful consideration. It is, in some part, the story of the forging of a single nation from a patchwork of small groups, and it is the sum of the stories of men such as Ida and Hengest, Ælfred and Guthrum, Hnæf and Hæsten and Penda.

During the period covered, few great technological changes took place. No new weapons were introduced, even though the use of some was replaced by that of others in certain places and at certain times. The sword Harold Godwinesson wielded at Hastings was not identical to the one with which Offa of Angeln slew his two challengers, but it was not so very different in its manufacture or use that either man would have failed to wield the other's weapon across an interval of 600 years. (Compare the modern infantryman's standard weapons to those in use at Crécy to get some idea of the pace of development in the modern world.)

Yet the societies which the two kings were defending were very different. Offa's *Angelcynn*, 'English folk', were numbered in thousands, Harold's perhaps as many as two million. Both Harold's and Offa's people were a strong, outward-looking nation on the edge of a major waterway, wealthy and hard-working and not afraid to make their mark in the world. Offa's folk moved out into the crumbling ruins of the Roman-dominated lands to the south and west, and through various changes of fortune came to reclaim one corner of it from the rule of a distant colonial power, to bring the religious and political centres closer to the societies they served, and to re-focus ambitions on achievable targets nearer home. The 'free peasant warrior-farmers' of the English conquest are something of a misconception, but the society created by the early English in Britain held immense opportunities for the right men in the right place at the right time. Lowly origins and lack of pedigree were no barrier to advancement when the occasion demanded only courage, commitment, immense energy and a generous helping of luck. (The poets and storytellers could always trace the kindred back to Wōden if one's lineage looked embarrassing in later life.)

Harold's society, by contrast, was already heavily stratified, with many grades of unfree, partly-free, and largely-free men. It was one where life for most people was heavily regulated, with long lists of duties and services which had to be rendered, to both church and state. All important matters were written down, and the records could be used to the benefit of the establishment as required. His was a land in which bureaucracy was already flourishing, and in which changes in leadership meant increasingly little to the bulk of the population, whose aims were divorced from those of the king and his court. In short, later Anglo-Saxon England was not very different

215

from the Norman state which partially replaced it. Significantly, although William removed virtually all the native English nobility from their positions of power, he left the governmental machinery firmly in place – it was one of the main tools with which he would benefit from the newly-won land.

The nature of English warriorhood changed dramatically during the period covered, as did the society's view of heroism. The early Germanic material deals rather with situations than with personalities; the last stand of the *werod* around their fallen lord, held together not so much by respect for their leader as loyalty to each other, is a powerful and noble image, made the more tragic for the knowledge that the stated aims – vengeance for the lord and that immortality by proxy which comes from personal fame – were not guaranteed even by such terrible and desperate acts of heroism. Their only satisfaction was that of a clear conscience, of having refused to be cowed into surrender, even in the face of death; they might have lost but they were not beaten, because they refused to submit to the last. Yet the northern poets loved these awful, anxious, soul-rending situations in which a man could not emerge with both honour and life; they loved the bitter, overwhelming, sad and desperate inevitability of failure even in victory.

The Christian church tapped into this respect for *wyrd* 'the course of events, the way of the world' and transformed it into a new brand of heroism – not the physical and emotional courage of the Germanic tragic warrior-hero, but the moral courage of the religious 'soldiers of Christ' who also faced up to overwhelming forces with nothing more than an unbending will and a determination to emulate the founders of the church.

These two views of heroism were not irreconcilable in principle, although in practice men who felt spiritually unrewarded by the battlefield often turned to the fight against the Devil in later life. The mental rearrangement which the introduction of the Christian faith caused was so thorough that we can only dimly perceive how such longings might have been satisfied in the society in heathen times. The elder gods did not insist on total and unconditional belief from their followers; they were satisfied if a man needing their help brought gifts to buy their favours, much as he might go about winning over a powerful human ally. And like human beings, they might decide to help this or that man for reasons of their own quite unconnected with how devoted or sincere he was.

At no time in its history was the English nation ever able to support huge field armies of the kind available to contemporaries such as Charlemagne. Winning out by the brutal arithmetic of 'weight of numbers' was not an option for the early English in either their early, expansive role against the Romano-British, or their later defensive one against the successive generations of invasive Scandinavians. It follows, then, that where quantity was not available, quality must have been crucial to success. That the quality of English arms and men was sufficient to the task was evidently often true – often enough for England to have spread from small footholds on the east coast to cover virtually the entire lowland area of Britain, to have almost lost political control more than once but each time to have won it back. And, finally, when forced to play a long and tiresome game of watching and waiting, then instant mobilization, the English forces under Harold were more than a match for the best that Scandinavia or Normandy could throw at them; sadly, though, not when obliged to fight both enemies at opposite ends of the country within days of each other. It is doubtful that any European army could have fought Harold's last campaign and emerged victorious; certainly no other of comparable size could have hoped to do more than he did.

And now the reputations those warriors eagerly sought and laid down their lives earning are all but lost. The Conquest destroyed much of the best of early English life; the Reformation, and especially the anti-papist zeal of the rising middle classes, destroyed much more. There was wholesale destruction of records which had been left undisturbed for centuries: commemorative landmarks such as village crosses were thrown down as idolatrous monuments, books and manuscripts were torn apart and burnt, or sold by the shipload for 'recycling'. The nation had not only turned its back on its pre-Conquest past, it seems it had actively set out to expunge all record of it. Only a handful of collectors and antiquaries had any idea of English literature and material culture from pre-Conquest times, and they most often had only the dimmest awareness of what might be the significance of the relics and manuscripts they acquired. The *Beowulf* manuscript came close to destruction in a disastrous, accidental fire in 1731; had it not been copied some short while before the original manuscript was burnt, *The Battle of Maldon* would now be unrecoverable – not only would we know next to nothing of the battle, its circumstances and significance (only a handful of other references to the events of 991 exist), but there would actually be no surviving example of 'heroic' verse in Old English from the later period – we would assume, in all likelihood, that martial poetry died out with the absorption of the vikings into England and its 'new' Christian culture after the Benedictine Reform.

A poem like *Maldon* then, should be the more precious since the handful of English warriors mentioned therein must stand as the sole representatives of their kind, almost the only pre-Conquest fighters of other than royal stock whose names are known, the Anglo-Saxons' own 'Tommy Atkins' figures, if you will, symbolic of a particular struggle and the folk of the period in which it took place.

For this reason, if for no other, it is important to keep alive the great wealth of Old English literature and learning, and to continue studying, recording and publishing finds from cemeteries and grave mounds, so that what little remains may be understood as completely as possible and treasured that much more. Many of these early English warriors, farmers and nobles had precious little dignity in life, or impact on the world about them beyond the immediate – we owe it to them and to ourselves to do all we can to understand them, their society and their times.

Appendix I

The Battle of Brunanburh

Here King Athelstan – the lord of heroes,
the warrior's ring-giver, and his brother likewise,
Atheling Edmund – lifelong glory
4   they won in the fray with swords' edges
around *Brunaburh*. They clove the shieldwall,
hammers' leavings[1] hewed the war-linden
– the scions of Edward as it was natural for them
8   from their ancestry, that in warfare they often
protected the land against every foe,
their hoard and homes. The attackers fell,
the folk of the Scots and the seafarers
12   dropped, doomed, the field streamed
with blood of men, from when the sun
in the morning – the splendid star
– glided over the lands – bright candle of God,
16   the everlasting Lord – until that noble creation
sank to its rest. There many a man lay
struck down by spears – the man from the north,
shot down through his shield, likewise the Scot too,
20   weary, sated with war. Forward, the West Saxons
the whole day long in mounted troops
stayed on the track of the hated peoples,
hewed the fugitive foes cruelly from behind
24   with mill-sharpened[2] swords. The Mercians did not refuse
hard hand-play to any of the fighters
who across the mingling waves with Anlaf,
sought out the land on a ship's bottom,
28   came fated to the fight. Lay still five
young kings on the battlefield,
slain with swords, likewise seven
of Anlaf's *jarls*, untold raiders,
32   seamen and Scots. There was put to flight
the Northmen's ruler, forced by need
to the ship's keel with a small bodyguard;
the vessel rushed on the sea, the king sped off
36   on the dark deeps, he saved his life.
Thus there the old man also came with his fleeing men
north to his homeland, Constantine,

The Battle of Brunanburh

Hēr Æþelstān cyning, eorla dryhten,
beorna bēahgifa and his brōþor ēac,
ēadmund æþeling, ealdorlangne tīr
4   geslōgon æt sæcce sweorda ecgum
ymbe Brunanburh. Bordweal clufan,
hēowan heaþolinde hamora lāfan,
afaran ēeadweardes swā him geæþele wæs
8   from cnēomægum þæt hī æt campe oft
wiþ lāþra gehwæne land ealgodon,
hord and hāmas. Hettend crungun,
Sceottta lēoda and scipflotan
12   fæge fēollan, feld dænnede
secga swāte siðþan sunne ūp
on morgentīd, mǣre tungol,
glād ofer grundas, godes condel beorht,
16   ēces drihtnes, oð sīo æþele gesceaft
sāh tō setle. Þǣr læg secg mænig
gārum āgēted, guma norþerna
ofer scild scoten swilce Scittisc ēac
20   wērig, wīges sæd. Wesseaxe forð
ondlongne dæg ēoredcīstum
on lāst legdun lāþum þēodum,
hēowan herefēman hindan þearle
24   mēcum mylenscearpan. Myrce ne wyrndon
heardes hondplegan hæleþa nānum
þǣra þe mid Anlāfe ofer ǣra gebland
on līdes bōsme land gesōhtun,
28   fæge tō gefeohte. Fife lægun
on þām campstede cyningas giunge,
sweordum āswefede, swilce seofene ēac
eorlas Anlāfes unrīm heriges,
32   flotan and Scotta. Þǣr geflēmed wearð
Norðmanna bregu, nēde gebēded,
tō līdes stefne lītle werode;
crēad cnear on flot, cyning ūt gewāt
36   on fealene flōd, feorh generede.
Swilce þǣr ēac se froda mid flēame cōm
on his cȳþþe norð Costontīnus

grey-haired fighter, he had no cause to gloat
40   at the closing-together of men; he was bereft of his kinsmen,
of his loved ones felled on the battlefield,
slain in strife and left his son behind
in the place of slaughter, laid low with wounds,
44   that youngster in war. He had no need to boast
of the sword-clash, that grizzled chief,
old opponent – no more had Anlaf;
they had no cause to laugh with the remnant of their forces,
48   that they were the better men in battle-work,
on the field of combat, in clash of banners,
meeting of spears, encounter of warriors,
strife of weapons – when on the slaughter-field
52   they played[3] with Edward's heirs.
The Northmen went in nailed ships,
the bloodied survivors of spears, on Dingsmere,
seeking Dublin across the deep water,
56   in sad mood back to Ireland.
Thus both the brothers together,
king and atheling sought out their native soil,
the land of the West Saxons, exultant in war.
60   Behind them they left the corpses to be shared
by the dark-coated one – the black raven
with curving beak – and the grey-coated one,
the eagle with white tail, the carrion to be enjoyed
64   by the greedy hawk of war and the grey beast,
the wolf in the wood. A greater slaughter was not
ever yet in this island
slain by an army before this
68   with sword's blades – as books tell us,
ancient scribes – since here from the east
the Angles and Saxons came over
across the broad sea – they sought Britain,
72   the proud war-makers overcame the Welsh,
the keen heroes won a homeland.   (ASC 'A', s.a.937)

---

[1] A poetic image to describe the smith's product, i.e. the sword.
[2] Although mechanization of industrial processes was not common in Anglo-Saxon times, water-driven trip hammers and the like do seem to have been in use. The reference here seems to be to a grinding-wheel powered by a watermill.
[3] Warfare is often described as "play" (OE *plega*), the original meaning of which seems to have been "contention, striving" hence "competition".

hār hilderinc, hrēman ne þorfte
40 mæca gemanan, hē wæs his mæga sceard
frēonda gefylled on folcstede,
beslagen æt sæcce and his sunu forlēt
on wælstōwe wunden forgrunden,
44 giiungne æt gūðe. Gelpan ne þorfte
beorn blandenfeax bilgeslihtes,
eald inwidda, ne Anlāf þȳ mā;
mid heora herelāfum hlehhan ne þorftun
48 þæt hēo beaduweorca beteran wurdun
on campstede cumbolgehnastes,
gārmittinge, gumena gemōtes,
wǣpengewrixles, þæs hī on wælfelda
52 wiþ ēadweardes afaran plegodan.
Gewitan him þā Norþmen nægledcnearrum,
drēorig daraða lāf on Dinges mere
ofer dēop wæter Difelin sēcan,
56 eft Īraland ǣwiscmōde.
Swilce þā gebrōþer bēgen ætsamne,
cyning and æþeling cȳþþe sōhton,
Wesseaxna land wīges hrēmige.
60 Lētan him behindan hrǣw bryttian
saluwigpādan þone sweartan hræfn
hyrnednebban and þane hasewanpādan
earn æftan hwīt, ǣses brūcan
64 grǣdigne gūðhafoc and þæt grǣge dēor
wulf on wealde. Ne wearð wæl māre
on þis eiglande ǣfre gieta
folces gefylled beforan þissum
68 sweordes ecgum þæs þe ūs secgaþ bēc,
ealde ūðwitan, siþþan ēastan hider
Engle and Seaxe ūp becōman
ofer brād brimu Brytene sōhtan,
72 wlance wīgsmiþas, Wealas ofercōman,
earlas ārhwate eard begēatan.

223

Appendix II

The Battle of Finnsburh

"... gables are burning."[1]
Hnæf shouted, the king young in war:
"Neither is it dawning from the east, nor does a dragon fly here
4 nor are the gables of this hall burning;
rather murderous men are bringing forward
their splendid armaments. The birds are singing
the greycoated [wolf] is baying; the war-rod resounds,
8 shield responds to shaft. Now this moon shines
wavering beneath the clouds, now deeds of woe arise
which will carry out this hatred within a people.
But waken now, my warriors!
12 Don your mailcoats, take thought of courage,
strive in the battle-line, be valiant!"
Then arose from his bed many a great-hearted,
gold-bedecked thane, girded on his sword,
16 then to the doors went the noble warriors,
Sigeferð and Eaha, drew their swords,
and at the other doors Ordlāf and Gūþlāf;
and Hengest himself followed in their path.
20 Still Gūðere advised Gārulf
that for the first time so dear a life as his
should not bear armour to the hall's door
now a harsh act of violence would take it away;
24 but he asked openly in front of all,
the brave-hearted hero, who held the door.
"Sigeferþ is my name" he said "I am a lord of the Secgan,
a widely-known adventurer; many woes have I undergone,
28 hard battles; it is now fixed for you,
whatever [fate] you wish to seek from me."
Then there was the roar of slaughter in the hall:
The ridged shield in the hands of brave men had to
32 break apart, the body's defence; the stronghold's floor resounded
until Garulf fell in the fighting,
first of all among land-dwellers,
Gūðulf's son, and many good men about him,
36 the corpses of the swift ones. The raven hovered,
drab and dark brown. The light of swords rose up
as if all Finnesburg were afire.

The Battle of Finnsburh

"... hornas byrnað"
Hnæf hlēoþrode heaþogeong cyning:
"Ne ðis ne dagað ēastan ne hēr draca ne flēogeð
4 *ne hēr ðisse healle hornas ne byrnað;*
ac hēr forþ berað feorhgenīðlan
fyrdsearufūslīc. Fugelas singað,
gylleð grǣghāma, gūðwudu hlynneð,
8 *scyld scefte oncwyð. Nū scȳneð þes mōna*
waðol under wolcnum, nū ārīsað wēadǣda
ðe ðisne folces nīð fremman willað.
Ac onwācnigeað nū wīgend mīne!
12 *Habbað ēowre hlencan, hicgeaþ on ellen,*
þindað on orde, wesað ōnmōde!"
Ðā ārās of ræste rūmheort mænig
goldhladen ðegn, gyrde hine his swurde
16 *ðā tō dura ēodon drihtlīce cempan,*
Sigeferð and Eaha, hyra sword getugon
ond æt ōþrum durum Ordlāf and Gūþlāf
and Hengest sylf hweraf him on lāste.
20 *Ðā gyt Gārulfe Gūðere styrde*
ðæt hē swā frēolīc feorh forman sīþe
tō ðǣre healle durum hyrsta ne bǣre
nū hyt nīþa heard ānyman wolde
24 *ac hē frægn ofer eal undearninga,*
dēormōd hæleþ, hwā ðā duru heolde.
"Sigeferþ is mīn nama" cweþ hē "ic eom Secgena lēod,
wreccea wīde cūð, fæla ic wēana gebād
28 *heardra hilda; þē is gyt hēr witod*
swæþer ðū sylf tō mē sēcean wylle."
Ðā wæs on healle wælslihta gehlyn,
sceolde celæs bord cēnum on handa
32 *bānhelm berstan, buruhðelu dynede*
oð æt ðǣre gūðe Gārulf gecrang
ealra ǣrest eorðbūendra,
Gūðulfes sunu ymbe hyne gōdra fæla,
36 *hwearflīcra hrǣw. Hrǣfen wandrode*
sweart ond sealobrūn. Swurdlēoma stōd
swylce eal Finnesburuh fȳrenu wǣre.

227

I have never heard in men's warring that more worthily
40   did sixty victorious fighters bear themselves better,
nor ever did henchmen better repay
their shining mead, hard companions,
than [when] his bodyguard repaid Hnæf.
44   They fought for five days so that none of them fell
the noble comrades, but they held the doors.
Then a wounded warrior went away,
said that his mailcoat was broken,
48   his steadfast warcoat, and his helm was split,
when the army's leader straightaway asked him
how the warriors were bearing their wounds
or which of the youths....

---

[1] Sadly this line is almost entirely missing, but from the context it is clear that the speaker has seen the glint of light outside the hall and suggested three possible explanations for this: – dawn breaking, a fire-breathing dragon or the hall's roof afire. These possibilities are rejected in turn by Hnæf who correctly foresees the glint of foemen's weapons.

> Ne gefrægn ic wurþlīcor æt wera hilde
40   sixtig sigebeorna sēl gebǣran
> ne nǣfre swānas sēl forgyldan
> hwītne medo, heardgesteallan,
> ðonne Hnæfe guldan his hægstealdas.
44   Hig fuhton fīf dagas swā hyra nān ne fēol
> drihtgesīða ac hig ðā duru hēoldon.
> Ðā gewāt him wund hæleð on wǣg gangan,
> sægde þæt his byrne ābrocen wǣre,
48   heresceorp unhrōr and ēac wæs his helm ðyrel
> ðā hē sōna frægn folces hyrde
> hū ðā wīgend hyra wunda genǣson
> oððe hwæðer ðǣra hȳssa....

229

Appendix III

The Battle of Maldon

... should be broken.
He then bade each of the warriors drive away his horse,
send it far away and go forwards,
4   think of his hands' work, and be of good heart.
Then Offa's kinsman first found out
that the *eorl* would not stand for slackness;
he let fly from his hand his dear one then,
8   – his hawk – to the woods, and strode to the fight.
From that one could tell that the youth would not
weaken in the warfare when he took to his weapons.
Eadric wished also to follow his leader,
12   his lord, to the battle; he began to bear
his spear to the fray. He had a firm resolve
while with his hands he could yet hold
his shield and broad sword; he fulfilled his vow
16   when he had to fight before his lord.
Then Byrhtnōð began to draw up the warriors there.
He rode along and advised them, showed the men
how they ought to stand and keep their place
20   and bade that they held their shields in the right way,
firm with their fists, and that they should have no fear.
When he had rightly arrayed the *folc*
he then alighted among the men dearest to him
24   where he knew his hearthband were most steadfast.
Then at the shore stood, calling out sternly,
the vikings' messenger: he uttered words,
he who threateningly delivered the seafarers'
28   message to the *eorl* where he stood on the bank:
"Bold seamen sent me to you,
bade me tell you that you may quickly send
rings for your protection, and it is better for you
32   that you buy off his clash of spears with your tribute
than that we should share in so hard a battle.
We need not destroy each other if you are wealthy enough:
in return for the gold we wish to make a firm peace.
36   If you, who are most powerful here, so decide
that you wish to free your folk by ransom,
give to the seamen – by their own judgement –

The Battle of Maldon

...brocen wurde.
Hēt þā hyssa hwæne hors forlǣtan,
feor āfȳsan and forð gangan,
4   hicgan tō handum and t[ō] hige gōdum.
Þ[ā] þæt Offan mǣg ǣrest onfunde
þæt se eorl nolde yrhðo geþolian,
hē lēt him þā of handon lēofne flēogan
8   hafoc wið þæs holtes, and tō þǣre hilde stōp;
be þām man mihte oncnāwan þæt se cniht nolde
wācian æt [þ]ā m w[ī]g e þā hē tō wǣpnum fēng.
Eac him wolde Eadrīc his ealdre gelǣstan,
12   frēan tō gefeohte: ongan þā forð beran
gār tō gūþe – hē hæfde gōd geþanc
þā hwīle þe hē mid handum healdan mihte
bord and brād swurd; bēot hē gelǣste
16   þa hē ætforan his frēan feohtan sceolde.
Ðā þǣr Byrhtnōð ongan beornas trymian:
rād and rǣdde, rincum tǣhte
hū hī sceoldon standan and þone stede healdan,
20   and bæd þæt hyra randan rihte hēoldon
fæste mid folman, and ne forhtedon nā.
Þā hē hæfde þæt folc fægere getrymmed,
hē līhte þā mid lēodon þǣr him lēofost wæs
24   þǣr hē his heorðwerod holdost wiste.
Þā stōd on stæðe, stīðlīce clypode
Wīcinga ār, wordum mǣlde.
Sē on bēot ābēadbrimlīþendra
28   ǣrænde tō þām eorle þǣr hē on ōfre stōd:
«Mē sendon tō þē sǣmen snelle,
hēton ðē secgan þæt þū mōst sendan raðe
bēagas wið gebeorge, and ēow betere is
32   þæt gē þisne gārrǣs mid gafole forgyldon
þon wē swā hearde [hi]lde dǣlon.
Ne þurfe wē ūs spillan gif gē spēdaþ tō þām:
wē willað wið þām golde grið fæstnian;
36   gyf þū þat gerǣdest, þe hēr rīcost eart,
þæt þū þine lēoda lȳsan wille,
syllan sǣmannum on hyra sylfra dōm

wealth in exchange for friendship and accept peace with us,
40   then with that money we mean to go to our ships,
put out to sea and leave you in peace."
Byrhtnōð spoke out – he raised his shield
and shook his slender spear – he uttered words,
44   angry and unbending he gave him his answer:
"Do you hear, seafarer, what this people says?
They want to send you spears as payment,
deadly point and ancient sword,
48   a *heriot* which will be of no use to you in battle.
Seamen's messenger – take this message back,
say to your people much more unwelcome tidings:
that here stands an *eorl* of no ill-fame with his wartroop
52   who means to defend this homeland,
Æþelred's kingdom, my lord's
people and territory. Fall they must
in battle, the heathens – it seems too shameful to me
56   that you should go to your ships with our wealth
unfought for now that thus far here
you have penetrated our land.
Not so easily should you come by riches –
60   point and edge should first decide the matter between us
– grim warplay – before we give tribute."
He bade shields be raised then and warriors go forward
so that they all stood on the riverbank.
64   Because of the water each troop could not reach the other.
The river came flowing there after the ebb-tide,
the waterways locked together. It seemed to them too long
until they could bring their spears together.
68   They stood about the Pant's stream in their war-might,
the East Saxon *ord* and the viking *here*;
none on either side could harm the others
except those who fell through the arrow's flight.
72   The waters drove outwards; the seamen stood ready,
many vikings eager for fighting.
The heroes' protector then bade the bridge be held
by a war-hardened warrior called Wulfstān,
76   a bold man like his kinsmen – he was Cēola's son –
who killed with his spear the first man
who most bravely stepped onto the bridge.
With Wulfstān stood undaunted fighters there,

feoh wið freode and niman frið æt ūs,
40 wē willaþ mid þām sceattum ūs tō scype gangan,
    on flot fēran and ēow friþes healdan.»
    Byrhtnōð maþelode, bord hafenode,
    wand wācne æsc, wordum mǣlde,
44 yrre and ānrǣd āg eaf him andsware:
    «Gehȳrst þū sǣlida, hwæt þis folc segeð?
    Hī willað ēow tō gafole gāras syllan,
    ǣttrynne ord and ealde swurd,
48 þā heregeatu þe ēow æt hilde ne dēah!
    Brimmanna boda, ābēod eft ongēan,
    sege þīnum lēodum miccle lāþre spell,
    þæt hēr stynt unforcūð eorl mid his werode
52 þe wile gealgean ēþel þysne,
    Æþelredes eard, ealdres mīnes
    folc and foldan. Feallan sceolon
    hǣþene æt hilde! Tō hēanlic mē þinceð
56 þæt gē mid ūrum sceattum tō scype gangon
    unbefohtene nū gē þus feor hider
    on ūrne eard in becōmon;
    ne sceole ge swā sōfte sinc gegangan:
60 ūs sceal ord and ecg ǣr gesēman,
    grim gūðplega, ǣr [w]ē gofol syllon!»
    Hēt þā bord beran, beornas gangan
    þæt hī on þām ēasteðe ealle stōdon.
64 Ne mihte þǣr for wætere werod tō þām ōðrum
    þǣr cōm flōwende flōd æfter ebban;
    lucon lagustrēamas; tō lang hit him þūhte
    hwænne hī tōgædere gāras bēron.
68 Hī þǣr Pantan strēam mid prasse bestōdon,
    Eastseaxena ord and se æschere;
    ne mihte hyra ǣnig ōþrum derian
    būton hwā þurh flānes flyht fyl genāme.
72 Se flōd ūt gewāt – þā flotan stōdon gearowe,
    Wīcinga fela, wīges georne.
    Hēt þā hæleða hlēo healdan þā bricge
    wigan wīgheardne sē wæs hāten Wulfstān,
76 cāfne mid his cynne; þæt wæs Cēolan sunu
    þe ðone forman man mid his francan ofscēat
    þe þǣr baldlīcost on þā bricge stōp.
    Þǣr stōdon mid Wulfstāne wigan unforhte,

80   Ælfhere and Maccus – two bold men
who did not mean to flee from the ford
but rather they steadfastly fought with their foes
for as long as they could wield their weapons.

84   When they recognised and clearly saw
that the bridge-keepers they found there were fierce,
the hated strangers began to use guile:
they proposed that they should be allowed to come over,

88   to cross the ford and to line up the infantry.
Then the eorl in his over-confidence began
to allow too much land to that loathsome folk;
he started to call out then over the cold water,

92   the son of Byrhtelm – the warriors listened:
"Now room has been made for you. Come quickly to us,
men to the fight. Only God knows
to whom shall fall control of this slaughter-place."

96   The war-wolves waded, did not worry about water,
the viking troop went west over the Pant,
over the bright stream they carried their shields,
the seamen bore the lindenwood to land.

100   Against the fierce men there stood ready
Byrhtnōþ and his warriors. With shields he bade
the war-wall be formed and the troop hold
firm against the foe. Battle then was nigh,

104   glory in fighting: the time had come
when doomed men were to fall there.
A shout went up in that place. Ravens circled round,
the eagle, carrion-eager; turmoil was on earth.

108   They sent file-hardened spears from their fists,
grimly-ground darts flying forth;
bows were busy, shield clashed with point.
Bitter was the rush of war; warriors fell

112   on both sides, youths lay still.
Wulfmær was wounded: he chose death in battle,
the kinsman of Byrhtnōþ – with swords he was
cruelly cut down – his sister's son.

116   A similar reward was given to the vikings then:
I heard that Eadweard struck one
mightily with his sword – he did not hold back the blow –
so that the doomed warrior fell at his feet;

120   for that his lord thanked him,

80   *Ælfere and Maccus, mōdige twēgen,*
þā noldon æt þām forda flēam gewyrcan,
ac hī fæstlīce wið ðā fӯnd weredon
þā hwīle þe hī wǣpna wealdan mōston

84   *Þā hī þæt ongēaton and georne gesāwon*
þæt hī þǣr bricgweardas bitere fundon,
ongunnon lytegian þā lāðe gystas,
bǣdon þæt hī upgangan āgan mōston,

88   *ofer þone ford faran, fēþan lǣdan.*
Ðā se eorl ongan for his ofermōde
ālӯfan landes tō fela lāþere ðēode;
ongan ceallian þā ofer cald wæter

92   *Byrhtelmes bearn; beornas gehlyston:*
«Nū ēow is gerӯmed, gāð ricene tō ūs,
guman tō gūþe! God āna wāt
hwā þǣre wælstōwe wealdan mōte.»

96   *Wōdon þā wælwulfas, for wætere ne murnon,*
Wicinga werod west ofer Pantan
ofer scir wæter scyldas wēgon;
lidmen tō lande linde bǣron.

100   *þǣr ongēan gramum gearowe stōdon*
Byrhtnōð mid beornum: hē mid bordum hēt
wyrcan þone wihagan and þæt werod healdan
fæste wið fēondum. Þā wæs f[e]ohte nēh,

104   *tir æt getohte; wæs sēo tid cumen*
þæt þǣr fǣge men feallan sceoldon.
Þǣr wearð hrēam āhafen, hremmas wundon,
earn ǣses georn – wæs on eorþan cyrm!

108   *Hī lēton þā of folman fēolhearde speru*
[grimme] gegrundene gāras flēogan.
Bogan wǣron bysige; bord ord onfēng;
biter wæs se beadurǣs. Beornas fēollon,

112   *on gehwæðere hand hyssas lāgon.*
Wund wear[ð] Wulfmǣr, wælræste gecēas;
Byrhtnōðes mǣg, hē mid billum wearð,
his swustersunu, swiðe forhēawen.

116   *Þǣr wær[ð] Wicingum wiþerlēan āgyfen:*
gehӯrde ic þæt Eadweard ānne slōge
swiðe mid his swurde – swenges ne wyrnde –
þæt him æt fōtum fēoll fǣge cempa.

120   *Þæs him his ðēoden þanc gesǣde*

the *būrþēn* [household officer], when he had the chance.
So they stood fast, those firm-minded
warriors in battle – they eagerly sought to see

124 who with his spearhead could first
win the life from a doomed man,
a beweaponed warrior. The slain fell to the ground.
They stood firm – Byrhtnōþ commanded them,

128 bade each man turn his thoughts to the struggle
who meant to win a good name against the Danes.
A war-hard viking then stepped up, raised his weapon
and shield for protection and strode forward towards the warrior.

132 Just as firmly went the *eorl* to the *ceorl*,
each of them meant harm to the other.
Then the seaman sent a southern spear
so that the lord of warriors was wounded;

136 he shoved with his shield so the shaft shattered
and the spear shivered so that it sprang away.
The warrior became angry – with his spear he stabbed
the proud viking who had wounded him;

140 the champion was experienced: he let his *franca* bite
through the youth's neck – his hand guided it
so that he took the life of his deadly attacker,
another he hastily hurled

144 so the byrnie burst apart – he was wounded in his breast
through the mailcoat, in his heart there lodged
the deadly point. The *eorl* was the gladder at this,
then the bold man laughed, thanked God

148 for the day's work which the Lord allowed him.
Just then a certain *dreng* sent a dart from his hand,
flying from his fist so that it sped forth
through Æþelred's noble thane.

152 At his side stood a boy, not yet fully grown,
a youth in warfare who most hastily
drew the bloody spear from the warrior
– that was Wulfmǣr the young, Wulfstān's son –

156 he sent the hardened spear back again,
the point pierced so that he lay dead
who had severely harmed the lord.
Then a mail-clad warrior went to the *eorl*,

160 he meant to take off the nobleman's rings,
his war-gear and jewels and patterned sword.

238

þām būrþene þā hē byre hæfde.
Swā stemnetton stiðhicgende
hysas æt hilde, hogodon georne

124   hwā þær mid orde ærost mihte
on fægean men feorh gewinnan,
wigan mid wǣpnum. Wæl fēol on eorðan;
stōdon stædefæste. Stihte hī Byrhtnōð,

128   bæd þæt hyssa gehwylc hogode tō wīge
þe on Denon wolde dōm gefeohtan.
Wōd þā wīges heard, wǣpen ūp āhōf,
bord tō gebeorge, and wið þæs beornes stōp;

132   ēode swā ānrǣd eorl tō þām ceorl,
ǣgþer hyra ōðrum yfeles hogode
Sende ðā se sǣrinc sūþerne gār
þæt gewundod wearð wigena hlāford:

136   hē scēaf þā mid ðām scylde, þæt se sceaft tōbærst
and þæt spere sprengde þæt hit sprang ongēan.
Gegremod wearð se gūðrinc: hē mid gāre stang
wlancne Wicing þe him þā wunde forgeaf.

140   Frōd wæs se fyrdrinc: hē lēt his francan wadan
þurh ðæs hysses hals – hand wisode
þæt hē on þām fǣrsceaðan feorh gerǣhte.
Ðā hē ōþerne ofstlīce scēat

144   þæt sēo byrne tōbærst: hē wæs on brēostum wund
þurh ðā hringlocan; him æt heortan stōd
ǣtterne ord. Se eorl wæs þē blīþra:
hlōh þā mōdi man, sǣde Metode þanc

148   ðæs dægweorces þe him Drihten forgeaf.
Forlēt þā drenga sum daroð of handa
flēogan of folman þæt sē tō forð gewāt
þurh ðone æþelan Æþelredes þegen.

152   Him be healfe stōd hyse unweaxen,
cniht on gecampe: sē full cāflīce
brǣd of þām beorne blōdigne gār:
Wulfstānes bearn, Wulfmǣr se geonga,

156   forlēt forheardne faran eft ongēan;
ord in gewōd þæt sē on eorþan læg
þe his þēoden ǣr þearle gerǣhte.
Ēode þā gesyrwed secg tō þām eorle:

160   hē wolde þæs beornes bēagas gefecgan,
rēaf and hringas and gerēnod swurd. .

Byrhtnōþ drew his sword from the sheath,
broad and bright-edged, and struck at his byrnie.
164   One of the seafarers was too quick, hindered him
when he wounded the *eorl*'s arm.
The golden-hilted sword fell to the earth:
nor could he hold the hard glaive,
168   wield the weapon. Yet he uttered words
the grey-haired warrior – he emboldened the fighters –
bade them go forwards, those good comrades.
He could no longer stand firm on his feet,
172   he looked to the heavens ...
"I thank you, Folk-ruler,
for all those joys which I have experienced in life.
Gentle Lord, I now have greatest need
176   that you grant mercy to my spirit,
so that my soul may journey to you,
Lord of Angels, and into your power
travel in peace. I beg of you
180   that Hell's harmful beings may not take it from here."
Then the heathen warriors cut him down
and both the fighters who stood beside him;
Ælfnōþ and Wulfmǣr both lay still,
184   alongside their lord they gave up their lives.
Those who no longer wished to be there then turned from the fight:
Odda's sons were first in flight from there,
Godric was away from the fray and abandoned the good man
188   who often in the past had given him a horse;
he leapt onto the steed – which his lord had owned –
in its trappings, which it was wrong to do;
and with him his brothers both ran –
192   Godwine and Godwīg – they did not care for fighting
but went away from the battle and sought the woods,
fled to refuge and saved their lives,
and more of the men than was in any way fitting
196   if they had taken thought of all the rewards
which he had bestowed upon them for their benefit.
Offa had said to him earlier that day
at the speaking-place when he held a meeting,
200   that many there spoke bravely
who later would not last out in the strife.
That folk's leader had then fallen,

Ðā Byrhtnōð brǣd bill of scēðe,
brād and brūneccg and on þā byrnan slōh.

164 Tō raþe hine gelette lidmanna sum
þā hē þæs eorles earm āmyrde.
Fēoll þā tō foldan fealohilte swurd,
ne mihte hē gehealdan heardne mēce,

168 wǣpnes wealdan. Þā gȳt þæt word gecwæð
hār hilderinc: hyssas bylde,
bæd gangan forð gōde geferan.
Ne mihte þā on fōtum leng fæste gest[a]ndan.

172 Hē tō heofenum wlāt, [hæleð gemǣlde:]
«Geþance þē, ðēoda Waldend,
ealra þǣra wynna þe ic on worulde gebād.
Nū ic āh, milde Metod, mǣste þearfe

176 þæt þū minum gāste gōdes geunne,
þæt min sawul tō ðē siðian mōte
on þin geweald, Þēoden engla,
mid friþe ferian. Ic eom frymdi tō þē

180 þæt hī helsceaðan hȳnan ne mōton!»
Ðā hine hēowon hǣðene scealcas,
and bēgen þā beornas þe him big stōdon,
Ælfnōð and Wulmǣr, [þæt hī on wæle] lāgon

184 ðā onemn hyra frēan feorh gesealdon.
Hī bugon þā fram beaduwe þe þǣr bēon noldon!
Þǣr wurdon Oddan bearn ǣrest on flēame,
Godrīc fram gūþe, and þone gōdan forlēt

188 þe him mænigne oft mēar gesealde;
hē gehlēop þone eoh þe āhte his hlāford,
on þām gerǣdum þe hit riht ne wæs.
And his brōðru mid himbēgen ær[n]don,

192 God[w]ine and Godwīg; gūþe ne gȳmdon
ac wendon fram þām wige and þone wudu sōhton;
flugon on þæt fæsten and hyra fēore burgon,
and manna mā þonne hitǣ nig mǣð wǣre,

196 gyf hī þā geearnunga ealle gemundon
þe hē him tō duguþe gedōn hæfde.
Swā him Offa on dæg ǣr āsǣde
on þām meþelstede þā hē gemōt hæfde,

200 þæt þǣr mōdelīce manega sprǣcon
þe eft æt þ[ea]r[f]e þolian noldon.
Ðā wearð āfeallen þæs folces ealdor,

241

Æþelred's warrior. They could all see
204 – the hearth-companions – that their leader was down.
Forward from there went the proud thanes,
the undaunted men eagerly made haste;
they all wished for one of these two things:
208 to give up their lives or to avenge the dear man.
So Ælfric's son egged them forward,
a warrior young in winters, he uttered a speech,
spoke of courage, Ælfwine said:
212 "Remember those words which we often spoke over our mead
when we put up boasts at the bench
about hard strife, we heroes in the hall:
now whoever is brave may prove it.
216 I wish to make my ancestry known to all:
that I come from a great family among the Mercians.
My grandfather was called Ealhelm,
a wise *ealdormann*, lucky in this world.
220 Thanes in the land shall not be able to blame me,
or say that I wished to leave this *fyrd*,
to seek my homeland, now my leader lies
cut own in the fighting. It is the greatest of griefs to me:
224 he was both my kinsman and my lord."
Then he went forward, bore his grief in mind
so that he wounded a man with his spearpoint,
a seaman in the host, so that he fell to the ground
228 slain by his weapon. The friends began to encourage each other
– those comrades, brothers-in-arms – so that they went forwards.
Offa shook his ash-spear and spoke:
"You have emboldened us all indeed, Ælfwine,
232 us thanes in time of danger. Now that our lord lies dead,
the *eorl* on the earth, it is necessary for us all
that each of us shall encourage the other
warrior to the warfare, while his weapons he can still
236 heave and hold: a hard blade,
a spear and good sword. Godric has
completely betrayed us, the cowardly son of Odda:
many a man believed, when he rode off on the horse
240 – on the proud steed – that it was our lord;
because of that the *folc* was split up in the field,
the shieldwall broken apart. Let what he may begin be destroyed!
because he has caused so many men here to flee."

242

Æþelredes eorl; ealle gesāwon

204 *heorðgenēatas þæt hyra heorra læg.*

Þā ðǣr wendon forð wlance þegenas,

unearge men, efston georne:

hī woldon þā ealle ōðer twēga,

208 *lif forlǣtun oððe lēofne gewrecan.*

Swā hī bylde forð bearn Ælfrīces,

wiga wintrum geong, wordum mǣlde;

Ælfwine þā cwæð, hē on ellen sprǣc:

212 *«Gemun[a] þā mǣla þe wē oft æt meodo sprǣcon*

þonne wē on bence bēot āhōfon,

hæleð on healle, ymbe heard gewinn.

Nū mæg cunnian hwā cēne sȳ!

216 *Ic wylle mine æþelo eallum gecȳþan,*

þæt ic wæs on Myrcon miccles cynnes;

wæs min ealda fæder Ealhelm hāten,

wis ealdorman, woruldgesǣlig.

220 *Ne sceolon mē on þǣre þēode þegenas ætwitan*

þæt ic of ðisse fyrde fēran wille,

eard gesēcan nū min ealdor ligeð

forhēawen æt hilde. Mē is þæt hearma mǣst –

224 *hē wæs ǣ g[ð]er min mǣgand min hlāford.»*

Þā hē forð ēode; fæhðe gemunde

þæt hē mid orde ānne gerǣhte

flotan on þām folce þæt sē on foldan læg

228 *forwegen mid his wǣpne. Ongan þā winas manian*

frȳnd and gefēran þæt hī forð ēodon.

Offa gemǣlde, æscholt āscēoc:

«Hwæt, þū, Ælfwine, hafast ealle gemanode

232 *þegenas tō þearfe. Nū ūre þēoden lið,*

eorl on eorðan, ūs is eallum þearf

þæt ūre æghwylc ōþerne bylde,

wigan tō wīge, þā hwile þe hē wǣpen mæge

236 *habban and healdan, heardne mēce,*

gār and gōd swurd. Ūs Godrīc hæfð,

earh Oddan bearn, ealle beswicene.

Wēnde þæs formoni man, þā hē on mēare rād,

240 *on wlancan þām wicge, þæt wǣre hit ūre hlāford;*

forþan wearð hēr on felda folc tōtwǣmed,

scyldburh tōbrocen – ābrēoðe his angin

þæt hē hēr swā manigne man āflȳmde!»

244 Lēofsunu spoke and raised up his lindenwood
   – his shield as protection – he said to the warriors:
   "I give my word that from this place I do not mean
   to flee one foot's space; rather will I go forward
248 to avenge my friendly lord in the fight.
   Steadfast warriors around Sturmer need not
   blame me in their speech together, now my friend is fallen,
   that I am going home lordless,
252 fleeing from the fight; rather shall a weapon take me,
   a spearpoint and an iron sword." He strode very angrily,
   fought resolutely; he scorned flight.
   Then Dunnere spoke and shook his dart,
256 the lowly *ceorl* called out over all,
   bade that each of the warriors should avenge Byrhtnōþ:
   "He must not draw back who thinks to avenge
   his lord on the foe, nor care for his life."
260 They moved forwards then, did not take heed for their lives;
   the warband's men began to fight hard
   – those fierce spear-wielders – and prayed to God
   that they should be allowed to avenge their friendly lord
264 and bring death to their foes.
   The hostage began to help them eagerly;
   he was from a hard kindred of the Northumbrians,
   his name was Æscferþ, Ecglāf's son,
268 he did not shrink back at the war-play,
   rather he sent forth arrows swiftly –
   sometimes he hit a shield, sometimes pierced a warrior;
   time and again he dealt out wounds
272 while he was able to wield his weapons.
   Eadweard the Tall still stood at the forefront
   ready and keen; he spoke boasting words
   that he did not mean to flee by one foot's length of land,
276 to turn back while a better man than he lay dead.
   He broke through the shieldwall and fought against the warriors
   until his ring-giver on the seamen
   he had worthily avenged, before he lay among the slain.
280 Æþeric, the noble comrade, did likewise –
   keen and eager to advance he fought single-mindedly,
   the brother of Sibryht; and very many others
   clove through the ridged shield – keenly they fought.
284 The shield's rim burst and the mailcoat sang

244   *Lēofsunu gemǣlde and his linde āhōf,*
        bord tō gebeorge. Hē þām beorne oncwæð:
        «Ic þæt gehāte þæt ic heonon nelle
        flēon fōtes trym, ac wille furðor gān,
248   *wrecan on gewinne minne winedrihten.*
        Ne þurfon mē embe Stūrmere stedefæste hælæð
        wordum ætwitan, nū min wine gecranc,
        þæt ic hlāfordlēas hām siðie,
252   *wende fram wīge, ac mē sceal wǣpen niman,*
        ord and iren!» Hē ful yrre wōd,
        feaht fæstlīce – flēam hē forhogode!
        Dunnere þā cwæð, daroð ācwehte,
256   *unorne ceorl, ofer eall clypode,*
        bæd þæt beorna gehwylc Byrhtnōð wrǣce:
        «Ne mæg nā wandian sē þe wrecan þenceð
        frēan on folce, nē for fēore murnan!»
260   *Þā hī forð ēodon, fēores hī ne rōhton.*
        Ongunnon þā hiredmen heardlice feohtan,
        grame gārberend, and God bǣdon
        þæt hī mōston gewrecan hyra winedrihten
264   *and on hyra fēondum fyl gewyrcan.*
        Him se gȳsel ongan geornlīċe fylstan:
        hē wæs on Norðhymbron heardes cynnes,
        Ecglāfes bearn. Him wæs Æscferð nama;
268   *hē ne wandode nā æt þām wīġplegan*
        ac hē fȳsde forð flān genēhe;
        hwilon hē on bord scēat, hwilon beorn tǣsde;
        ǣfre embe stunde hē sealde sume wunde
272   *þā hwile ðe hē wǣpna wealdan mōste.*
        Þā gȳt on orde stōd Eadweard se langa,
        gearo and geornful; gylpwordum spræc
        þæt hē nolde flēogan fōtmǣl landes,
276   *ofer bæc būgan, þā his betera leg.*
        Hē bræc þone bordweall and wið þā beornas feaht
        oð þæt hē his sincgyfan on þām sǣmannum
        wurðlīce wrec ǣr hē on wæle lǣge.
280   *Swā dyde Æþerīc, æþele gefēra,*
        fūs and forðgeorn, feaht eornoste,
        Sibyrhtes brōðor, and swiðe mænig ōþer.
        Clufon cellod bord – cēne hī weredon!
284   *Bærst bordes lærig and sēo byrne sang*

a song of terror. Then in the fighting struck
Offa at the seaman so that he fell to earth
and there Gadd's kinsman sought the ground.

288   Offa was quickly cut down in the battle,
yet he had carried out what his lord had bidden,
just as he had vowed before his ring-giver:
that they both would either ride into the stronghold,

292   come safely home, or all in the host,
die of wounds at the place of slaughter.
Loyally he lay beside his lord.
Then came the clash of shields. The seamen strode up,

296   angered by warfare. Often a spear went through
a doomed man's body. Wīstān then went forward,
the son of Þurstān, and fought against the foemen.
He was the slayer of three of them in the throng

300   before Wīgelm's kinsman lay among the slain.
It was a hard encounter there. They stood fast,
those warriors in the strife. Fighting men fell
weary from their wounds. Gore fell to the ground.

304   All the while Ōswold and Ēadwold
– both those brothers – encouraged the fighting men,
bade in their speech their beloved kinsmen
that they must hold out in their time of need there,

308   use their weapons without weakening.
Byrhtwold spoke up, he raised his shield
and brandished his spear – he was an old retainer;
with great courage he addressed the troop:

312   "Mind shall be the harder, heart the keener,
courage the greater as our strength dwindles.
Here lies our leader, cut down,
the good man in the dirt. May he ever grieve

316   who now thinks to turn from this war-play.
I am old in life: I do not wish to leave,
but rather beside my lord,
– beside so dear a man – do I think to lie."

320   Likewise they were encouraged by Æþelgār's son
Godric, onward to the struggle. Often he sent a spear,
a slaughter-shaft, spinning into the vikings;
thus he led the fighting in the battle,

324   hewed and slew, till he fell in the fight.
that was not the Godric who turned away from the strife ...

gryreleoða sum. Þā æt gūðe slōh
Offa þone sǣlidan, þæt hē on eorðan fēoll;
and ðǣr Gaddes mǣg grund gesōhte:

288   raðe wearð æt hilde Offa forhēawen;
he hæfde ðēah geforþod þæt hē his frēan gehēt
swā hē bēotode ǣr wið his bēahgifan
þæt hī sceoldon bēgen on burh ridan,

292   hāle tō hāme, oððe on here crin[c]gan,
on wælstōwe wundum sweltan;
hē læg ðeēenlīce ðēodne gehende.
Ðā wearð borda gebræc! Brimmen wōdon,

296   gūðe gegremode; gār oft þurhwōd
fǣges feorhhūs. For[ð] ðā ēode Wistān,
Þurstānes suna, wið þās secgas feaht.
Hē wæs on geþrang hyra þrēora bana

300   ǣr him Wīgel[m]es bearn on þām wæle læge.
Þǣr wæs stið gemōt; stōdon fæste
wigan on gewinne. Wīgend cruncon,
wundum wērige; wæl fēol on eorþan.

304   Ōswold and Ēadwold ealle hwile
bēgen þā gebrōþru beornas trymedon;
hyra winemāgas wordon bǣdon
þæt hī þǣr æt ðearfe þolian sceoldon,

308   unwāclīce wǣpna nēotan.
Byrhtwold maþelode, bord hafenode;
sē wæs eald genēat; æsc ācwehte.
Hē ful baldlīce beornas lǣrde:

312   «Hige sceal þē heardra, heorte þē cēnre,
mōd sceal þē māre þe ūre mægen lȳtlað.
Hēr lið ūre ealdor eall forhēawen,
gōd on grēote: ā mæg gnornian

316   sē ðe nū fram þis wīgplegan wendan þenceð!
Ic eom frōd fēores; fram ic ne wille,
ac ic mē be healfe minum hlāforde,
be swā lēofan men, licgan þence.»

320   Swā hī Æþelgāres bearn ealle bylde,
Godrič tō gūþe; oft hē gār forlēt,
wælspere windan on þā Wicingas.
Swā hē on þām folce fyrmest ēode,

324   hēow and hȳnde o[ð] þæt hē on hilde gecranc.
Næs þæt nā se Godric þe ðā gū[ð]e forbēah! . . . .

Bibliography

ABELS, R., *Lordship and Military Obligation in Anglo-Saxon England*, British Museum Publications, London, 1988

— English Tactics, Strategy and Military Organization in the Late Tenth Century, in *The Battle of Maldon, AD 991* Basil Blackwell, Oxford, 1991

ADKINS, L. & R., *Handbook of British Archaeology*, Macmillan Publishers, London, 1983

ALCOCK, L., *Arthur's Britain*, Penguin Books, Harmondsworth, 1971

ARBMAN, H., *The Vikings*, Thames and Hudson, London, 1960

BLOOMFIELD, M.W., Beowulf and Christian Allegory: an Interpretation of Unferth, in *An Anthology of Beowulf Criticism*, University of Notre Dame Press, Notre Dame, 1980

— Patristics and Old English Literature: Notes on Some Poems, in *An Anthology of Beowulf Criticism*, University of Notre Dame Press, Notre Dame, 1980

— **& DUNN, C.W.**, *The Role of the Poet in Early Societies*, D.S. Brewer, Woodbrige, 1989

BONE, P., Development of Anglo-Saxon Swords from the Fifth to the Eleventh Century, in Oxford University Committee for Archaeology Monograph No.21, Oxford, 1989

BRADY, C., Weapons in *Beowulf*: analysis of the nominal compounds and an evaluation of the poet's use of them, in *Anglo-Saxon England*, volume 8

BRANSTON, B., *The Lost Gods of England*, Thames & Hudson, London, 1957

BROOKE, C., *The Saxon and Norman Kings*, Fontana, London, 1967

BROOKS, N., Weapons and Armour, in *The Battle of Maldon, AD 991* Basil Blackwell, Oxford, 1991

BROWN, T., *English Martial Arts*, Anglo-Saxon Books, Hockwold, forthcoming

BRUCE-MITFORD, R., The Sutton Hoo Helmet, in *Aspects of Anglo-Saxon Archaeology*, Victor Gollancz, London, 1974

— A note on the word *wala* in *Beowulf*, in *Aspects of Anglo-Saxon Archaeology*, Victor Gollancz, London, 1974

— **& LUSCOMBE, M.R.**, The Benty Grange Helmet, in *Aspects of Anglo-Saxon Archaeology*, Victor Gollancz, London, 1974

— Other 'Helmets' Found in Britain, in *Aspects of Anglo-Saxon Archaeology*, Victor Gollancz, London, 1974

BURNE, LT.COL. A.H., *More Battlefields of England*, Methuen & Co., London, 1952

CABANISS, A, Beowulf and the Liturgy, in *An Anthology of Beowulf Criticism*, University of Notre Dame Press, Notre Dame, 1980

CAMERON, M.L., *Anglo-Saxon Medicine*, Cambridge Studies in Anglo-Saxon England, Cambridge University Press, 1993

CARE EVANS, A., *The Sutton Hoo Ship Burial*, British Museum Press, London, 1986

CARVER, M.O., The Anglo-Saxon Cemetery: An Interim Report, in *Bulletin of the Sutton Hoo Research Committee*, No. 8, Sutton Hoo Research Trust, London, 1993

CHADWICK HAWKES, S., Weapons and Warfare in Anglo-Saxon England: an Introduction, in Oxford University Committee for Archaeology Monograph No.21, Oxford, 1989

— & PAGE, R.I., Swords and Runes in South-East England, in *The Antiquaries Journal*, London, 1967

CHAMBERS. R.W., *Widsith: A Study in Old English Heroic Legend,* Cambridge University Press, Cambridge, 1912

— & WYATT, A.J., *Beowulf with the Finnsburg Fragment,* Cambridge University Press, Cambridge, 1920

CLARK HALL, J.R., *A Concise Anglo-Saxon Dictionary,* Mediaeval Academy Reprints, University of Toronto Press, London, 1984

CUNLIFFE, B., *Wessex to AD 1000,* Longman, Harlow, 1993

DAMICO, H., The Valkyrie Reflex in Old English Literature, in *New Readings on Women in Old English Literature,* Indiana University Press, Indianapolis, 1990

DAVIS, N. ed., *Sweet's Anglo-Saxon Primer,* Oxford University Press, Oxford, 1961

DAVIS, R.H.C., Did the Anglo-Saxons have Warhorses?, in Oxford University Committee for Archaeology Monograph No.21, Oxford, 1989

DICKINSON, T. & HÄRKE, H., *Early Anglo-Saxon Shields,* Society of Antiquaries, London, 1993

DIXON, PHILIP H., *The Reading Lathe,* Cross Publishing, Newport, 1994

DOUGLAS, A., *The Beast Within – Man, Myths and Werewolves,* Orion Books, London, 1993

DUMÉZIL, G., *From Myth to Fiction,* University of Chicago Press, Chicago, 1973

DUNNING, G.C. & EVISON, V.I., The Palace of Westminster Sword, *Archaeologia* 98, The Society of Antiquaries, London 1961

EARL, J.W., *Thinking about Beowulf,* Stanford University Press, Stanford, 1994

EKWALL, E., *The Concise Oxford Dictionary of English Place-names,* Oxford University Press, Oxford, 1977

ELLIOTT, R.W.V., *Runes: an Introduction,* Manchester University Press, Manchester, 1971

ELLIS DAVIDSON, H.R., The Sword at the Wedding, in *Patterns of Folklore*, D.S. Brewer, Ipswich,1960

— *Pagan Scandinavia,* Thames & Hudson, London, 1967

— *Gods and Myths of Northern Europe,* Penguin Books, Harmondsworth, 1976

— *The Sword in Anglo-Saxon England,* Boydell & Brewer, Woodbridge, 1994

— The Training of Warriors, in Oxford University Committee for Archaeology Monograph No.21, Oxford, 1989

ENGSTROM, R., LANKTON, S.M. & LESHER-ENGSTROM, A., *A Modern Replication based on the Pattern-welded Sword of Sutton Hoo,* Mediaeval Institute Publications, Western Michigan University, Kalamazoo, 1989

EVISON, V.I., The Dover Ring-Sword and Other Sword-Rings and Beads, *Archaeologia* 101, Society of Antiquaries, London, 1967

— Sword Rings and Beads, *Archaeologia* 105, Society of Antiquaries, London, 1975

— Sugar-loaf Shield Bosses, *The Antiquaries Journal* 43, Society of Antiquaries, London, 1963

FLETCHER, R., *Who's Who in Roman Britain and Anglo-Saxon England,* Shepheard-Walwyn Publishers, London, 1989

FOOTE, P. & WILSON, D.M., *The Viking Achievement,* Sidgwick & Jackson, London, 1974

GALE, D.A., The Seax, in Oxford University Committee for Archaeology Monograph No.21, Oxford, 1989

GARMONSWAY, G.N., *An Early Norse Reader,* Cambridge University Press, Cambridge, 1928

GIRVAN, R., *Beowulf and the Seventh Century,* Methuen, London, 1971

GLOSECKI, S.O., *Shamanism and Old English Poetry,* Garland Reference Library of the Humanities, Volume 905, Garland Publishing, New York, 1989

GLOB, P.V., *The Bog People,* Paladin Books, St. Albans, 1971

GOLDSMITH, M.E., The Christian Perspective in Beowulf, in *An Anthology of Beowulf Criticism,* University of Notre Dame Press, Notre Dame, 1980

GRATTAN, J.H.G. & SINGER, C., *Anglo-Saxon Magic and Medicine,* The Wellcome Historical Medical Museum, Oxford University Press, Oxford, 1952

GREEN, B., ROGERSON, A. & WHITE, S.G., Morning Thorpe Anglo-Saxon Cemetery, Norfolk, Volumes I and II, *East Anglian Archaeology Report* No.36, Norfolk Archaeology Unit, Dereham, 1987

GRIFFITH, P., *The Viking Art of War,* Greenhill Books, London, 1995

HALSALL, G., Warfare and Society, in Oxford University Committee for Archaeology Monograph No.21, Oxford, 1989

HAMP, E.P., Beowulf 2863a *sec(g),* in *Homage to Georges Dumézil,* Journal of Indo-European Studies Monograph, Washington, 1982

HANDFORD. S.A. (trans.), *Caesar: The Conquest of Gaul,* Penguin Books, Harmondsworth, 1951

HÄRKE, H., Early Saxon Weapon Burials, in Oxford University Committee for Archaeology Monograph No.21, Oxford, 1989

HARRISON, M. & EMBLETON, G., *Anglo-Saxon Thegn 449-1066 AD,* Osprey Warrior Series, No.5, Reed Consumer Books, London, 1993

HART, C., The Ealdordom of Essex, in *An Essex Tribute,* Leopard's Head Press Ltd. London, 1987

HAYMES, A., *Anglo-Saxon Kinship,* forthcoming

HAYWOOD, J., *Dark Age Naval Power – A Reassessment of Frankish and Anglo-Saxon Seafaring Activity,* Routledge, London, 1991

HEATHER, P. & MATTHEWS, J., *The Goths in the Fourth Century,* Liverpool University Press, 1991

HEDEAGER, L., *Iron Age Societies,* Basil Blackwell, Oxford, 1992

HERBERT, K., *Looking for the Lost Gods of England,* Anglo-Saxon Books, Pinner, 1994

— *Spellcraft. Old English Heroic Legend,* Anglo-Saxon Books, Pinner, 1993

— *Peace-weavers and Shield-maidens*, Anglo-Saxon Books, Hockwold, forthcoming

HIGHAM, N.J., *The English Conquest. Gildas and Britain in the Fifth Century*, Manchester University Press, Manchester, 1994

HINES, J., The Military Context of the *Adventus Saxonum*: some Continental evidence, in Oxford University Committee for Archaeology Monograph No.21, Oxford, 1989

HODGES, R., *Dark Age Economics: The Origins of Towns and Trade AD 600-1000*, Duckworth & Co., London, 1989

HOLTHAUSEN, F., *Altenglisches Etymologisches Worterbuch*, Carl Winter Universitatsverlag, Heidelberg, 1974

HOOPER, N., *The Anglo-Saxons at War*, in Oxford University Committee for Archaeology Monograph No.21, Oxford, 1989

KAUL, F., MARAZOV, I., BEST, J. & DE VRIES, N., *Thracian Tales on the Gundestrup Cauldron*, Najade Press, Amsterdam, 1991

KLUGE, F. (translated by Francis Davis, J.), *Etymological Dictionary of the German Language*, George Bell & Sons, London, 1891

KRAPP, G.P. & VAN KIRK DOBBIE, E. (eds.), *The Exeter Book*, Columbia University Press, New York, 1942

LANG, J. & AGER, B., Swords of the Anglo-Saxon Periods in the British Museum: a Radiographic Study, in Oxford University Committee for Archaeology Monograph No.21, Oxford, 1989

LEYSER, K., Early Mediaeval Warfare, in *The Battle of Maldon: Fiction and Fact*, The Hambledon Press, London, 1993

LINCOLN, B., *Death, War and Sacrifice: Studies in Ideology and Practice*, University of Chicago Press, London, 1991

LOWRY, R.M.P., The Consumption and Symbolism of Alcohol in Anglo-Saxon England, in *Medieval Life* 1, 1995

LUND, N., Danish Military Organisation, in *The Battle of Maldon: Fiction and Fact*, The Hambledon Press, London, 1993

MACNAMEE, M.B., Beowulf – an Allegory of Salvation?, in *An Anthology of Beowulf Criticism*, University of Notre Dame Press, Notre Dame, 1980

MAGOUN, F.P., The Oral Formulaic Character of Anglo-Saxon Narrative Poetry, in *An Anthology of Beowulf Criticism*, University of Notre Dame Press, Notre Dame, 1980

MANLEY, J., The Archer and the Army in the Late Saxon Period, in *Anglo-Saxon Studies in Archaeology and History* 4, 1985

MATTINGLY, H. (trans.) revised by HANDFORD, S.A., *Tacitus: The Agricola and the Germania*, Penguin Books, Harmondsworth, 1970

METZNER, R., *The Well of Remembrance*, Shambala Publications, Boston, 1994

MILLER, D.A., Two Warriors and Two Swords: The Legacy of Starkað, in *Journal of Indo-European Studies* Vol.19, 1991

MYRES, J.N.L., *The English Settlements*, Oxford University Press, Oxford, 1986

NEEDHAM, G.I., *Ælfric: Lives of Three English Saints*, University of Exeter, Exeter, 1976

NEWTON, S., *The Origin of Beowulf and the Pre-Viking Kingdom of East Anglia,* D.S. Brewer, Cambridge, 1993

OWEN-CROCKER, G.R., *Dress in Anglo-Saxon England,* Manchester University Press, Manchester, 1986

— Hawks and Horse-Trappings, in *The Battle of Maldon, AD 991* Basil Blackwell, Oxford, 1991

PADGETT HAMILTON, M., The Religious Principle in Beowulf, in *An Anthology of Beowulf Criticism,* University of Notre Dame Press, Notre Dame, 1980

PÁLSSON, H. & EDWARDS, P., *Egil's Saga,* Penguin Classics,Harmondsworth,1976

PEDDIE, J., *Alfred the Good Soldier: His Life and Campaigns,* Millstream Books, Bath, 1989

PEPPER, G., "Tothill Street, Westminster and Anglo-Saxon Civil Defence" in *London Archaeologist*, vol.7 no.16, (Spring 1996)

PLUMMER, C. & EARLE, J., *Two of the Saxon Chronicles Parallel ,* Oxford University Press, Oxford, 1892

POLLINGTON, S. , "Heart Shall Be the Keener" – The Argument of Courage at Maldon, in *Maldon 991-1991: Reflections on a Battle*, Runetree Publications, London, 1993

— *Rudiments of Runelore,* Anglo-Saxon Books, Hockwold, 1995

— *The Warrior's Way,* Blandford Press, London, 1989

POLOMÉ, E.C., Isoglosses and the Reconstruction of the IE Dialectal Split, in *The Journal of Indo-European Studies*, vol.22 (1994)

— Introduction to *Homage to Georges Dumézil*, Journal of Indo-European Studies Monograph. Washington, 1982

POOLE, R.G., *Viking Poems on War and Peace,* University of Toronto Press, Toronto, 1991

RAVETZ, A. & SPENCER, G., Excavation of the Battle Ditches, Saffron Walden, *Transactions of the Essex Archaeological Society* (reprint), Part II, Vol.I, 3rd series

ROSÉN, H., Latin *Sacēna* Hebrew *Sakkīn* and the Mediterranean Substrate, in *Journal of Indo-European Studies* Vol.22 (1994)

SCOTT LITTLETON, C., *The New Comparative Mythology – An Anthropological Assessment of the Theories of Georges Dumézil*, University of California Press, Berkeley, 1973

SCRAGG, D. (ed.), *The Battle of Maldon,* Manchester University Press, Manchester, 1981

— (ed.), *The Battle of Maldon, AD 991,* Basil Blackwell, Oxford, 1991

SIMEK, R., *Dictionary of Northern Mythology,* D.S. Brewer, Cambridge, 1993

SWANTON, M.J., *The Spearheads of the Anglo-Saxon Settlements,* Royal Archaeological Institute, London, 1973

TAYLOR, A., *Anglo-Saxon Cambridgeshire,* The Oleander Press, Cambridge, 1978

THORPE, L., *The Bayeux Tapestry and the Norman Invasion,* The Folio Society, London, 1973

TOLKIEN, J.R.R., *Beowulf – The Monsters and the Critics,* George Allen & Unwin, London, 1983

— & **BLISS, A.** (ed.), *Finn and Hengest, The Fragment and the Episode,* George, Allen & Unwin, London 1982

TYLER, S., The Anglo-Saxon Cemetery at Prittlewell, Essex: an Analysis of the Grave Goods, in *Essex Archaeology and History,* 1988

VAN KIRK DOBBIE, E. (ed.), *The Anglo-Saxon Minor Poems,* Columbia University Press, New York, 1942

WEBB, J.F. & FARMER, D.H. (trans.), *The Age of Bede ,* Penguin Books, Harmondsworth, 1983

WEBSTER, L. & BACKHOUSE, J., *The Making of England: Anglo-Saxon Art and Culture AD 600-900,* British Museum Press, London,1991

WENHAM, S.J., Anatomical Interpretations of Anglo-Saxon Weapon Injuries, in Oxford University Committee for Archaeology Monograph No.21, Oxford, 1989

WHITELOCK, D. (ed.), *Sweet's Anglo-Saxon Reader,* Oxford University Press, Oxford 1967

WHITLOCK, R., *Warrior Kings of Saxon England,* Book Club Associates, London, 1977

WILSON, D.M. (ed.), *The Archaeology of Anglo-Saxon England,* Cambridge University Press, Cambridge, 1976

WOOD, M., *Domesday – A Search for the Roots of England,* BBC Publications, London 1986

— *In Search of the Dark Ages,* Ariel Books, London 1981

WOOLF, R., The Ideal of Men Dying With Their Lord in the *Germania* and the *Battle of Maldon,* in *Anglo-Saxon England,* volume 5

WRIGHT, A.C., Three Anglo-Saxon Blades from Prittlewell, in *South East Essex Archaeology* No.4, 1982

YORKE, B., The Kingdom of the East Saxons, in *Anglo-Saxon England,* 14

— *Kings and Kingdoms of Early Anglo-Saxon England,* Seaby, London, 1990

ZETTERSTEN, A. (ed.), *Waldere,* Manchester University Press, Manchester, 1979

Index

(Note: Æ follows A, Đ/Þ follows T; the Appendices are not included here.)

Lincoln, 214
Lincolnshire, 203
Loki, 67
London, 33, 105, 149, 177, 201, 202
Long Man of Wilmington, 53
longbow, 152, 153, 187
lord, lordship, 24, 31, 33–37, 44, 46, 47,
  50, 54, 65, 67, 75–78, 84–90, 92, 105,
  126, 153, 156, 158, 168, 176, 179–81,
  185, 186, 193, 204, 206, 210, 213, 216
Low Countries, 82
loyalty, 34, 37, 44, 54, 77, 82, 85, 88, 89,
  91, 168, 170, 184, 216
luck, 22, 32, 39, 44–46, 75, 91, 113, 168,
  215
Lund, 55
Lydford, Dorset, 200
Lyminge, Kent, 126
Lymn, River, 200

M

mace, 157, 158
magic, 46, 76, 112, 187
Magonsætan, 180
mail, 35, 41, 42, 58, 71, 75, 91, 93, 95,
  100, 118, 138–41, 145, 146, 148, 150,
  159, 174, 193, 197, 205, 209, 210
Maldon (battle), 75, 85, 118, 126, 138,
  155, 175, 177, 185, 186, 189, 212
Maldon, Essex, 83, 197
Malmesbury, Wiltshire, 199
maple (wood), 136
market towns, 28, 55
marksmanship, 48
marshall, 192
mask, 73, 98
māððum (treasure), 26, 35, 39, 96, 116,
  205
Maxims, 22, 53, 56, 71, 172, 189
mead, 36, 87
Medway, River, 179
meerschaum (pipe-clay), 106
Mercia, Mercian, 168, 172, 177, 178,
  180, 185, 195, 197, 213
Mersea Island, Essex, 201
Merton, Dorset, 207, 208
military service, 26, 31, 78, 79, 82, 83,

85, 88–92, 139, 151
military training, 22, 65
Milton, Kent, 200
missiles, 95, 102, 117, 118, 121, 126,
  150, 154, 156, 157, 166, 182, 184, 213
Mjolnir, 51, 157
morale, 185, 192
Morningthorpe, Norfolk, 96
Mucking, Essex, 27, 61, 132
Myrgings, 40

N

Naður (sword), 112
neck-plate (helmet), 141, 143
neckring, 72
nefa (nephew), 65
Neolithic, 23, 60, 61, 103
nephew, 65
Nerthus, 60
night attacks, 49
Norman, 50, 79, 82, 84, 92, 108, 130,
  152, 154, 157, 185, 186, 193, 203, 216
Normandy, 27, 158, 217
Norse, 26, 43, 45–47, 49–55, 64, 66, 67,
  70–73, 77, 106, 110, 113–14, 116, 117,
  121, 127, 145, 148, 155, 157, 169, 173,
  175, 176, 180, 182
Norsemen, 27, 75, 76, 82, 128, 168, 175,
  180
North Sea, 27, 28, 58, 59, 141, 157
North Sea Germanic, 28, 59, 141
Northumbria, Northumbrian, 52, 66, 85,
  88, 159, 175, 179, 196, 200, 208
Norwegians, 90, 112, 155, 167
Norwich, Norfolk, 82
Nottingham, 214
numeri (troops), 30
Nydam, 60, 118, 151

O

oak (wood), 136
oaths, 34, 35, 44, 46, 90, 105, 175, 176,
  200
Oberflacht, Germany, 151, 153
obsessio montis badonici (siege of Mount
  Badon), 62
Odin (Óðinn), 46, 45–47, 51, 52, 55, 67,

An Introduction to
the Old English Language and its Literature

Stephen Pollington

The purpose of this general introduction to Old English is not to deal with the teaching of Old English but to dispel some misconceptions about the language and to give an outline of its structure and its literature. Some basic knowledge of these is essential to an understanding of the early period of English history and the present form of the language.

UK £3·95   ISBN 1–898281–06–8   48pp

The Battle of Maldon
Text and Translation

Translated and edited by Bill Griffiths

The Battle of Maldon was fought between the men of Essex and the Vikings in AD 991. The action was captured in an Anglo-Saxon poem whose vividness and heroic spirit has fascinated readers and scholars for generations. *The Battle of Maldon* includes the source text; edited text; parallel literal translation; verse translation; a review of 103 books and articles.

This new edition has a helpful section about Old English verse – alliteration, English as an inflected language, auxiliary verbs, compounds.

£5·95   ISBN 0–9516209–0–8   96pp

Beowulf
Text and Translation

Translated by John Porter

The verse in which the story unfolds is, by common consent, the finest writing surviving in Old English, a text that all students of the language and many general readers will want to tackle in the original form. To aid understanding of the Old English, a literal word-by-word translation is printed opposite the edited text and provides a practical key to this Anglo-Saxon masterpiece.

£7·95   ISBN 0–9516209–2–4   192pp

An Introduction to Early English Law

Bill Griffiths

Much of Anglo-Saxon life followed a traditional pattern, of custom, and of dependence on kin-groups for land, support and security. The Viking incursions of the ninth century and the reconquest of the north that followed both disturbed this pattern and led to a new emphasis on centralized power and law, with royal and ecclesiastical officials prominent as arbitrators and settlers of disputes. The diversity and development of early English law is sampled here by selecting several law-codes to be read in translation - that of Æthelbert of Kent, being the first to be issued in England, Alfred the Great's, the most clearly thought-out of all, and short codes from the reigns of Edmund and Æthelred the Unready.

UK £6·95   ISBN 1–898281–14–9   96pp

The Hallowing of England
A Guide to the Saints of Old England and their Places of Pilgrimage

Fr. Andrew Philips

In the Old English period we can count over 300 saints, yet today their names and exploits are largely unknown. They are part of a forgotten England which, though it lies deep in the past, is an important part of our national and spiritual history. This guide includes a list of saints, an alphabetical list of places with which they are associated, and a calendar of saint's feast days.

UK £4·95   ISBN 1–898281–08–4   96pp

Wordcraft
Concise English/Old English Dictionary and Thesaurus

Stephen Pollington

This book provides Old English equivalents to the commoner modern words in both dictionary and thesaurus formats. The Thesaurus presents vocabulary relevant to a wide range of individual topics in alphabetical lists, thus making it easily accessible to those with specific areas of interest. Each thematic listing is encoded for cross-reference from the Dictionary. The two sections will be of invaluable assistance to students of the language, as well as to those with either a general or a specific interest in the Anglo-Saxon period.

UK £9·95   ISBN 1–898281–02–5   256pp

A Handbook of Anglo-Saxon Food
Processing and Consumption
Ann Hagen

For the first time information from various sources has been brought together in order to build up a picture of how food was grown, conserved, prepared and eaten during the period from the beginning of the 5th century to the 11th century. Many people will find it fascinating for the views it gives of an important aspect of Anglo-Saxon life and culture. In addition to Anglo-Saxon England the Celtic west of Britain is also covered. Now with an extensive index.

UK £8·95   ISBN 0–9516209–8–3   192pp

A Second Handbook of Anglo-Saxon Food & Drink
Production and Distribution
Ann Hagen

Food production for home consumption was the basis of economic activity throughout the Anglo-Saxon period. This second handbook complements the first and brings together a vast amount of information on livestock, cereal and vegetable crops, fish, honey and fermented drinks. Related subjects such as hospitality, charity and drunkenness are also dealt with. There is an extensive index.

UK £14·95   ISBN 1–898281–12–2   432pp

Spellcraft
Old English Heroic Legends
Kathleen Herbert

The author has taken the skeletons of ancient Germanic legends about great kings, queens and heroes, and put flesh on them. Kathleen Herbert's extensive knowledge of the period is reflected in the wealth of detail she brings to these tales of adventure, passion, bloodshed and magic.

The book is in two parts. First are the stories that originate deep in the past, yet because they have not been hackneyed, they are still strange and enchanting. After that there is a selection of the source material, with information about where it can be found and some discussion about how it can be used.

UK £8·95 net   ISBN 0–9516209–9–1   292pp

Alfred's Metres of Boethius   Edited by Bill Griffiths

In this new edition of the Old English *Metres of Boethius*, clarity of text, informative notes and a helpful glossary have been a priority, for this is one of the most approachable of Old English verse texts, lucid and delightful; its relative neglect by specialists will mean this text will come as a new experience to many practised students of the language; while its clear, expositional verse style makes it an ideal starting point for all amateurs of the period.

In these poems, King Alfred re-built the Latin verses from Boethius' *De Consolatione Philosophiae* ("On the Consolation of Philosophy") into new alliterative poems, via an Old English prose intermediary. The text is in effect a compendium of late classical science and philosophy, tackling serious issues like the working of the universe, the nature of the soul, the morality of power – but presented in so clear and lively a manner as to make it as challenging today as it was in those surprisingly Un-Dark Ages.

The text is in Old English without Modern English translation

£14·95   ISBN 1–898281–03–1 B5   208pp

Monasteriales Indicia Edited with notes and translation by Debby Banham
The Anglo-Saxon Monastic Sign Language

The *Monasteriales Indicia* is one of very few texts which let us see how life was really lived in monasteries in the early Middle Ages. Written in Old English and preserved in a manuscript of the mid-eleventh century, it consists of 127 signs used by Anglo-Saxon monks during the times when the Benedictine Rule forbade them to speak. These indicate the foods the monks ate, the clothes they wore, and the books they used in church and chapter, as well as the tools they used in their daily life, and persons they might meet both in the monastery and outside. The text is printed here with a parallel translation. The introduction gives a summary of the background, both historical and textual, as well as a brief look at the later evidence for monastic sign language in England.

£6·95   ISBN 0–9516209–4–0   96pp

Anglo-Saxon Runes
John. M. Kemble

Kemble's essay *On Anglo-Saxon Runes* first appeared in the journal *Archaeologia* for 1840; it draws on the work of Wilhelm Grimm, but breaks new ground for Anglo-Saxon studies in his survey of the Ruthwell Cross and the Cynewulf poems. It is an expression both of his own indomitable spirit and of the fascination and mystery of the Runes themselves, making one of the most attractive introductions to the topic. For this edition new notes have been supplied, which include translations of Latin and Old English material quoted in the text, to make this key work in the study of runes more accessible to the general reader.

£6·95   ISBN 0–9516209–1–6   80pp

An Index of Theme and Image
to the Homilies of the Anglo-Saxon Church
Robert DiNapoli

For many decades the Old English homilies have been carefully studied for their theological, linguistic and historical content, but they have yet to receive their full measure of attention as literary artefacts (however odd the notion might have seemed to their authors), in part because of the extraordinary labours involved in getting acquainted with them fully.

This is an index and does not contain the texts of the homilies. It is a practical and useful guide to the homilies of Ælfric, Wulfstan, and the Blickling and Vercelli codices, allowing both the researcher and the general reader to range more freely across the mental landscape of these crucial texts than has been possible before.

£9·95   ISBN 1–898281–05–X   128pp

Anglo-Saxon Verse Charms, Maxims
and Heroic Legends
Louis J. Rodrigues

The Germanic tribes who settled in Britain during the fifth and early sixth centuries brought with them a store of heroic and folk traditions: folk-tales, legends, rune-lore, magic charms against misfortune and illness, herbal cures, and the homely wisdom of experience enshrined in maxims and gnomic verse. Louis Rodrigues looks at the heroic and folk traditions that were recorded in verse, and which have managed to survive the depredations of time.

UK £7·95   ISBN 1–898281–01–7   176pp

Anglo-Saxon Riddles
Translated by John Porter

This is a book full of ingenious characters who speak their names in riddles. Here you will meet a one-eyed garlic seller, a bookworm, an iceberg, an oyster, the sun and moon and a host of others from the everyday life and imagination of the Anglo-Saxons. Their sense of the awesome power of creation goes hand in hand with a frank delight in obscenity, a fascination with disguise and with the mysterious processes by which the natural world is turned to human use.

This edition contains all 95 riddles of the Exeter Book.

UK £4·95   ISBN 1–898281–13–0   112pp

Looking for the Lost Gods of England
Kathleen Herbert

Kathleen Herbert sifts through the royal genealogies, charms, verse and other sources to find clues to the names and attributes of the Gods and Goddesses of the early English. The earliest account of English heathen practices reveals that they worshipped the Earth Mother and called her Nerthus. The tales, beliefs and traditions of that time are still with us and able to stir our minds and imaginations.

UK £4·95   ISBN 1–898281–04–1   64pp

Rudiments of Runelore
Stephen Pollington

The purpose of this book is to provide both a comprehensive introduction for those coming to the subject for the first time, and a handy and inexpensive reference work for those with some knowledge of the subject. The *Abecedarium Nordmannicum* and the English, Norwegian and Icelandic rune poems are included in their original and translated form. Also included is work on the three Brandon runic inscriptions and the Norfolk 'Tiw' runes.

UK £5·95   ISBN 1–898281–16–5   Illustrations 88pp

English Martial Arts

by Terry Brown

Techniques included in this book are for bare-fist fighting, broadsword, quarterstaff, bill, sword and buckler, sword and dagger. Explanations of the techniques are accompanied by over 250 photographs. The theory behind the techniques is explained in a chapter on The Principles of True Fighting.

The author has for many years been a highly skilled practitioner of kung fu but when, several years ago, he discovered that the English had their own system of martial arts he set about collecting together information about its history and the techniques employed. The results of that research, which are published here for the first time, reveal a highly organized body of martial artists who practised a system that ranks as high in terms of effectiveness and pedigree as any in the world.

In the first part of the book the author investigates the history and development of the English fighting system and in doing so looks at some of the attitudes, beliefs and social pressures that helped shape it. He describes the weapons used and looks at available evidence for clues as to how the design and use of the weapons evolved. The tales of great skill and courage revealed here bring to life the people who helped shape the development of not only English martial arts but also the outlook and attitudes of the English people. That inheritance is still with the English and other Anglo-Saxon peoples throughout the world.

The second part of the book deals with various techniques and methods, all of which are explained in detail and accompanied by photographs. These instructions should lay to rest the mistaken but commonly held belief that English martial arts bear any resemblance to the 'methods' that are often displayed in film and television productions. Experienced martial artists will immediately recognise that the criteria upon which the techniques, methods and principles of this system are based are as valid as those that underlie the system with which they are familiar.

English martial arts have an impressive history. Unlike some systems they are not the fighting arts of a family or village, but the indigenous and empirical fighting arts of an entire nation. While nearly all of the recorded fighting techniques and other information are from a later period, the roots of the system are to be found in the heroic traditions of Anglo-Saxon warfare and culture. The warriors produced by that culture were renowned throughout Europe for their skills and ferocity and were only equalled, perhaps, by the Northmen who so frequently fought against them. The merging of Danish and other Scandinavian settlers into the English population introduced additional areas of martial expertise into the English system, an example of this being the two-handed battle-axe which the English, already fond of the equally lethal two-handed bill, adopted with relish. This merging of military skills created a unique and effective fighting art which had, as its final ingredient, the belligerently defended independent character of the English people.

ISBN 1-898281-18-1   To be published October /November 1996

We accept payment by cheque, Visa, Eurocard and Mastercard. For orders of less than £7 please add 50 pence for p & p in the UK; £7–£14 add £1 p & p; over £14 add £1·50. For a full list of publications see URL: http://www.ftech.net/~regia/as-books.htm or send a s.a.e. to:

Anglo-Saxon Books

Frithgarth, Thetford Forest Park, Hockwold-cum-Wilton, Norfolk IP26 4NQ
Tel/Fax: 01842 828430   e-mail: 100636.2512@compuserve.com

Most titles are available in North America from:
Paul & Company Publishers Consortium Inc.
c/o PCS Data Processing Inc., 360 West 31 St., New York, NY 10001
Tel: (212) 564-3730 ext. 264

Þa Engliscan Gesiðas

Þa Engliscan Gesiðas (The English Companions) is a historical and cultural society exclusively devoted to Anglo-Saxon history. Its aims are to bridge the gap between scholars and non-experts, and to bring together all those with an interest in the Anglo-Saxon period, its language, culture and traditions, so as to promote a wider interest in, and knowledge of all things Anglo-Saxon. The Fellowship publishes a journal, *Wiðowinde,* which helps members to keep in touch with current thinking on topics from art and archaeology to heathenism and Early English Christianity. The Fellowship enables like-minded people to keep in contact by publicising conferences, courses and meetings that might be of interest to its members. A correspondence course in Old English is also available.

For further details write to:
The Membership Secretary, Þa Engliscan Gesiðas
BM Box 4336, London, WC1N 3XX England.

Regia Anglorum

Regia Anglorum is a society that was founded to accurately re-create the life of the British people as it was around the time of the Norman Conquest. Our work has a strong educational slant and we consider authenticity to be of prime importance. We prefer, where possible, to work from archaeological materials and are extremely cautious regarding such things as the interpretation of styles depicted in manuscripts. Approximately twenty-five per cent of our membership, of over 500 people, are archaeologists or historians.

 The Society has a large working Living History Exhibit, teaching and exhibiting more than twenty crafts in an authentic environment. We own a forty foot wooden ship replica of a type that would have been a common sight in Northern European waters around the turn of the first millennium AD. Battle re-enactment is another aspect of our activities, often involving 200 or more warriors.

For further information see URL: http://www.ftech.net/~regia or contact:
K. J. Siddorn, 9 Durleigh Close, Headley Park, Bristol BS13 7NQ, England
e-mail: regia@hrofi.demon.co.uk

West Stow Anglo-Saxon Village

An early Anglo-Saxon Settlement reconstructed on the site where it was excavated consisting of timber and thatch hall, houses and workshop. Open all year 10a.m.–4.15p.m. (except Yule). Free taped guides. Special provision for school parties. A teachers' resource pack is available. Costumed events are held at weekends, especially Easter Sunday and August Bank Holiday Monday. Craft courses are organised.

Details available from:
The Visitor Centre, West Stow Country Park
Icklingham Road, West Stow
Bury St Edmunds, Suffolk IP28 6HG
Tel: 01284 728718